TECHNOLOGY AND MANAGEMENT
IN LIBRARY AND INFORMATION SERVICES

Technology and Management

in Library and Information Services

F. W. Lancaster & Beth Sandore

1997

University of Illinois
Graduate School of Library and Information Science
501 East Daniel Street
Champaign Illinois 61820-6211

Distributed exclusively by the University of Illinois
Graduate School of Library and Information Science Publications Office
501 E. Daniel Street
Champaign IL 61820-6211
USA

ISBN 0-87845-099-8

Designed and typeset by Robert Chapdu, IntelliText Corporation,
Champaign IL 61826 USA
Printed and bound by Thomson-Shore Inc.,
Dexter MI 48130 USA

CONTENTS

IOIOIOIOIOIOIOIOIOIOIOIOIOIOIOIOIOIOIOIOIOIOIOIOIOIOIOIOIOIOIOIOIOIOIOIOIOIOIOIOIOIOIOIOIOIOIOIOIOIOIOIOIOIOIOIOIOIOIOIOIOI

IOI

THIS BOOK deals with the logical intersection of "technology" and "management" in the context of libraries and other information centers. While the major thrust is the management of technology, the reverse relationship—the use of computer and related technologies to facilitate or improve management—is also covered.

The larger the library, the more complex are all aspects of management, including the management of technology. Therefore, the text is likely to have greatest relevance to the managers of large libraries or library systems, particularly those in the academic arena—where most of the research and development tends to occur. Nevertheless, much of the discussion should also be of interest to librarians in management positions in smaller institutions. While the word "library" is given special emphasis in the book, we hope the managers of information centers in general will find it of interest and value. "Library," then, should be regarded as a shorthand for "library and information center."

Because the area dealt with is obviously one that is changing very rapidly, we have tried to restrict ourselves to the major "issues" confronting managers relative to the application of technology within library and information services. No attempt is made to evaluate particular "systems." Indeed, wherever possible, we have avoided reference to specific systems, particularly those that are commercially available. The major issues examined in this book reflect the rather fundamental changes in library operations and services that are being brought about by technology.

Because a comprehensive text in this area would occupy several volumes, we have been somewhat selective in our coverage. For example, we have avoided discussion of many of the legal ramifications (relating to licensing agreements, copyright in the electronic environment and suchlike), which are outside our areas of experience and would comprise a text in themselves, as well as more general issues, such as "fee versus free," which are not exclusively linked to technology. The topics that are treated are not treated at an equal level of detail. This is less a reflection of our own priorities than of the amount of research and literature that exists on the various topics. Wherever possible, we have included references to sources of further information for those readers who wish to pursue a topic in more detail.

The book is intended primarily for use by managers of library and related information services. However, it could also serve as a text for a course in graduate schools of library and information science since, we believe, it is the management of technology rather than the technology itself that should now be a major focus of our professional curriculum.

F. W. Lancaster
Beth Sandore
University of Illinois
October 1996

ACKNOWLEDGMENTS

IOIOIOIOIOIOIOIOIOIOIOIOIOIOIOIOIOIOIOIOIOIOIOIOIOIOIOIOIOIOIOIOIOIOIOIOIOIOIOIOIOIOIOIOIOIOIOIOIOIOIOIOIOI

THE AUTHORS would like to thank Richard W. Meyer, Ann Bishop, Mary Jane Petrowski, and Mary E. Jackson for reviewing various chapters in draft form, as well as Kathy Painter for the secretarial work that was so important to the completion of the book. Reprint permissions from several publishers are acknowledged throughout the text.

IOI

THERE ARE MANY POSSIBLE WAYS in which this book could be organized and no single sequence is necessarily "the best." Indeed, we have changed the sequence several times before we settled on the one actually used.

As the contents page reveals, we deal first with some broad management issues that affect virtually all libraries and information services in their applications of technology. The second section of the book focuses primarily on various effects of technology on the users of library and information services.

Finally, we look at some more specialized issues in the management of technology, try to summarize the major content and conclusions of the book, and end with a discussion of possible future trends.

Clearly, these sections are not mutually exclusive. For example, the chapter on training includes both training of staff and training of users, while the chapter on CD-ROM deals with management issues as well as impact on users. Nevertheless, we hope that the majority of readers will find the presentation to be both logical and useful.

IOI

F. WILFRID LANCASTER is Professor Emeritus in Library and Information Science at the University of Illinois at Urbana-Champaign. He is the author of ten earlier books, six of which have received national awards from the American Society for Information Science and the American Library Association, and the editor of many others. Since 1986 he has been editor of *Library Trends*.

BETH SANDORE is Coordinator for Imaging Projects and Associate Professor of Library Administration at the University of Illinois at Urbana-Champaign. She is the author of a number of articles on technology in libraries and systems evaluation.

LIST OF FIGURES

IOIOIOIOIOIOIOIOIOIOIOIOIOIOIOIOIOIOIOIOIOIOIOIOIOIOIOIOIOIOIOIOIOIOIOIOIOIOIOIOIOIOIOIOIOIOIOIOIOI

TECHNOLOGY AND MANAGEMENT
IN LIBRARY AND INFORMATION SERVICES

CHAPTER 1

Why Libraries Apply Technology

IOIOIOIOIOIOIOIOIOIOIOIOIOIOIOIOIOIOIOIOIOIOIOIOIOIOIOIOIOIOIOIOIOIOIOIOIOIOIOIOIOIOIOIOIOIOIOIOIOI

SOME POSSIBLE REASONS for applying technology to library operations are listed in Figure 1. The first three, which are inter-related, all involve staffing needs. When automation was first introduced into libraries, a major justification was that it would save money by reducing the number of staff required or, at least, allowing the library to cope with increasing demands without the need for extra people.

---

1. To cope with increasing demands
2. To reduce staff or prevent staff increases
3. To allow more activities to be performed by clerical and paraprofessional staff
4. To improve existing services
5. To provide new services
6. To collect better data to aid overall management of the library

---

FIGURE 1
Possible reasons for applying technology in libraries

In actual fact, there is little evidence that automation has reduced staff size (Craghill et al., 1989). While it may have drastically downsized certain departments—most notably cataloging—in many libraries, this has not usually led to shrinkage in the library as a whole. More often, it has meant the redeployment of staff, with new departments emerging and others growing in size. At the same time, of course, the staffs of the larger libraries have been expanded by the addition of people specifically involved in technological applications. In the early days, it was often thought that such appointments would be temporary; once the library was automated, the need for those people would disappear. Instead, these temporary appointments have become permanent and the proportion of the staff dealing primarily with the application of technology has increased steadily in many libraries. In her survey of major research libraries in North America, Johnson (1991) found that, whilenumber of support staff may have decreased overall, the supervisory or managerial positions have actually grown with the increasing applications of technology.*

Nevertheless, while automation may not have eliminated positions overall, it probably prevented further increase in numbers. Put differently, it is unlikely that most libraries would be able to offer the level of services they now offer at present personnel levels without the aid of technology. Moreover, cuts in budgets or purchasing power, threatening staff positions, may well have provided a major impetus for automation in the first place.

If technology has not reduced the overall size of staff, it has certainly had a profound effect on professional/nonprofessional relationships. Many activities formerly performed by professional librarians are now performed in a computer-assisted mode by other members of the staff, and more of this reallocation is likely to occur in the future. As paraprofessional and clerical employees have taken on greater responsibilities, this has often brought about the upward grading of their jobs.

Items 4 and 5 of Figure 1 relate to the services that libraries offer. Improvement of existing services has been a justification for automation activities from the beginning, although it always seems to have been a secondary consideration, after that of cost cutting or cost containment.**

By embracing automation in the form of computer and telecommunications technologies, libraries are now able to offer services that they were quite unable to offer earlier. However, the feasibility of offering new services was not a major justification for automation twenty or so years ago.

---

*It is worth noting that most libraries participating in the recently completed TULIP project (TULIP, 1996), which was designed to deliver electronic journals to the desktops of users, seem to feel that the digital libraries of the future will need more librarians than those of today.

**A typical project objective from the late 1960s is this one from Dartmouth College:

> To develop a prototype automated circulation desk which will eliminate typical manual procedures used in most libraries; will do so in an economic manner and will relieve present circulation desk staff of many repetitive clerical tasks while at the same time improving overall circulation service (*Current Research*, 1969, page 436).

Sweeney (1994) claims that libraries have not achieved great productivity increases through technology because they have used it primarily to automate existing operations rather than to provide new services:

> In the past, library leaders asked how to use technology to accomplish existing tasks such as circulation and cataloging. The post-hierarchical library leader asks how technology can accomplish something totally new. For example, how can a library provide remote searching and retrieval of articles from home? (Page 80)

The last reason for applying technology, as identified in Figure 1, relates to the overall management of the library. One could make a strong case for claiming that the major justification for automated systems is that they can yield data, difficult or impossible to collect otherwise, that allow better management of the library and its resources. The most obvious example relates to data on the use of the library collections. In other words, one can regard an automated system within a library as primarily a management information system or a decision support system (Lancaster, 1983). Regrettably, most libraries do not consider better management/decision making as a major reason for automation, and the system vendors certainly fail to emphasize their capabilities in this area.

Johnson (1990b, 1991) reports on a survey of heads of technical services of academic libraries that are members of the Association of Research Libraries. The 54 respondents (response rate about 45%) ranked their automation objectives on a three-point scale of very important, some importance, and not important. The results are presented in Figure 2. Especially noteworthy is the lack of emphasis given to the management information aspect and the fact that improvement in services, rather than cost reduction or cost containment, is now accepted as the major reason for automation. As Johnson (1990b) says, "... libraries are still concentrating on using automation to replicate and enhance previously manual tasks." (Page 6)

The respondents to Johnson's survey also used a three-point scale to judge the effects of automation in their libraries. The results, shown in Figure 3, indicate that these libraries consider that automation has been most valuable in improving service to users and, possibly, improving the library's image. It has not had much effect in improving the overall management of the library or in reducing costs of operation.

Automation objectives		Value	
	1	2	3
1. Improve patron services	94.4	5.6	0.0
2. Offer new patron services	77.7	16.7	5.6
3. Supply more information	76.0	24.0	0.0
4. Increase speed of operations	64.8	31.5	3.7
5. Replace obsolete systems	64.8	13.0	22.2
6. Improve technical services operations	55.5	38.9	5.6
7. Keep up with increasing volume of work	53.7	35.2	11.1
8. Supply more accurate information	44.4	48.2	7.4
9. Reduce operating costs	27.7	51.9	20.4
10. Achieve a management information system	24.1	25.9	50.0
11. Increase staff satisfaction	18.5	63.0	18.5
12. Tighten audit and control	18.5	44.5	37.0

KEY: 1 = Very important
2 = Some importance
3 = Not important

FIGURE 2

Objectives for automating activities in 54 major academic and research libraries in North America as reported by Johnson (1991). The values are the percentage of respondents giving each objective a particular value on the three-point scale.

Reprinted with permission of G. K. Hall & Co., an imprint of Simon & Schuster Macmillan, from *Automation and Organizational Change in Libraries* by Peggy Johnson. Copyright © 1991 by Margaret Ann Johnson.

While technology was first applied to improve internal library operations and the daily lives of staff members, the potential for enhancing user services is more widely recognized today, a point made forcefully by Lowry (1995b):

> In some measure, we have "crammed" automation down the throats of library patrons as a by-product of technical services activities, although with very good intentions . . . But we have now begun to take hold of events and consciously and deliberately start shaping automation to the human needs of our patrons. (Page 299)

The remaining chapters of this book will address the various subjects implied by the contents of Figures 1-3, namely the effects of automation on the organization and management of the library; effects on staff, services, and users; automated systems as a source of management information; and the evaluation of automated systems in libraries. Current trends and possible future developments will also be dealt with.

Automation results	Value		
	1	2	3
1. Service to patrons	75.9	24.1	0.0
2. Offered new patron services	57.4	38.9	3.7
3. Speed of operation in processing data	53.7	33.3	13.0
4. Library's image	48.1	50.0	1.9
5. Use of staff	44.4	53.7	1.9
6. Speed of operations in general	40.7	46.3	13.0
7. Quality of information	33.3	57.4	9.3
8. Reduction in clerical workload	29.6	29.6	40.8
9. Management control	11.1	75.9	13.0
10. Management decision-making	9.2	24.1	66.7
11. Decreased cost of operations	3.7	35.2	61.1

KEY: 1 = Greatest improvement
2 = Some improvement
3 = Little or no improvement

FIGURE 3

Achievements of automation as reported by respondents from 54 major academic and research libraries in North America.

Reprinted with permission of G. K. Hall & Co., an imprint of Simon & Schuster Macmillan, from *Automation and Organizational Change in Libraries* by Peggy Johnson. Copyright © 1991 by Margaret Ann Johnson.

CHAPTER 2

Effects of Technology on Management and on Organizational Structures

IOIOIOIOIOIOIOIOIOIOIOIOIOIOIOIOIOIOIOIOIOIOIOIOIOIOIOIOIOIOIOIOIOIOIOIOIOIOIOI

CONCURRENTLY with their increasing application of technology over the last twenty-five years, many of the larger libraries have experienced significant changes in their organizational structure and form of management, The more obvious areas of effect are identified in Figure 4.

---

1. Composition and size of departments
2. Centralization/decentralization
3. Staff responsibilities and job descriptions
4. Autonomy at branch and divisional levels
5. Management style and management skills

FIGURE 4
Areas affected by organizational/managerial changes accompanying the increasing automation of libraries

Organizational Structure

As mentioned in the preceding chapter, automation has resulted in the abolition of some departments and the downsizing of others, as well as the emergence of new entities. Perhaps more significantly, the traditional divisional/departmental structure of large libraries has become less rigid: the automated library tends to make more use of a matrix organization of temporary structures, such as task forces or project groups, causing a blurring of divisional or departmental boundaries.

Automation may also contribute to the increasing decentralization of a number of professional activities. In large public and academic libraries, it has long been traditional to centralize the technical services but to decentralize the public services through branch or departmental libraries. Because technological developments tend to facilitate the process, more of the professional functions, especially original cataloging, have been decentralized in some of the larger academic libraries. Gorman (1987), in particular, has been a strong proponent of this approach.

Gorman illustrates his views by a description of changes made at the Library of the University of Illinois at Urbana-Champaign:

> In practical terms, at the macro level, "Technical" and "Public" services have been replaced by "General" and "Departmental Library" services. General Services comprises all the processing units (order, claiming, and receipt; copy cataloging; database maintenance and management; circulation and book-stacks; binding) and a number of other central services (central reference; special collections libraries; special languages libraries; area and special bibliographers). The first group of units is staffed overwhelmingly by clerical staff and has a high degree of automation in its activities. The second is staffed preponderantly by professional librarians and paraprofessionals. Departmental Library Services comprises all the departmental and branch libraries and the Undergraduate Library. Within each of these units, the professional librarians are responsible for the execution of all professional tasks connected with the subject area (e.g., biology), departmental subject focus (e.g., modern languages and linguistics), or service (e.g., to undergraduates) for which those libraries exist. The professional tasks for which the librarians are responsible include: materials selection; bibliographic verification (in the minority of cases in which it is necessary); original cataloging (across the board approximately 15% of our acquisitions require original cataloging ...); reference services; and bibliographic instruction.
>
> In theory, all librarians in a unit should engage in all of these activities, and, in many cases they do. However, the transfer to decentralized libraries of librarians who used to be catalogers and bibliographers, and the relative unfamiliarity with modern bibliographic control of many of the ex-public services librarians has meant that some aspects of compartmentalization remains [sic]. Time and increasing ease with what used to be unfamiliar will remedy this temporary problem, and the ideal of comprehensive professionalism limited not by a professional specialty but by a clientele served will be realized completely. Within that "client-centered library" (to use Charles Martell's felicitous phrase), each element of professional work will enrich and inform each other element thus providing a much more rewarding work experience for the librarians and a much greater level of service to the library's patrons. (Pages 164-165)

However, while Gorman's argument in favor of the "holistic librarian" is attractive in theory, the increasing decentralization of certain activities presents problems of implementation when imposed upon existing organizations. For example, a report of a task force at the University of Illinois (*Final Report*, 1990) identified the following concerns:

Because of the daily pressure exerted by patrons in public service areas, cataloging, by default, receives low priority in many units. Added to this is the fact that there is not a sufficient quantity of cataloging done in many units to develop and maintain expertise . . . To maintain expertise in cataloging, continuing education is needed. With the low staffing levels at our library, it is difficult to find the time both to give frequent enough continuing education and to attend such training. Furthermore, decentralization has visibly diminished the quantity, quality and uniformity of cataloging . . . it is common knowledge that some librarians simply do not want to catalog. If one is forced by circumstances to catalog, a poor product results. In addition, the inability to "talk shop" with colleagues who catalog on a regular basis is sorely felt . . . the argument that a decentralized approach insures greater familiarity with the material and better subject control over it is largely specious. If 80-90% of the material received in departmental libraries is OCLC cataloging, then the 10-20% over which the librarian can exercise subject control is negligible. (Pages 3-4)

The task force recommended the abandonment of decentralized cataloging except in a handful of units where the nature of the materials dealt with demands specialized knowledge (e.g., units dealing with rarer languages or special formats such as music or maps). The library would return to a centralized cataloging section. However, because much of the material received does not require original cataloging, this unit can now be much smaller than it was before the library began to make extensive use of OCLC and other utilities—perhaps as few as five or six professionals.

While there may be obstacles complicating the implementation of the holistic librarian philosophy, the fact remains that automation has brought greater diversity in the work of many professional librarians. That is, the librarian of today is more likely to be engaged in several professional activities rather than specialized in a single area—cataloging, collection development, reference work, or whatever. Consequently, advertisements for professional positions, and the corresponding job descriptions, have become increasingly similar. Xu (1996) studied advertisements for cataloger and reference librarian positions in academic libraries in the period 1971 to 1990. The advertisements were drawn from *American Libraries*. She concluded that, as libraries became more automated, the requirements for the two positions grew more similar in terms of education and previous work experience, with growing demand for computer skills in both groups, although differences still existed in the specific skills required.

Automation brings with it the need for greater standardization. Without standardization it is impossible to implement effective integrated systems within libraries or programs for resource sharing among libraries. The requirement for greater standardization has meant that the departments or branches of a large library may now have less autonomy than they did before. One manifestation is the fact that files of information that were once the exclusive domain of a single department (e.g., a "books on order" file) may now be widely accessible to all staff members and even, perhaps, to library users. As a result, some librarians now feel more vulnerable since errors or inefficiencies (e.g., processing delays) are easily observed (Somers, 1989).

While standardization may have increased staff vulnerability to criticism due to errors, technology has greatly enhanced the ability of staff to identify and correct errors using more systematic and less labor-intensive methods, such as global maintenance or software programs designed to spot errors and replace them with correct forms.

Standardization brings other costs with it. Allen (1995) suggests that standardization has an "insidious effect" in stifling creativity. In particular, he claims, the standard approaches to cataloging are not very effective in dealing with networked resources.

Nevertheless, standardization in cataloging has contributed to improved and expanded online access points to materials in and across library collections. Also, the need for greater standardization has been the impetus for collaborative innovation in some cases. For example, members of the ILCSO (Illinois Library Computer Systems Organization) consortium of online libraries devised an approach to bibliographic and authority file maintenance that benefits all institutions in the network without requiring any one library to 'reinvent the wheel' in designing authority control for an online local system (Preece and Henigman, 1994).

Management Style

As libraries have applied technology over the last twenty-five years, the way in which they are managed has also changed. The autocratic management approach, coupled with a rigid hierarchical organization, has given way to more participative management in a less formal hierarchical structure (Marchant and England, 1989).

In general, staff working in the less hierarchical structures, with greater participation in management decisions, are found to be more open to technology in the library and perhaps more innovative. Olsgaard (1984) discovered that attitudes of librarians towards automation are strongly related to their perceptions of how the library is managed—the more they feel involved in management, the more receptive they are to automation—and his findings have been replicated in a less developed country (Su, 1993).

Creth (1989) points out that ease of communication in the automated library environment, through electronic mail and electronic bulletin boards, contributes to the breaking down of traditional top-down communication. Members of the staff are now more able to communicate in all directions—up, down and sideways—and perhaps to cross departmental or divisional lines. Also, junior members of the staff may today have access to information formerly held only by managers. Most observers seem to consider that this multilevel communication is highly desirable. However, the advantages/disadvantages seem not to have been investigated in any systematic way. Does the increasing breakdown of rigid hierarchical structures create strength or instability in the organization? Does it really promote innovation or does it lead to chaos? The results from Johnson (1991), shown in Figure 3, suggest that librarians in large academic libraries do not feel that automation has improved management control.

It is generally agreed that the library manager of today needs rather different skills from the manager of yesterday, and perhaps greater managerial sophistication. The fact that libraries now operate in a technological and social environment that is changing rapidly demands a more flexible approach to management. The manager needs to be visionary and able to provide true leadership. Communication skills are extremely important: the manager needs to deal not only with the staff of the library but also with an increasing variety of external entities—library networks, vendors, university computer centers, and others—and thus must be effective in a boundary spanning role.

Allen (1995) stresses the need for libraries to develop organizational flexibility in order to foster innovation and creativity and to ensure that the competencies of staff members are the competencies needed today.

As an example, he points to the fact that new positions for "online search specialists" were established in many libraries in the 1970s but that the need for such positions has greatly diminished as this expertise has spread to other members of the staff. The same situation will apply, he feels, to the "network librarians" now being appointed in some libraries.

Sweeney (1994) has provided perhaps the most complete discussion of what the organizational structure needs to look like today if the library is to be responsive to society's needs. He coins the term "post-hierarchical library" to refer to a flexible, nonbureaucratic entity that "can change its organizational structure fundamentally and rapidly in order to offer new and better services to meet rapidly changing user needs." The post-hierarchical library is designed "to satisfy user knowledge and information needs rather than provide a collection of documents in a building." Such a library could incorporate several different substructures—a confederation of teams, a vendor-library alliance, a more conventional departmental structure—where such diversity seems optimum to achieve the required results.

Writing from a European perspective, van Gils (1995) is another author who has emphasized the need to create a more flexible organizational structure if the library is to survive in an increasingly electronic operating environment:

> It is not possible to build a digital future properly from a traditional organisational environment with its closely related logistic processes. One of the most essential features of the electronic revolution in supply of information is the rapidly expanding *interaction* between the various participants in the information system: publishers, intermediaries, readers. This interaction is highly promoted by the many means of technology which are at our disposal. If libraries want to play a significant role in this scientific information flow, they will have to adopt a very *active* attitude instead of a reactive one, in their offer of services and products and in their selection of strategic alliances with, for example, researchers and other academic professionals. (Page 535)

> ... We have to leave behind an organisation in which processes take place subdivided into parts via various departments. We have to aim at working in integrated teams that are responsible for a special service or product, for example electronic document delivery. In such teams, knowledge of traditional library tasks such as acquisition and cataloguing should be completely integrated with new aspects such as information technology and marketing. (Page 536)

IOI

> . . . I conclude that an integration of traditional operation processes in terms of *product teams* will be the future for libraries. This is the only way to obtain a necessary balance between *contents* and *technology*. Many scientific libraries will have to cooperate strategically with the computer centres of universities, instead of competing with them. (Page 537)

Of course, a more fluid organizational structure may cause some staff members, at all levels, to feel less secure. Creth (1995), however, believes that this can actually be good for the profession. Unless librarians become more "vigorous and imaginative," their role in society will decline:

> Professionals should be less concerned with an organization that reflects order and symmetry, comfort, and familiarity than with encouraging action and decision-making, risk, and innovation throughout the organization. (Page 93)

Nevertheless, the flexible structure advocated by Sweeney and others is not now in place in the great majority of libraries and, indeed, de Klerk and Euster (1989) suggest that organizational changes in academic libraries have not yet been as radical as many had predicted.

CHAPTER 3

Effects of Technology on Library Staff

IOIOIOIOIOIOIOIOIOIOIOIOIOIOIOIOIOIOIOIOIOIOIOIOIOIOIOIOIOIOIOIOIOIOIOIOIOIOIOI

C ERTAIN EFFECTS of technology on individual members of the library staff were touched upon earlier. This chapter deals with the subject in greater detail. Figure 5, identifying eight aspects of the effects of technology, provides the framework for the discussion.

---

1. Demands placed on the individual
2. Skills required
3. Professional/nonprofessional relationships
4. Training needs
5. Job satisfaction and self image
6. Contact with the public
7. Deprofessionalization
8. Employee fears and acceptance of automation

FIGURE 5
Aspects of the effects of technology on individual members of staff

Demands on Members of the Staff

It seems generally agreed in the library profession that technological applications have placed greater demands on members of the staff. Most obvious is the fact that they have had to learn to use various computer-based systems, and this requirement has become more onerous with the increase in number and diversity of the systems. For example, a reference librarian may now need to search databases accessible online through several different vendors, as well as some available in the library on CD-ROM, and this will require knowledge of different software and search capabilities.

For each of the overt demands associated with a particular technology, some more covert demands may also be created. For example, the librarian may have to instruct users in database searching techniques, which adds a new dimension to the requirement: a good searcher is not necessarily a good teacher.

Librarians involved in database searching must also be effective communicators since they need to interact with users to fully understand what it is they are looking for. While the ability to communicate has always been a requirement of public service librarians, the database searching situation enhances this requirement: in general, greater communication skills are needed in the database searching situation than in other aspects of reference service. Moreover, effective database searching may also require more knowledge of the subject matter dealt with, especially its terminology, which implies a greater need for some level of subject specialization. Furthermore, some librarians now provide reference service to remote users, who communicate with the library through electronic mail, and this presents a special challenge since it precludes the traditional face-to-face reference interview.

There is another less obvious requirement associated with this particular technology. As well as knowing how to search databases, the librarian must have a good knowledge of the range of databases available in order to select the one most likely to satisfy a user request. This may in fact be the most stringent requirement associated with the growth of database searching. It is well illustrated by the case of the librarian of a small special library in industry who, thirty years ago, had only five or six databases available to search (printed indexing/abstracting services) but today has several hundred accessible through online networking. It is perhaps little wonder that librarians do not always select the database most appropriate but, instead, return frequently to the source or sources with which they are most familiar (see, for example, Hu (1987)).

Technology has increased demands on library staff in other ways. Automated systems require greater accuracy and rigor in use, due in part to the fact that more standardization is needed to facilitate intra-institutional and inter-institutional resource sharing. Moreover, automation exposes the individual's work to wider scrutiny. The most obvious manifestation is the contribution of original cataloging to a large bibliographic utility, but other examples also exist since files that were once the exclusive domain of a particular department may now be accessed by all library staff members and even, perhaps, by members of the public.

Library users also place greater demands on the staff because they tend to expect more from the automated library than they did before. These heightened expectations range from better recordkeeping (e.g., users may expect the automated circulation system to indicate which books they have borrowed and when they are due) to a higher level of information service. Stoffle et al. (1996) have put this situation clearly and provocatively:

> Despite the fact that libraries have over time conditioned their customers to expect little, faculty and students are less willing to accept slow or shoddy service or to accept personal responsibility for failure in getting what they need. Expectations of traditional library service and response times have escalated, fueled by a culture of instant gratification. (Page 219)

Different Skills

Some of the new or enhanced skills implied by the automated library environment have already been alluded to. Others can also be recognized. For example, the librarian of today may need to understand the principles of marketing in order to develop new user-responsive services and to promote them within the community. (See Weingand (1995) for a broad overview of the marketing of library services.)

As mentioned in Chapter 2, staff members must now be more flexible and versatile since they are likely to engage in a greater variety of tasks than they did in the past. However, a somewhat anomalous situation has arisen: while they are expected to be more interchangeable, they may also be expected to develop more specialized skills—e.g., in database searching—and even to acquire a stronger background in a particular subject area.

All of this suggests that the librarian of today needs to know more, and to possess a greater variety of skills, than the librarian of twenty or thirty years ago. This has led to dissatisfaction among some staff members who feel that they now face greater pressures and responsibilities without a commensurate increase in status or financial reward.

The librarian must now be more adaptable in another way. The library and the library profession are going through a period of considerable change. Indeed, electronic networks can radically alter one's ideas about what constitutes a "library" and what is involved in "librarianship."

In this environment the librarian must be flexible in attitude of mind—able to keep pace with and adapt to dramatic changes in the library itself and in the technological and social environments in which it operates.

In the larger libraries, a split may occur between the staff members who enthusiastically embrace technology and those who do not. This can lead to resentment because the former, who may be younger and have less experience, might advance more rapidly in position and salary.

Professional/Nonprofessional Relationships

As mentioned in Chapter 2, automated systems allow some of the tasks formerly performed by professional librarians to be passed down to paraprofessionals, clerks or, in some cases, library users themselves. This trend is well represented in the philosophy put forward by Gorman (1987):

- no professional should do a task which can be performed by a paraprofessional;
- no paraprofessional should do a task which can be performed by a clerical staff member;
- no human being should do a task which can be performed by a machine. (Page 158)

Some library tasks, such as the generation of overdue notices and notices of books being held for users, have been taken over by the computer, while others have actually been taken on by library users in some places—e.g., the charging out of books or the initiation of interlibrary lending activities.

On the other hand, while some clerical tasks have been eliminated by automation, others have emerged, including tasks associated with data input, the conversion of records, and system backup and maintenance activities.

At the same time, while professional librarians have passed certain activities down to paraprofessionals, they have taken others on—in system development and implementation, in learning system capabilities, in teaching, and in the design and operation of new services. In general, more of the professional functions of today occur in the public services arena rather than that of technical services.

Training Needs

Automation has brought with it the need for more on-the-job training of staff and for the upgrading of their skills, especially when new technologies are introduced or significant changes are made to an existing system. Such training activities can be a major component of total automation costs—as much as fifty percent by some estimates. While some staff members will be eager to learn new skills and acquire additional experience, others may feel that too much of their time is spent in adapting to a changing technological environment, at the expense of direct service to the public, and that automation has brought about training overkill. Creth (1995) points out how important it is for the manager to "develop a culture in which the process of continuous learning and an acceptance of change by staff is the norm." Training is dealt with in detail in the next chapter.

Job Satisfaction and Self-Image

It seems widely accepted within the library profession that automation has improved job satisfaction and the self-image of the professional librarian and other members of the library's staff. This is understandable: the professional librarians have relinquished some of the jobs they consider less important, while the paraprofessionals and clerical staff have also given up some of the most routine tasks (to the computer) and taken on others that are more satisfying and that they perceive as more "professional."

One of the reasons why librarians have embraced technology with enthusiasm is the expectation that this will improve their image with library users and perhaps eventually increase their status within the communities served. Recent surveys of attitudes towards libraries and librarians (see Slater (1984) for a prime example) suggest that no improvement of this kind has actually occurred.

A number of surveys have looked at the effects of automation on the attitudes of library workers towards their jobs. Among the more interesting is a study of attitudes among four groups in Australian academic libraries, as reported by Waters (1988).

The group-by-group results of the Waters study are shown in Figure 6 and the attitudes of professional staff members are compared with those of nonprofessionals in Figure 7. While the results do reveal some agreement that automation has made library work more challenging and interesting, support for this is not very strong. In fact, more of the 64 respondents feel that the challenge of their jobs has remained the same, or even declined, than feel that the challenge has increased. Rather surprisingly, although automation should have increased the challenge and interest for nonprofessionals, since they may now be handling more of the tasks previously handled by professionals, this is not strongly supported by the data in Figure 7. Indeed, more nonprofessionals feel that creativity has been reduced than that it has increased. Bothwell and Lovejoy (1987), also dealing with academic libraries in Australia, report similar results in the sense that, while some employees feel that their jobs have become more interesting as a result of automation, the majority report no change or even a decline in interest. However, the 75 staff members surveyed, in three university libraries, were more in agreement that automation had increased efficiency.

The results of Prince and Burton (1988) are more positive but show that major differences may exist from one library to another. While 45% of the staff in one British academic library report that their jobs are now more interesting (50% report no change), only 33% do so in a second library (67% no change) and 23% in a third. In the last case, 31% report that the work has become less interesting.

Based on a survey in three academic libraries in the United States, Jones (1989) reports that support staff (paraprofessional and clerical) are generally positive toward technology. In fact, many of the more than one hundred respondents feel that automation has been introduced too slowly. However, she reports overwhelming agreement that the support staff should have greater involvement in decisions made on the acquisition of new systems or capabilities.

A more recent study, by Edwards et al. (1995), used questionnaires, interviews, and other sources to study attitudes of staff in six academic libraries in the United Kingdom. While many support staff felt that "electronic information" had reduced their workload, the majority of professional librarians disagreed, although all groups reported an increase in job satisfaction and that they felt more effective in their work. The majority, professional librarians and support staff alike, find it difficult to keep up with new developments and are frustrated by their "lack of technical expertise." There was strong agreement that technology does not foster isolation—either from library users or other staff members—and that it is unlikely to lead to loss of jobs. A somewhat surprising find-

		Varied	Interesting	Closely Supervised	Regimented	Challenging	Simple	Independent	Hectic	Fragmented	Routine	Repetitive	Creative	Exciting
GROUP 1 (17)	% Increased	53	47	12	24	53	25	35	24	35	35	35	29	35
	% Same	18	24	70	53	24	44	41	65	59	29	35	35	35
	% Decreased	29	29	18	24	24	31	24	12	6	35	29	35	29
GROUP 2 (13)	% Increased	38	62	31	56	54	38	23	62	31	38	23	31	46
	% Same	46	31	54	33	38	23	31	38	62	31	38	54	38
	% Decreased	15	8	15	17	8	38	46	0	8	31	38	15	15
GROUP 3 (12)	% Increased	58	100	27	17	58	33	8	50	25	17	17	42	25
	% Same	33	0	45	58	42	17	75	42	42	50	58	42	67
	% Decreased	8	0	27	25	0	50	17	8	33	33	25	17	8
GROUP 4 (22)	% Increased	23	41	18	9	32	36	19	38	18	32	36	18	14
	% Same	36	32	50	68	45	18	57	48	64	45	50	41	68
	% Decreased	41	27	32	23	23	45	24	14	18	23	14	41	18
All respondents	% Increased	41	58	21	22	47	33	22	41	27	31	30	28	28
	% Same	33	23	56	56	38	25	51	49	58	39	45	42	53
	% Decreased	27	19	24	22	16	41	27	10	16	30	25	30	19

FIGURE 6

Changes in thirteen aspects of the nature of work since the introduction of automated systems.
From Waters (1988) by permission of the State Library of New South Wales and of the author

{ 19 }

		Varied	Interesting	Closely Supervised	Regimented	Challenging	Simple	Independent	Hectic	Fragmented	Routine	Repetitive	Creative	Exciting
Professional	% Increased	54	58	13	13	50	22	21	52	29	17	17	33	33
(24)	% Same	33	38	58	58	46	26	58	48	54	46	46	54	63
	% Decreased	13	4	29	29	4	52	21	0	17	38	38	13	4
Non-	% Increased	33	58	26	28	45	40	23	35	25	40	38	25	25
Professional	% Same	33	15	54	54	33	25	46	50	60	35	45	35	48
(40)	% Decreased	35	28	21	18	23	35	31	15	15	25	18	40	28

FIGURE 7

Differences in attitudes of professionals and nonprofessionals based on Figure 6 data.
From Waters (1988) by permission of the State Library of New South Wales and of the author

ing is that, while respondents are enthusiastic about working with electronic tools, they seem to feel little confidence in them.

Contact with Users

It is sometimes claimed that the librarian of today must be more extrovert than the librarian of yesterday. The implication behind this claim is that the librarian now spends more time in direct contact with library users. There is some justification for this belief in the sense that more professional hours are now devoted to public services, rather than the behind-the-scenes technical services, than was true in the past. Nevertheless, the fact that librarians now spend more time being trained and in committee or task force meetings, coupled with the fact that paraprofessionals may now provide more of the public service functions, or library users perform them for themselves, suggests that hours of direct contact between professional librarians and the public may actually have declined. In some libraries, contact between users and nonprofessional members of the staff may also have declined as users take on more activities for themselves. At least, a decline in contact with the public may be a perception of many nonprofessionals, who may feel that the library, as a result, has become a less congenial working environment (Sykes, 1991).

Deprofessionalization

Not all librarians are of the belief that technology will improve their image and status. Harris (1992) points out that improvements in the ability of librarians to exploit technology may have caused a deterioration in other expertise. She is supported in this by those reference librarians who complain that the amount of time they now spend with electronic resources threatens their familiarity with the printed sources. Drawing upon the work of sociologist Toren (1975), Harris claims that deprofessionalization occurs when a profession loses control over its knowledge base and service ideal.

Lancaster (1991, 1993b) has suggested that the profession may well be losing its service ideal because he believes that many librarians have become mesmerized by the glamour of technology, seeing automation as an end in itself rather than a means of improving range, scope, and quality of services.

Harris (1992), on the other hand, sees the profession losing control over its knowledge base. Skilled professional catalogers have been replaced by network copy cataloging and, she believes, end user searching of CD-ROM and other databases will mean less demand for the services of a search specialist. Harris contends that

> ... the loss of the service ideal and loss of control over a knowledge base through the routinizing of professional functions, will lead to deprofessionalization. In other words, the changes underway in librarianship are likely to lead to its demise as a profession. (Page 14)

A debate held at the 1995 annual meeting of the Medical Library Association posed various questions to library administrators that do reflect concerns relating to staff morale, loss of the service ideal, and the possible transfer of tasks to other types of professionals. Among these questions, focused specifically on reference services, were the following:

- How do you maintain staff morale in a constantly changing environment, where responsibilities are fluid, additional services are added, and staff are reduced?
- Is a "reference librarian" needed to develop and provide instruction for electronic resources? Can't systems staff do this better?
- How do we bring other staff (nonlibrarians) into our reference/ teaching activities and still keep clear lines among responsibilities, rewards, position levels, etc? Or, do we want to have those lines? ...
- Are public services librarians losing their commitment to user service? Are they becoming overly fascinated and involved with the electronic world and forgetting how to apply it to their specific users' needs?
- How is service to users affected when reference desk hours are shortened so that staff can have more time to evaluate new electronic resources and develop print and on-screen guides for users? (Nagle, 1996, page 662)

Employee Fears

Fine (1986) has pointed out that about twenty percent of the members of the staff may be resistant to technology even today. Much of this resistance stems from fear, which may be associated with the introduction of a new system or with changes in an existing system.

A rather complete discussion of fear of technology in the library context can be found in Bergen (1988), and the human factors have also been dealt with by Cargill (1987), Rimmer and Miller (1987), Dyer (1991) and Sykes (1991), among others. Possible reasons for employee fear are summarized in Figure 8.

In some cases the fear is of the technology itself, and its possible effects, such as the fear that books will be replaced.

A second fear is that of making a mistake that will damage the equipment, wipe out a file, or otherwise prove costly to the organization. Older employees in particular may be afraid that they will be unable to learn how to use a new system. There may well be some justification for this because organizations rarely have enough resources to train all staff members adequately, especially in a situation in which the system is in a period of rapid change.

Some employees may fear that their jobs are threatened although, as already discussed, automation in libraries has led to redeployment of staff and changing responsibilities rather than actual staff reductions. A related fear, also touched upon earlier, is that of deprofessionalization and the loss of traditional skills (e.g., the fear that print-related skills will decline as more reference work involves use of electronic resources).

Other fears relate to reduced socialization—if tied to a terminal for a large part of the day, one will have less contact with other staff members or with the public—and to the Big Brother phenomenon (is the computer spying on me?).

Finally, there may exist fear of possible health hazards. While extreme cases may reflect simple paranoia, some justification exists for concerns relating to less serious effects such as backache and eyestrain. Useful summaries of the health and ergonomic aspects can be found in Dainoff (1986), Bergen (1988) and Dyer (1991).

Most fears are best handled by giving employees greater involvement with the technology through demonstrations, workshops, and visits to institutions in which the technology to be introduced is already in place.

Resistance to technology can take various forms (see, for example, Fine, 1986): decline in quality or quantity of work, unwillingness to change or to learn, absenteeism or lateness, behavioral problems (apathy, boredom, negativism, withdrawal or even aggression), and, in extreme cases, physiological problems such as headache, nausea or high blood pressure.

Olsgaard (1985) has identified the factors that determine whether or not technology is introduced successfully into an organization. These are summarized in Figure 9 as a series of problems that must be solved.

1. Technology itself
2. Cost of error
3. Ability to learn
4. Job security
5. Reduced socialization
6. Big Brother phenomenon
7. Health effects

FIGURE 8
Possible reasons for employees fearing technology.
Based largely on Bergen (1988)

The problems occur in a logical progression from those that are purely technological to those that are behavioral. First, and most obviously, the system adopted must be effective in doing what it is supposed to do. Second, the transition to the new system must be well planned and the staff well trained. The management must be strongly committed to the system and able to convey the strength of this commitment throughout the organization. Finally, management must work to minimize conflict among individuals or departments—related, for example, to changing responsibilities and organizational structure—and to minimize the effects of resistance in those individuals opposed to the change.

Jackson (1993a) points out that the addition of a new technology, if it is to be well accepted,

> ...must be carefully planned and integrated into existing procedures. If not, it will probably be relegated to infrequent use or used only in extreme rush situations...(Page 21)

She was referring specifically to new document delivery systems but the principle applies equally to other technologies.

Fine (1986) suggests that it may be a good thing that some employees resist technology. The manager should not necessarily dismiss such people as mere problems. Sometimes those who resist have been able to see undesirable consequences of a proposed change that others have completely overlooked. She feels that healthy growth in an organization can result from the tension that exists between those pulling for technology and those resisting.

Olsgaard (1985) points to the fact that there exist two opposing views on the behavioral effects of technology:

1. The more experience one has with technology, the more positive one is about its capabilities.
2. The more one uses the technology, the more aware one is of its limitations and dangers.

While most librarians seem to fall into the first group, this situation may be changing. The introduction of computers into libraries at a significant level, in the 1970's, was met with hostility, skepticism or indifference among many members of the profession. This eventually gave way to somewhat pervasive overenthusiasm and overoptimism regarding the benefits of technology. While this still exists to a very large extent, it is encouraging to find that some librarians are now more realistic in judging the effects of technology. Recently, for example, Ewing and Hauptman (1995) and LaGuardia (1995) imply that reference librarians at least may have lost more than they have gained. Ewing and Hauptman put it this way:

> ... technologies incorporated into libraries to economize or to make access easier have rarely done either; what they have done is to transmute the reference librarian's ostensible intellectual endeavors into manual tasks. Microformat readers and printers, photocopiers, desktop computers and workstations, and associated printers, output devices, CD-ROM drives, and debit card systems all require varying degrees of maintenance, [and] repair, and often demand immediate assistance and/or instruction. (Page 4)

LaGuardia believes that the major problem is a different one:

> The truth is, technology has not yet delivered on all its promises to us. Instead of saving our patrons and us time, it demands more and more of us. The logistical stuff, paper jams, ink cartridge replacements, and CD-ROM swapouts consume time at a reference desk, but they are still small considerations in comparison to the systems that are requiring major investments of time and effort to learn and pass on to our users, either at the desk or in library classes. We find ourselves working full-tilt just to keep up with the basic tools we need to know. We cannot access everything that is now available to us via networks and in print, but we are complicit with others in the information industry in creating a new myth: the myth that we *can* do it all, under present operating conditions. (Page 7)

On the other hand, based on "in-depth interviews" with librarians from several universities, Tenopir and Neufang (1992) claim that the majority feel that reference work is now more exciting and rewarding, so it is obvious that significant differences of opinion still exist on the impact of technology on the profession.

1. System capabilities (technology problem)
2. Planning and implementation of transition (organizational problem)
3. Management commitment (organizational problem)
4. Minimization of conflict (organizational and behavioral problem)
5. Minimization of resistance (behavioral problem)

FIGURE 9
Factors affecting successful introduction of technology.
Based on Olsgaard (1985)

CHAPTER 4

Instruction and Training

IOIOIOIOIOIOIOIOIOIOIOIOIOIOIOIOIOIOIOIOIOIOIOIOIOIOIOIOIOIOIOIOIOIOIOIOIOIOIOI

THE PROCESS of integrating technology into libraries has added a new dimension to our understanding of how information is organized and how we go about finding it. Likewise, technology has had an impact on how we educate patrons, staff, and librarians to find and use information. The printed, linear format of information has formed the core of principles that libraries have traditionally used for classifying and organizing knowledge. In the print library, the librarian inevitably knew more than the patron about where to find materials and how to exploit them. Understanding bibliographic organization principles requires a level of motivation and effort that most users lack unless compelled by a critical research or other information need. Computers and networking have made librarians and patrons more equal in gaining access to, storing, retrieving, and representing information in novel and efficient ways, to the extent that fundamental changes in the relationships among libraries, users, and information have occurred.

First, remote access to the library's electronic resources using computers, modems, and networking has made the library more accessible, and has potentially attracted a new population of users who have the capability to use libraries without physically entering them. Second, and perhaps more important, remote seekers of information can gain direct access to what have traditionally been classified as "library" information resources, without depending on the library's intermediary role. Patrons themselves are now capable of being information providers and publishers, using the Internet and the World Wide Web. Until recently, this was a role that was occupied primarily by publishers and professional societies, with the primary access mechanism to the published literature being the library. Third, users now have at their disposal the software and computing tools to store and manage significant amounts of electronic information—in a sense, to create their own personal libraries. Consequently, there is a growing convergence between the strategies and skills that librarians and users alike need in order to navigate their way around digital and print-based libraries.

Some have argued that user-friendly online systems and self-service information technology reduce or eliminate the need for user education and training programs. Others argue with equal conviction that changes like these raise the prerequisite technology learning curve, thus presenting an even more compelling need for strengthening and transforming the education and training role of libraries. Such diverse views compel us to look closely at the significance of technological changes and their potential impact on the education and training of both library users and library staff.

Impact on the Goals of Instruction and Training

The library's role in education and training can be said to involve the fostering of two major skills: ability to find relevant information and ability to evaluate its content in a critical fashion. Simple as these may seem, understanding the organization of information in its various forms presents a daunting challenge for even the accomplished researcher in the traditional print-based library.

Skilled information retrieval in the print library requires at least some knowledge of the catalog, classification schemes, indexing and abstracting services, citation indexes, specialized reference works, and a myriad of other access tools. The evaluation of information is rarely accomplished using only a set of rational and objective criteria. The recommendations of a student's academic advisor, an expert in a particular field, may serve as the authoritative source of information on that topic. A central goal of professional library education programs is to teach librarians how to categorize objectively and to evaluate the sources and the authoritativeness of information, based on a set of time-honored principles. User education programs address this same critical evaluation issue, albeit to a lesser degree, with programs that are tailored to the special subject needs of the information seeker.

Technology has overlaid new prerequisite concepts and skills upon those that have been required for effective use of the print-based library. In the electronic library, users and staff must both employ or acquire technical skills to use online resources. Further, they must understand on some level how the information is organized within a database, and which commands work best, in order to be successful in retrieving the desired information. With the advent of Internet and World Wide Web publishing, it has become increasingly critical that users and librarians alike be able to distinguish between verified and unverified sources of information, and weigh the implications of using each type of information according to their own needs. Users of information, regardless of where it is located, must expand their information-seeking habits, according to the type of information they seek, to include both print- and electronically-based materials in order to have a comprehensive overview of available information.

Trends in Instruction and Training

Several important factors have interacted to bring about significant changes in the library approach to instruction and training programs within the past twenty years. In addition to technology, these factors include: the widespread inclusion of cognitive and behavioral learning theories as the foundation of instruction programs; the information literacy movement; and extensive integration of educational theory and practice to enhance library instruction programs to align them more closely with concurrent learning activities (e.g., active learning, writing across the curriculum, and critical thinking skills).

Until the 1980s, many bibliographic instruction and training programs were based on procedural training. Kobelski and Reichel (1981) introduced the use of conceptual models in the bibliographic instruction program, based on the work of significant cognitive and behavioral theorists in the fields of education and psychology. Kobelski and Reichel's approach posited that, through the use of conceptual models, librarians could teach concepts and skills that would ideally impart to users an internal model that could help them learn similar points without having to begin over again with each new point. The information literacy movement of the 1980s recognized the library's mandate to expand its instructional role, and served as an impetus to transform library instruction from the traditional one-hour classroom presentation into various approaches geared toward the needs of different user groups. It prompted librarians to identify the basic information needs of diverse user groups and to determine how instruction and public service programs could best meet these needs and instill lifelong information-seeking skills in users. Within the past decade, librarians have incorporated additional approaches to teaching that are designed to bring the learner and the information-seeking process more closely in line with what he or she is studying or learning. In the academic setting, approaches based on critical thinking have emphasized the importance of developing evaluative skills in both the research and the writing process. Active learning has been employed as a method to engage learners in the process of discovering what it is that they need to know, as well as learning it, in order to increase retention and stimulate further learning.

On the one hand, technology has provided the tools to make instruction more effective and more interesting. On the other, the continuing and rapid introduction of new technologies into the library itself places significant further demands on those staff members directly involved in instructional programs. Technology can play an important facilitator role and thus have a significant impact on instruction and training. Networking and computer-assisted instruction courses have transformed the classroom from a mere physical environment to a virtual learning environment. Self-paced instruction software and Internet chat fora or listservs are now used to teach basic information-seeking skills to students who commute or who attend courses at night. The same technologies are being used to reach segments of the student or public population that were previously unreachable through classroom instruction. Conversely, the need to incorporate the concepts of electronic information storage and retrieval into our professional and user training programs has pushed the library to develop more flexible approaches to teach and train users and staff how to find and evaluate information. For example, models can be developed to enable an instructor to incorporate both print-based and electronic information retrieval as parts of the whole process of information seeking, within and beyond the library walls.

The Impact of Technology on the Direction of User Education

In his discussion of alternative professional models for reference librarians in the Information Age, Nielsen (1982) expressed the concerns that bibliographic instruction needed to address information retrieval issues, ought to be delivered more flexibly, and that instruction librarians were perhaps myopic in their view of instruction as an end in itself, rather than as an extension of core reference services:

> Much of what is being taught in bibliographic instruction programs is mind-deadening. Teaching about the problem of information retrieval can be intellectually challenging, as the problem touches on some of the most difficult questions in philosophy, linguistics, psychology, and sociology. The bibliographic instruction curriculum should be broadened to treat more thoroughly and creatively basic principles, including such things as set theory for online searching. At the same time, it should take the teaching of technique out of the classroom and into self-instructional learning packages, hands-on experience, and other less expensive mediated methods. Above all, advocates of the teaching role should not make a cult out of teaching. Librarians provide many helpful and necessary services besides teaching, and the totality of that contribution deserves recognition in its own right. Attempts to emulate academic faculty roles can be just as dysfunctional as attempts to mold reference into a doctor-patient model. The teaching cult also tends to divide instruction librarians from all other librarians, which is harmful to all librarianship. For all of these reasons, librarians must work toward defining a new role for reference service. (Page 188)

Nielsen's exhortations of fifteen years ago succinctly represent the areas that many user instruction programs and reference departments have attempted to address. It is clear from Nielsen's statement that technology has affected not only the content of what is taught in user education programs, but has also caused a re-examination of the role of reference and public service librarians. While it is not the intent of this chapter to discuss the impact of technology on the professional roles of instruction and reference librarians, the point is significant because it signaled the importance of technology as a catalyst for change in the traditional distinctions between reference and instruction and even, on a broader scale, between public and technical services roles. In the 1980s the major push to integrate automation, especially within academic libraries, transformed both access to information and approaches to teaching access principles:

> Automation, which was barely recognized in 1981 as a factor in instructional programs . . . permanently changed the nature of user interaction with libraries—on all levels. By the end of the decade, computer technology was a major factor in determining how library users obtained information (Baker et. al., 1992, pp. xiii-xiv.)

Some ten years after Nielsen's exhortations, similar points were made in the proceedings of the second ACRL Bibliographic Instruction Think Tank. The editors were concerned that user instruction programs were still focusing primarily on print-based research strategies, missing a significant shift in how users approached the electronic resources in the library:

> The combined events of the 80s produced a perspective of value on information, and convenience of access to information, which now stands foremost in the minds of users. In the field of library and information science, a positive outlook toward the mission of literacy has been adopted. Juxtaposed with the concerns of the authors of *A Nation at Risk* is the popular ALA slogan, "A nation of readers," created with the intention of promoting readership. However, the real concern of BI librarians about users' lack of critical information seeking and evaluation skills might be summed up in the phrase "A nation of readers at risk." Across U.S. campuses, the risk of losing the opportunity to promote student readership and critical thinking skills increases steadily as librarians fail to evaluate and change current print-based instruction methods in libraries (Baker et. al., 1992, pp. xiv-xv.)

Despite criticisms and concerns within the profession, significant changes in bibliographic instruction have occurred in many academic libraries within the past thirty years. Approaches have included the use of printed guides, manuals, the one-hour formal classroom lecture on either a tool or a research topic, instruction integrated into the syllabus of a for-credit course, computer-assisted instruction as a stand-alone program, hypermedia, and Internet- or Web-accessible self-paced instruction. Perhaps the greatest impact of technology in this area has been to enable the provision of network-accessible instruction and training to users when they need it in the convenience of their homes or workplaces, in the form of CAI (computer-assisted instruction) or other hypermedia-based software. The interaction between the librarian and the user is still maintained, but it becomes asynchronous. For example, a user completes an instructional software module at 10 p.m. at home and sends the assignment back to the librarian through FTP across the Internet; the librarian reviews the assignment and any corresponding questions during the next business day, provides answers or advice, then returns the work electronically to the user.

Tiefel (1995) traces the evolution of instruction programs, noting the considerable impact of technology and societal change and its effect on the path of instructional development:

> Dramatic changes in technology and society are having a considerable impact on libraries and their instruction programs. These changes have created an urgency to teach users how to become more effective, efficient, and independent in their information searching. In response to this, the goals of library user education have expanded from teaching tools to teaching concepts and from library instruction to information literacy and lifelong learning (Page 318).

She believes that user education will become an even more valued component of library service because of the continuing effects of technology, economic constraints, and the current trend toward self-sufficiency and end-user access. She cites several evaluation studies that have linked higher course completion rates and long-term library use skills to library instruction. Tiefel advocates a continued focus on developing concept-based approaches to user education, while at the same time devising innovative ways to reach increasing numbers of students, and suggests that technology will help librarians accomplish these challenging goals, especially those related to reaching larger segments of the population. She outlines the requirements for an expanded user education program in libraries:

> An expanded library user education program will include teaching the structure of information, use of new electronic formats, and applying critical thinking to information. Librarians will have to maximize the use of technology to teach more skills to greater numbers of users. More complex expert systems will be developed to help users with in-depth use of complex abstracting and indexing services. The emphasis will be on problem-solving and on obtaining and accessing information rather than on ownership . . .
>
> Libraries will need increasingly to help users become more independent in locating and retrieving information. Users should be able to accomplish this using systems that are easy and transparent to use (Page 329).

There is also a growing recognition that instruction programs in libraries are subject to budget cuts and downsizing, and that these programs must begin to exploit computer-assisted instruction and more effective online user interface development as channels to increase library/user interaction without increasing the total number of staff assigned to the program. Tiefel, a long-time advocate of public service participation in interface development, describes the Ohio State University Library's Gateway to Information, an interface to the online and CD-ROM resources on the campus, which serves over 53,000 students. The Gateway is designed around a research strategy approach that enables students to learn usable research strategies as they perform their own course-related information seeking. The Ohio State University Gateway to Information represents a good example of how online interface development has rapidly become the shared purview of systems designers *and* public services librarians, especially those involved in instruction.

A number of libraries have developed programs of computer-aided instruction for use with staff members or with the public. At the University of Tennessee-Knoxville library, supervisors responsible for training new library staff developed CBT (computer-based training) modules using Hypercard software (Bayne et al., 1994). Teams of staff members worked on different training modules and the CBT was implemented and evaluated using a team approach to judge its effectiveness. The training modules covered the following topics: computers in libraries, the Library of Congress classification system, periodical access, introduction to reference services, interlibrary loan, and acquisitions and cataloging. Bayne et al. note that staff involvement in the project was high, as was acceptance of the training modules, and that the approach alleviated the basic training burden on supervisors in a library in which staff turnover rate is high.

In a study of the most effective ways to convey different types of training at OCLC, Mushrush (1990) identified several advantages in the use of CBT for teaching procedural information, including: the ability to learn at one's own pace; savings in travel funds to acquire the same learning, and being trained on the same equipment on which the staff member would be working; trainees receive consistent content delivery; and many staff can be trained from the same software program. She notes, however, that conceptual points are best conveyed by an instructor, and suggests that a combination of both approaches can result in effective staff training programs and prudent use of staff time for training.

As the use of networks and electronic information increases, librarians are exploring ways to teach users how to integrate their use of print and electronic resources. Petrowski et al. (1995) describe a credit course for first-year undergraduates, "Designing the Electronic Village," the goal of which was to enable students to work collaboratively to design a rural information network, using assignments that would familiarize them with networked information tools, as well as building an understanding of the foundations of the research process. Assignments included joining and participating in a listserv, researching a particular Free-net, analyzing readings on various Internet topics as well as scholarly ethics, how to do research, how to organize Free-nets, and teaching other students how to use the Web.

At the University of Illinois at Urbana-Champaign, a joint task force of the Library and the Graduate School of Library and Information Science recently recommended that a combination of instructional approaches be established to provide students with a modular approach to learning the campus information infrastructure (Task Force on Library Instruction, 1995). Several approaches to instruction were proposed, including course-integrated instruction, workshops, short courses, and a credit course on information strategies and skills. The syllabus for "Information Seeking Strategies and Skills" integrates strategies for finding and evaluating print and networked information resources; the intended audience is primarily upper-division undergraduate students (see Appendix 2).

From a professional development standpoint, networking technology has enabled librarians involved in instruction to carry on continuing conversations on important practical and philosophical issues with colleagues all over the world through listservs such as BI-L and NETTRAIN. Professional organizations involved with instruction, such as the LOEX Clearinghouse, the ACRL Instruction Section, and ALA's LIRT (Library Instruction Round Table) now make resources available through the Internet and the Web that could previously be shared only through regular mail or less frequently at conferences.

All of this suggests that technology has had a profound impact on the direction of user instruction in libraries, perhaps enough to have changed the course of user education programs and to have elevated their importance in the library's organizational structure. Next, we shall examine some current conceptual and practical approaches to instruction for electronic resources.

Instruction for Electronic Access to Information

Online catalogs, end-user searching of journal citation databases, and CD-ROM systems represent perhaps the most fully developed area of technology-related instruction because they have been in existence the longest. Wanger (1979) presented an early review of the literature on the training and education of users of online systems. In the 1980s, the first online catalog instruction programs were typically one-shot workshops that focused on the mechanics of searching the online catalog, including formatting and executing commands and manipulating search results. Reports on these offerings suggest that, while attendance was usually low, attendees were enthusiastic about searching the online catalog. Many such programs have incorporated formal classroom sessions, printed guides, point-of-use materials, manuals, and assignments that are reviewed after the session.

With time, it became clear to librarians that users were not interested in learning how to search the online system as an end in itself, but rather as a means to the end of finding information on a topic of interest. In order to be complete in presenting information about the library's collections in the card catalog and in the online catalog, instruction sessions needed to focus on concepts rather than mechanics. Baker (1986) developed one of the first programs for the concept-based teaching of online catalog use. Research performed at Northwestern University Library revealed that undergraduate students who participated in a concept-based online catalog instruction program performed better on bibliographic searching tests than those who received no instruction or simple procedural instruction (Nielsen and Baker, 1987).

Lippincott (1987) identified five concepts that a user needs to understand to be able to exploit any electronic database:

- What a database is.
- What a bibliographic record is and what its fields and access points are.
- How to divide a topic into component parts (sets) for development of a search strategy.
- How to use controlled vocabulary and free text terms effectively.
- How Boolean operators or connectors are used to link terms or sets.

Lippincott emphasized the importance of teaching concepts in conjunction with skills or procedural knowledge. Although these points may now seem obvious, a significant amount of experimentation was devoted in the early 1980s to the identification of the most important elements to include in online system instruction and to the shaping of instruction modules around these. The development of gateway interfaces that provide access to numerous systems—including the online catalog, journal article databases, full text databases, and reference works—supports the need for instruction that emphasizes the commonality of approaches for accessing information as well as the differences in the contents of the various electronic sources.

Informal observation and experience with users who encounter searching problems has prompted the incorporation of various approaches to resolve either specific or general problems through instruction. Lancaster's early work with MEDLARS online revealed that users experienced difficulty in conceptualizing their information needs, choosing appropriate terminology, and developing search strategies to exploit the maximum retrieval power of the online system (Lancaster, 1972). Geffert (1995) suggests that problems in subject searching in online catalogs are due to users' lack of familiarity with the MARC format. He claims that users can perform more efficient searches if they understand several basic points about record and field structure:

- subject searches require specific and exact terminology,
- there is rarely any single heading that will elicit all relevant material,
- it is possible to limit searches by format, language, etc.,
- searching under different spellings sometimes brings up different records, and
- searches occasionally find records that apparently do not contain words from the search statement. (Pages 27-28)

Geffert describes an instruction program at St. Olaf College that includes a description of the MARC fields that are important for subject access (e.g., 245, title; 6xx subjects and LCSH) and an explanation of how to format searches to exploit these successfully. Much of online catalog instruction in the last decade or so has focused on similar issues related to concept-based instruction.

Newkirk and Jacobson (1994) suggest that it may not be profitable to emphasize relatively sophisticated search strategies when dealing with unsophisticated users. They found that students make little use of Boolean operators and field delimiters in searching CD-ROM databases and frequently retrieve too many items to be even browsable. Perhaps it would be more effective to realign instruction efforts toward helping such users refine their application of the simpler functions that they are more likely to employ in formatting a search.

The proliferation of CD-ROM databases with various search interfaces has necessitated the creation of numerous point-of-use guides or "cheat sheets" that a searcher can use as a reminder of the basics of how to format a search and which menu choices are appropriate in the various databases. Ironically, such simple printed guides offer perhaps the most direct and effective way of addressing the need to have instructions at the user's fingertips while executing a search in a CD-ROM or other electronic database. Online help has met with mixed response. Studies of OPAC transaction logs show that help screens are rarely consulted voluntarily. While the development of context-sensitive searching help in commercial CD-ROM products has somewhat improved the situation, it is clear that users rarely take the time to read online help screens unless the assistance is specific to their current problem.

Reese (1994) reports that the introduction of CD-ROM databases in her academic library caused a marked decline in requests for online searches and a considerable increase in requests for one-on-one instruction in the use of the databases, a situation common to many other institutions. Reese's study evaluates the use of several instructional tools, including one-on-one instruction, group instruction, point-of-use written guides, CAI tutorials, online help, and videotapes. Since most of the CD-ROM publishers develop CAI, online help, and videotapes to accompany their products, these teaching tools can be used flexibly by librarians without significant time spent on developing in-house approaches. She recommends that each library needs to determine the appropriate combination of instructional tools that are suitable for various user groups.

At the University of Houston, Wilson (1989) found that approximately one-half of all CD-ROM uses required staff intervention of some kind, which prompted the library to provide sixty hours a week of assistance to users in CD-ROM searching and to experiment with an expert systems approach to assisting users to find information at the point of need—the Intelligent Reference Information System (Bailey, 1992).

In 1994, the University of Washington and Apple Computer launched UWired—a cooperative project to promote student use of computers and networked information resources both inside and outside of the classroom. Several freshmen students were supplied with laptop computers, which they used in conjunction with course work and research. The Undergraduate Library and its staff at the University of Washington served as the locus for many of the instructional activities that comprised the program. The project is considered a success due to the ability of its planners to integrate fundamental information seeking and evaluation concepts into a technological setting (Sharpe, 1995).

Remote Users

The training of remote users represents both a challenge and an opportunity to reach new segments of the population. With the growth of remote access to online catalogs in the 1980s, many libraries assumed some responsibility for teaching users how to get connected and how to search the tools once they were successfully logged on. Davis (1988) describes an instructional effort at Indiana State University that included standard printed instructional materials as well as a "loaner kit" comprising an ASCII terminal, a modem, and a set of LCSH volumes. Faculty (groups or individuals) could check out the "Travelling LUIS" kit to learn more about remote access to ISU's online catalog. This unusual degree of library involvement in the technical aspects of access provision demonstrates the breadth and depth of concern that some librarians have applied to both user and staff training issues associated with remote access, and emphasizes the yet unresolved issues of who provides what type of help in a networked environment—the library, the computer center, or both?

At Texas A & M University Library, it was decided that the best approach to comprehensive remote access instruction was to create a user training manual containing instructions for connecting to the library's online system as well as a guide to searching for information in the online catalog. Jaros (1990) notes that care was also taken to design effective on-screen help to anticipate the questions or problems that might arise for remote users while searching the online catalog. After an initial mailing of information about remote access to faculty, the library experienced numerous telephone calls for technical assistance from users. It took two approaches to enable staff to respond to these requests for help: group training sessions were offered to users and all staff members were trained in remote access methods in order to be familiar with the various types of communications software that patrons were likely to be using.

More recently, libraries have begun using the Internet and the Web to deliver self-paced instructional modules to users and to foster interaction with remote users. Acting on the assumption that users with network connections are least likely to avail themselves of in-library instruction, Jensen and Sih (1995) targeted engineering faculty and students at two University of California campuses for a six-part self-paced tutorial on searching INSPEC delivered through e-mail. E-mail announcements to all faculty and graduate students in the physical science departments on the UC-San Diego and the UC-Berkeley campuses brought 377 requests for the tutorial within a week. Feedback from the participants was generally positive although only 20% reported that they had read all six of the assignments. Anecdotal comments suggested that the method may suit remote users better than other methods since several valued the opportunity to keep the modules and to refer to them when they had questions about searching the INSPEC database. Jensen and Sih, who have made the instructional modules freely available through FTP or the Web, also indicate that both campuses are moving to incorporate further Internet and Web-based instructional modules for remote users.

While progress has been made in this area, the instruction of remote users remains a significant problem. Engel (1991) highlights some of the difficulties when she points out that there are various degrees of "remoteness" among remote users. Users who obtain remote access to locally-accessible resources have the benefit of support connections from the local library or computing center. However, a user who is connecting to the online system of another institution may not have sufficient background information to search the catalog effectively. Engel describes several of the technical and content problems that are faced by remote searchers:

- database descriptions and new user help seldom provide the information needed to determine the actual contents of the databases on the system

  . . .

- special files are available only to the local community of each system because they are licensed from database producers for specific uses . . .

- Password requirements are confusing ... especially when the system requests "your library ID number" or when the user's local system also requires passwords ...
- locating collections unique to a remote system is difficult when items from special collections are cataloged with other holdings in a single database.*

(Pages 148-149)

Training of Library Staff

In the commercial sector, training, re-training, and client education programs are commonplace for those who work with computers, networking, and software. Staff acquire new technology skills that enable them to compete effectively in the work force and to enrich the work of their organizations. The category "information professional" is shared by individuals with numerous types of backgrounds, including librarians, all of whom manage information, either in the traditional, print-based world, in the networked world, or, increasingly, in both. Senge (1990) suggests that the most critical factor in its struggle for survival and success is the ability of the organization to learn continually and to transform its mission on the basis of new ideas and developments. Nevertheless, in most libraries, staff training programs do not occupy a permanent line in the organizational budget.

The shift away from building physical collections and toward providing access to information, increasingly networked information, which differs markedly in format from print-based information, makes it critical for library directors to identify training and retraining as a key element in their retooling of services for the twenty-first century. Jennings (1992) identifies the "regrowing" of staff as a management priority to ensure the long-term success of the university library in the networked information environment. She identifies a shift in values away from the traditional physically-based roles that demand new skills from library staff:

> ... libraries need to move away from a production mode of service to a facilitator mode. The process of selection, acquisition, cataloging, storage, and lending of library-owned collections will continue, but decline in importance in relation to new services that will enable clients to undertake the production process themselves with ease and efficiency in the electronic environment. The library's increasingly important new roles will be to provide clients with

---

*Special collections holdings are rarely indicated online.

advice about electronic information and to help them develop skills in accessing, using, and managing this information. There is no doubt that the staff profile of university libraries will change if the present production-based service declines as print collections are replaced by electronic publishing, delivery, and access. (Page 83)

Jennings also points out that "University libraries will be servicing both the traditional information gathering behavior of students and academic staff as well as their new needs as they participate in the scholar's workstation environment." She claims that changes are occurring too rapidly to be adequately addressed in the literature, in library school curricula, or in professional continuing education programs. Hence the need to work directly with staff in libraries to exact the needed changes in the approach to work and the range of information handled. She identifies specific areas in which librarians need training: the provision of access to finding tools, in print and electronic form; repackaging information that is considered essential for the institution; providing access to either on-site or remote information that is directly relevant to the needs of clients; facilitating on-demand access to information through fast and easy document delivery; advising clients in the identification, location, selection and management of their own repositories of information; and collaborating with related information professionals to provide cohesive access to a "campus information environment." Jennings recommends several approaches to training, including structured training programs, staff support and team learning, and performance feedback, as well as encouraging staff to explore networked resources and to learn on their own.

Holt (1995a) outlines what he believes are the ten most pertinent staff training issues of the 1990s. Several of these are related to the need for staff to become conversant with, and to stay at the forefront of, new technologies as they are introduced into the mainstream of library services:

> ... staff—especially professional staff—need to be trained to recognize that their employment opportunities will endure only so long as their skills are up to date
> . . . Cataloging may give way to abstracting; reference may give way to answering E-mail queries . . . All these changes require extensive re-training.
> . . . public librarians need to be trained in the skills of organizational effectiveness, including job empowerment.
> . . . training must make clear the real purpose of instituting a quality movement in a public library.

... public-library training needs to be built on correct assumptions about adult education.

... public librarians need to be trained to work increasingly with nonlibrarians. Specialists in computing, networked communications, literacy, education, training ... As library dependence on networked computing increases, shifting job roles and changing work will make regular retraining a survival imperative for all public librarians.

... public libraries will have to provide advanced and ongoing training in new technology. . . . technology training will become more technology based . . . . Already universities are using computer-based training modules on various library functions, including periodical access, resource sharing, reference, acquisition, and cataloging.

... increasingly, public libraries will train their constituents in the use of information technology. (Pages 559-560)

While many in the profession criticize the lack of proper support for permanent training programs, librarians have developed numerous approaches to training and re-training themselves in the uses of technology, with many rich and useful examples easily located in the literature. Many training programs develop at the operational level, organized by staff who are responsible for integrating technology. Other programs are organized by committees or task forces charged with devising, implementing, and periodically reviewing these programs. Yet others have been developed by professional associations or commercial enterprises.

Hickox (1994) surveyed 180 academic librarians in the AMIGOS consortium to determine how well current training programs were preparing them to use the Internet. He concluded that: "Academic librarians are generally dissatisfied with quality of received training for network use. Quality of training was uniformly ranked very low by respondents."

In a survey of the impact of technology on over two thousand support staff in the academic libraries of Wisconsin, Palmini (1994) reports that thirty-eight percent of respondents feel that on-the-job training in the use of technology is inadequate despite the fact that half of them spend fifty percent or more of their day working at a computer. Figure 10 shows the types of computer applications used by support staff as reported in Palmini's survey. It is noteworthy that two of the highest frequency functions—e-mail and word processing—are relatively new requirements and represent more general networking and office automation activities for which libraries have not traditionally organized training programs. In the past, training programs for library staff have centered upon specific functions and operations that need to be accomplished but the results of Palmini's survey suggest that training may need to be more broadly based to encompass prerequisite skills that fall outside the traditional scope of library staff training. Kriz and Queijo (1989) point out that pre-automation staff training programs were constructed around many physical cues involved in the processing of print-based materials. In an automated environment, the physical cues are no longer evident, which further complicates the training requirements:

> In a manual information system, the physical environment provides cues to action. Process control was guided by the handling of objects (such as pieces of paper in the form of order slips, invoices, books, and printed indexes) housed in a specific physical location (such as the acquisitions department or on the index tables.)
>
> When a library becomes heavily automated, the physical cues are no longer present or apparent. Information processing is converted from a physical to an abstract process. The employee no longer moves through a physical space and no longer manipulates physical objects containing the information ... today's library employee must learn to move through a virtual information space rather than a physical information space. To a large extent, the employee must build a mental map of that space in order to perform a job. (Page 63)

Developing a plan to address the actual training needs of staff working in an electronic environment, or a combination print/electronic environment, requires careful study and planning. Glogoff (1989) describes a program at the University of Delaware Library that includes formal needs assessment and training, a statement of goals, training a core group to train others, evaluation, self-paced workbook learning, manuals, and general orientation sessions.

A survey of the impact of training on the technology used in public libraries in Canada and in England (Cowan and Usherwood, 1992) revealed several needs for technology training for staff and for managers:

- learn how to operate equipment;
- keep informed of ongoing technology developments;
- learn how to develop databases for organizing and storing information;
- anticipate user needs

Automated System	% of Support Staff
Online catalog	75
E-mail	66
Word processing	63
Circulation system	46
OCLC	46
Cataloging system	37
Other (spreadsheet, data-manager, graphics, etc.)	31
CD-ROM databases	22
Acquisition system	22
Serials system	13
Interlibrary loan system	13

FIGURE 10

Types of automated systems used by support staff in Wisconsin academic libraries.

From Palmini (1994) by permission of the American Library Association

Tennant (1995) argues that library staff who work with electronic resources need to know not only what the resources are but also how to successfully apply them in their daily work:

> Staff is a library's single most expensive resource and should be treated that way. Any investment made in retooling staff skills to meet the challenges and opportunities of the electronic age will be repaid many times over in better service to clientele and a vital and engaged workforce. (Page 46)

Tennant advocates the establishment of a strong in-house training program for staff with leadership provided by an individual highly qualified in instructional methods. Training documentation should be developed and made available electronically to staff; they should use both traditional and electronic means of current awareness about technology developments, including listservs, SDI searches on specific topics, and email filters to route mail to topic-specific folders.

Technology has brought about considerable advances in the education and training programs offered by libraries, although technology itself has been the focus of a considerable portion of that instruction. Some are concerned that, in their willingness to adopt new technologies, librarians are not using instruction programs to represent the full scope and content of information resources in an objective way, putting undue emphases on those in electronic form. Oberman (1995) is one who has warned of this danger:

> A real unmasking of technology—stripping away the glamour, appeal, and convenience surrounding its use in librarianship—leads to the realization that librarians should really be striving, as always, for the creation of an environment in which access to information, knowledge, and ideas can flourish. By this, I do not mean the *illusion* of access—which I fear is what most users now understand to be access. Searches must be preceded by a thorough understanding of the variety of resources available and the differences among them in content, authority, and viewpoint. The risk is to allow technology to become the dominant player in information-seeking behavior, thereby limiting the type of information to which users are exposed and denying them an opportunity to learn the politics of information . . . Librarians should resist allowing a technology to preconstruct our mode of thinking and teaching . . . (Page 38)

CHAPTER 5

Management Data from Automated Systems

IOIOIOIOIOIOIOIOIOIOIOIOIOIOIOIOIOIOIOIOIOIOIOIOIOIOIOIOIOIOIOIOIOIOIOIOIOIOI

ONE COULD MAKE A STRONG CASE to support the claim that the major potential benefits of automated systems in libraries are the data they can provide to improve the management of the library's resources (Lancaster, 1983). In other words, the automated system should be seen primarily as a management information or decision support system. Speaking specifically of automated acquisitions systems, Hawks (1986) has said:

> Not the least of the benefits of automating . . . is the enhanced ability to mon-itor processes, to collect, structure, analyze, and report critical or useful data previously unavailable or extremely difficult or costly to obtain. (Page 246)

But the Johnson (1991) survey, discussed in Chapter 1, clearly shows that better management information is not seen as a major objective of automation in academic libraries and that automation is not considered to have had much effect in improving management control or decision making.

By the same token, the vendors of automated systems for libraries do not emphasize this capability and perhaps fail to recognize the true potentials of their own systems in this respect. In 1992, one of the authors sent a letter to the major vendors of automated library systems in North America, requesting information on their "management infor-mation" capabilities. Responses indicated that vendors tend to see their "management reports" in rather pedestrian terms, providing fairly routine statistical and financial data, of the type common to business systems in general, rather than more sophisticated reports specific to library needs (e.g., to aid in collection development decisions).*

---

*This is not to suggest that these routine data—budget data, typical circulation data, and so on—are not important, but that we have chosen to deal in this book with management data that are less common and especially with data that apply only to the library field.

Available Management Reports

Hawks (1986, 1988) provides a useful summary of fairly routine data that can be obtained from present automated systems. She identifies five major types of management reports. While she is dealing specifically with acquisitions systems, the areas she identifies are applicable, in a broad sense, to automated library systems in general:

1. Fund accounting
2. Vendor performance
3. Collection management
4. Order control
5. Systems management

Of these, only the collection management reports are unique to the library situation (and even these can be considered as merely special forms of inventory control reports); the other types are widely used beyond the library environment.

Systems management reports are reports providing data on the system itself—how much it is used, how it is used, where it is used from, and so on. This aspect will be dealt with in Chapter 14 since it is related to the topic of systems evaluation.

While Hawks includes collection management reports among the types that present systems can produce, the reports that can be routinely generated by commercially available systems today are relatively unsophisticated. The subject of collection management is dealt with in detail in the next chapter.

Fund accounting reports (how much money was allocated to a particular fund, how much is already spent, how much is committed, how much remains) and order control reports (what items are on order, from where, when the order was placed, and so on) are completely routine today in libraries of all sizes. They are not unique to the library situation and need not concern us further here.

The vendor performance reports are less routine and, indeed, it was very difficult to collect data of these kind in a systematic way prior to the adoption of automated acquisitions systems. Figure 11 shows a vendor record, displayable on a terminal, from the INNOPAC acquisitions module. Note how the data recorded can be used to generate reports relating to vendor performance—what proportion of the items ordered is delivered within X period of time, what proportion is never delivered at all, what level of discount is provided, and so on. A more complete record of bookseller performance, allowing comparisons to be made over different time periods, is shown in Figure 12.

```
Vendor : hall                        BASIC DATA

     Address1 1: G.K. Hall & Company          Address2 1: G.K. Hall & Company
              2: 70 Lincoln Street                     2: P.O. Box 6000
              3: Boston, MA 02111                      3: Boston, MA 02100
     Alternative code: 89764
     Claim Cycle : b
        NOTES:
     ────────────────────── VENDOR STATISTICS FOR G.K. HALL ──────────────────

                    Orders :        10      Open orders:                   13
                    Claims :         2      Amount of open orders : $40.50
           Orders claimed :          2      Percent Claimed :             20%
          Orders canceled :          0      Percent Canceled :             0%
          Orders received :          8      Avg. weeks to deliver :        3
             Amount paid :     $227.14      # of Copies Received :         8

                         INVOICES PAID TO G.K. HALL

   NO.    INV. NO.    AMOUNT    INV. DATE    PAID DATE    VOUCHER    # OF ITEMS
   1      160655      $22.50    11/06/92     12/15/92      334          1
   2      122647      $257.76   03/04/93     03/18/93      1653         6
   3      56754       $19.38    07/08/93     08/20/93      2286         1
   4      22715       $30.00    10/06/93     11/20/93      3856         2
```

FIGURE 11

Example of vendor record from an automated acquisitions module.
Reproduced by permission of Innovative Interfaces Inc.

Carried to its logical conclusion, a vendor performance module might be used to select a vendor automatically based on past performance in the supply of publications of a particular type. Such a capability would be especially valuable in the acquisition of materials that are less routine—conference proceedings, certain technical reports, publications in certain languages, publications from certain countries, and so on.

Pontigo et al. (1992) have described a type of expert system designed to select vendors in this way. The system described has a learning capability: the performance factors associated with each vendor are updated automatically as the system gathers further data on vendor performance. In fact, the system is designed to rank potential vendors by the probability that they will be able to supply a particular item needed.

Mean number of weeks from order to receipt or report

Order placed	No. rec'd	Wks to receipt	No. rep'd	Wks to report	Vols ordered	% rec'd	% rep'd unavail.
Financial year 1982/3	2741	12.1	143	16.2	2930	94	5
1983/4[a]	776	12.0	36	12.5	820	95	4
1984/5	2076	12.6	54	15.9	2194	95	2
Quarter Apr.–Jun. 1985	33	8.3	0		40	82	0
Jul.–Sep. 1985							
Oct.–Dec. 1985							
Jan.–Mar. 1986							
Overall	5626	12.3	233	15.5			
% of all suppliers	29	113	44	85			

Note:
(a) 1983/4 figures adjusted to alleviate the effect of lost data.

Pattern of receipt or reporting

Months to receipt or report	Financial year 1983/4			Financial year 1984/5			Financial year 1985/6		
	No.	%	Cum. %	No.	%	Cum. %	No.	%	Cum. %
Within 1 month	7	1	1	66	3	3	0	1	1
1–2 months	243	30	31	297	14	17	13	38	39
2–3 months	401	50	81	966	45	62	20	61	100
3–4 months	46	6	87	515	24	86		0	100
4–5 months	19	2	89	166	8	93		0	100
5–6 months	10	1	90	82	4	97		0	100
6–7 months	16	2	92	25	1	98		0	100
7–8 months	6	1	93	27	1	99		0	100
8–9 months	16	2	95	7	0	100		0	100
9–10 months	25	3	98	2	0	100		0	100
10–11 months	3	0	99	1	0	100		0	100
11–12 months	6	1	99	0	0	100		0	100
12–13 months	5	1	100	1	0	100		0	100
More than 13 months	8			1					
Total for less than 13 months	803			2 155			33		

FIGURE 12

Bookseller performance data from an automated system.

Reprinted from Lantz (1986) by kind permission of Bowker-Saur,
a division of Reed Business Information, and the Institute of Information Scientists

A similar system, known as the Monographic Acquisitions Consultant, was developed at Iowa State University (Zager and Smadi, 1992;
Hawks, 1994). The system was designed to optimize the decision on
which vendors to go to for particular types of monographs. The knowledge base of the system includes both descriptive and evaluative data
on each supplier. Descriptive data deal with type of publisher (foreign,
university press, publisher of science materials) and relationship with
the library (blanket order, approval plan, standing order, on exchange
list), while the evaluative data cover aspects of service (delivery time, accuracy, discounts, shipping and handling charges, and so on). The eval-

uative elements can be weighted and the system can thus assign a composite numerical score to each vendor based on the company's previous performance for the library. As Hawks (1994) describes:

> In the selection process, the vendor with the highest score who can supply a given type of material is recommended. Once a certain number of orders has been sent to that vendor in a given time period, the vendor with the next highest rating will be selected instead, supporting the library's goal of using multiple vendors. (Page 208)

This system and the one developed in Mexico by Pontigo et al. (1992) were implemented as prototypes but have not been used on a full production basis. Hardware problems and the cost involved in updating the knowledge base were mentioned as problems preventing full adoption in Iowa, although it was shown that the system could save a considerable amount of professional time in the actual selection of vendors.

Along the same lines, but somewhat less ambitious, is a system developed at Pennsylvania State University to determine whether or not a particular title is likely to be received through one of the library's many approval plans (Brown, 1993). Criteria incorporated into the knowledge base, and used to determine probability of receipt, are publisher, subject, price, year of publication, and place of publication. Again, while a prototype was developed and tested, the system has not been fully implemented.

Other expert systems, designed to help library users satisfy their own needs, have also included document ordering aids (e.g., Bianchi and Giorgi, 1986; Waldstein, 1986).

Desirable Reports

If the automated systems now in place in libraries appear rather modest in their management information capabilities, Chaudhry (1993) has gone to the opposite extreme in his list of management reports *expected* (emphasis ours) from automated systems. His list is reproduced in Figure 13.

Chaudhry's checklist is useful because it is comprehensive and serves to remind the librarian of data that might be valuable in support of management decisions as well as data that could be generated by an automated system. Nevertheless, the list ranges from data of extreme importance to data that are relatively trivial, from data that virtually all

Collection Use Analysis

1. Circulation statistics
   - number of transactions by patron type
   - number of transactions by location
   - number of transactions by type of material
   - number of transactions by call number

2. In library use
   - ability to record in building use by scanning labels of materials being reshelved
   - supply of information on utilization of collection for staff scheduling

3. Photocopy support
   - statistics on volume of photocopying done
   - provision for photocopy statistics for titles
   - information on number of copies made by titles
   - generation of reports of photocopies

4. Circulation history data
   - provision for retention of historical data on title use
   - statistics on the number of times an item (copy or title) has circulated

5. Use exception reports
   - reports on items not circulated in a specified time
   - reports on items circulated for less than a specified number
   - reports on items circulated for more than a specified number

6. Reserve statistics
   - number of holds placed and items recalled
   - reserve statistics by user and material type
   - automatic printing of purchase alerts (when holds against a title reach a specified level)
   - statistics on material booking
   - reports by hour, day, week and month

7. Interlibrary loan
   - statistics on requests received and filled
   - statistics on requests sent and material received
   - average turnaround time
   - total number of items loaned
   - lending/borrowing ratio

Use of Facilities

1. Discussion rooms
   - inventory of availability of meeting rooms
   - use of special seats/carrels

2. Equipment
   - booking and issue frequency statistics by type of equipment: (AV, microforms, etc.)

3. Terminals
   - amount of time terminals are in active use

Continued

FIGURE 13

Data useful to the library manager, some of which could be generated automatically.

From Chaudhry (1993) by permission of the International Federation of Library Associations and Institutions

4. Printers
- number of records printed online/offline
- printer use by terminal and/or location
- printer use statistics by the hour, day, week. etc.

Searching

1. Searching statistics
- number of searches performed by search type: author, title, subject, series
- number of searches by terminal, group of terminals, library units

2. Response time
- High, low, and mean response time for each search/type of search

3. Searches in progress
- daily high, low and mean number of searches in progress in any one hour

4. Public catalogue use statistics

Collection Development Reports

1. Summary of orders
2. Subject selection lists
3. Selector performance reports
4. Desiderata reports
5. Material notification
6. Reports of order types
7. Subscription lists
8. Standing order reports
9. Aging reports: outstanding orders and claims
10. Reports on withdrawals and transfers
11. Holdings and new additions: by location, call number, and language and other library-specified formats
12. Gifts and exchange reports

Cataloguing Reports

1. Online records used for cataloguing
2. Records input from other sources
3. Local/original records input
4. Records created/items processed
5. Records created online
6. Catalogue cards, bar coded labels, spine labels produced
7. Authority subscription activities:
- source of authority records, number of authority records input and number of records modified

Financial Reports

1. Fund control reports
2. Accounting information
3. Payment information
4. Year end processing
5. Next year projections
6. Currency conversion reports
7. Fine reports
8. Missing/lost books cost

FIGURE 13 *continued*

Systems Transactions

1. Transaction log
   - activity log automatically printed
   - error messages by terminal/system wide
   - help messages by terminal/system wide

2. Database statistics
3. Dial-up access statistics
4. Down time statistics

Vendor Performance Reports

1. Orders placed and completed
2. Claims sent and responded
3. Delivery time
4. Returns
5. Pricing discrepancies
6. Discount percentages

Staff Productivity Reports

1. Performance reports
2. Personnel action summaries
3. Staff productivity data
4. Quality control reports

FIGURE 13 *continued*

libraries now collect to data that are very difficult to collect, and includes data that could not be generated routinely as a byproduct of the operation of automated systems.

CHAPTER 6

Automated Systems in Collection Management

IOIOIOIOIOIOIOIOIOIOIOIOIOIOIOIOIOIOIOIOIOIOIOIOIOIOIOIOIOIOIOIOIOIOIOIOIOIOIOIOI

Automated systems can provide data on the use of library collections that are more complete than those available in the pre-automation era. Consequently, collection development policies, and collection management in general, should now be better than they were in the past. "Better" here implies decisions that are more effective or more cost-effective: buying more of the things that patrons really need, buying fewer that will never be used or used only rarely, buying more items whose cost-per-use will be low.

Various aspects of the use of automated systems in collection management have been dealt with in the literature. Perhaps the most complete overview is that of Nutter (1987). Figure 14 shows ways in which various electronic databases can be used to yield data of potential value in collection management decisions.

1. Analysis of present holdings
2. Comparison with external databases
3. Analysis of present circulation
4. Building of special databases
5. Comparison of data relating to holdings, circulation, acquisitions and interlibrary loan
6. Monitoring OPAC interactions

FIGURE 14
Possible ways in which automated systems can yield data useful in collection development

Analysis of the Collection

As Nutter (1987) points out, the online catalog, representing what the library now owns, can be used to produce a detailed analysis of the present collection. Tabulations can be produced for such variables as language, country of publication, date of publication, subject, and publication type, and useful correlations can also be made—for example, between subject and language or subject and date of publication. Simple but detailed analyses of this type might in themselves suggest strengths and weaknesses in the collection, and the data can be used to monitor changes over time. In an academic setting, the analyses of holdings can be compared with "profiles" of the various academic departments or faculties, where these profiles are defined by numbers from the scheme of classification used to organize the collection.

A good example of the analysis of the holdings of academic libraries can be found in the work of Kountz (1991), who compared holdings data with data on student course enrollment to measure the extent to which collections match "constituency interests."

Comparison with External Databases

Nutter (1987) suggests that one approach to the evaluation of a collection is to compare it with external databases to identify strengths, weaknesses, items that should probably be acquired, and so on. This seems particularly appropriate to the special library situation. For example, a medical library might compare its monograph acquisitions over, say, the last five years with the acquisitions of the National Library of Medicine (NLM) in the same time period, as represented in NLM's monographic database. Comparisons could be made on the basis of class numbers, where the local library makes use of NLM's classification, or subject headings. The ratio of local library acquisitions to NLM acquisitions in various subject areas could be taken as an indicator of areas in which the local library appears strong and areas in which it appears weak.

Another type of holdings/database comparison involves the use of databases searched online on behalf of library users. The bibliographic references actually retrieved in such searches presumably reflect the interests of library users, or at least those who make use of the database searching service. By downloading the references retrieved by all searches performed during a particular period of time, a useful database can be created. Analyses can then be performed on the resulting data. Most obviously, one can produce a list of journals ranked by the number of times they have been retrieved, and this may reveal certain titles that should perhaps be added to the collection because they seem to match current community interests rather closely. Again, this type of analysis is likely to be more valuable in the special library than in the general library. Lancaster et al. (1991) present an example of how search results can be used in this way in an academic library setting.

Circulation Analysis

Although it has always been possible to perform analyses of circulation records to study use of the collection, at least on a sampling basis, studies of this kind are greatly facilitated when circulation is automated. Records representing all circulations, rather than a sample, can be manipulated by computer program to produce data on subject distribution of the circulation, to identify the most heavily used titles, and (if the data are collected for a sufficiently long period) to measure rate of obsolescence. The most obvious application of circulation data is to produce analyses of use of the collection by subject according to the various subdivisions of the classification scheme in use in the library.

Jain (1965-1969) pointed out that librarians should be less concerned with establishing the absolute use of portions of a collection than with determining "relative" use. What this really means is that one should use circulation data to reveal differences between actual and "expected" behavior. Suppose, for example, that books on physics make up 12% of a particular collection. Probability alone suggests that physics books should account for 12% of the circulation. If they do, that portion of the collection is behaving exactly as expected. On the other hand, if physics books account for only 8% of the circulation, one can say that the class is "underused" (used less than expected) whereas it would be "overused" if it accounts for, say, 15% of all circulation. An overused class is one in which items are used more than expected (in a probabilistic sense) relative to the proportion of the collection occupied by that class. An underused class is one in which items are used less than expected relative to the proportion of the collection occupied by that class.

If data on the library's holdings in various classes are built into an automated circulation system, printouts or displays can be generated to show for each class what proportion of the collection it occupies and what proportion of the circulation it accounts for. An example is given in Figure 15.

The table shows that circulation in 620 and 640 is close to what is expected, while classes 610 and 650 are heavily overused and 630 is heavily underused. An automated circulation system could be used to generate such data in a more useful format; e.g., identify those classes that deviate most from the expected behavior—those most overused and those most underused (see Dowlin and Magrath, 1983, for an example based on public library circulation).

| | Collection | | Circulation | |
Class	Number of books	% of collection	Number of items borrowed	% of circulation
610	172	.17	65	.45
620	309	.31	48	.33
630	524	.52	27	.19
640	602	.60	73	.52
650	144	.14	35	.25

FIGURE 15

Hypothetical "relative use" data for selected subdivisions of Dewey class 600

The assumption is that the most deviant classes are those that need most attention. The circulation data merely highlight the deviant classes; they do not tell the librarian how to deal with them. One could argue that both overused and underused classes may fail to meet user needs. If a class is heavily overused (true of 610 in Figure 15 which gets almost three times the expected volume of use), the implication is that the library lacks the strength in this area to meet the present volume and variety of demands. The more overused a class, the lower the probability that any particular book will be on the shelf when looked for by a user. Moreover, the more overused the class, the less valuable it will be to the browser because of the phenomenon of "shelf bias." Shelf bias refers to the fact that, all other things being equal, the shelves of a library will tend to display books that nobody wants to borrow. The phenomenon was identified explicitly by Buckland (1972) and Buckland and Hindle (1969), who referred to it as "collection bias." "Shelf bias" seems more descriptive of what is actually taking place. Buckland (1975) expresses the bias in terms of the proportion of the material absent from the shelves at a particular time. Thus, if 80 books out of 240 were absent, the bias would be 33%.

A heavily underused class may be just as disturbing as one heavily overused. The class appears not to be of much interest to the community. This may reflect changing interests over time. On the other hand, it may indicate that the selection of books is just not a good one. Perhaps the library is buying the wrong books (e.g., too technical or too theoretical) or that it owns too many books that are out-of-date and should be discarded. It is possible that use of the class would increase substantially if it were thoroughly weeded and more attractive, up-to-date items added.

Circulation data can bring "problem" classes to the librarian's attention. It is then the librarian's task to look more closely at such classes to decide why they are behaving as they are and what corrective action appears to be necessary.

The degree of discrepancy between holdings and circulation can be expressed in several ways. The simplest, perhaps, is the "circulation/inventory ratio" (C/I) used by Wenger et al. (1979), which is nothing more than the number of circulations occurring in a class during a particular period of time divided by the number of items in that class. Thus, a class with seven items and twenty circulations receives a C/I ratio of 2.9 (20/7), i.e., approximately 2.9 uses per item per x period of time (usually a year).* Dowlin and Magrath (1983) also use this but refer to it as "inventory use ratio." The Public Library Association (PLA), in its output measures for public libraries (Van House et al., 1987), uses the term "turnover rate" for the same measure (i.e., uses per item per year). Following the recommendations of the PLA, and of various state library agencies, many public libraries in the United States collect turnover data, although few seem to make intelligent use of them. In fact, the turnover rate for a complete

---

*They also suggest the introduction of a time variable, incorporating in the equation the number of days the library was open during the period represented by the use data. Thus

$$\frac{20 \text{ circulations}}{(7 \text{ books}) \times (64 \text{ days})}$$

yields a figure of 0.00446 circulations per book per day.

collection is of very little interest (except, perhaps, in comparing the performance of similar libraries). What is of interest is the turnover rate for various parts of the collection. Figure 16 gives turnover rates for different classes of adult nonfiction for a small public library in Illinois. The turnover rate for adult nonfiction as a whole (1.11) masks the fact that the turnover ranges from a low of .51 (about one half of a use per book per year) for class 800 to 1.84 for class 400. The table shows how turnover rate correlates well with relative use. For example, class 400 has high relative use (circulation is almost twice what probability suggests it should be) and the highest turnover, and class 800, with the lowest turnover rate, is used at exactly half the level expected (10% of the collection and 5% of the use). The data from Figure 16 suggest that the classes in most immediate need of attention are 800 and 920 since both are heavily underused.

West Chicago Public Library District
July 1, 1989-June 30, 1990
Adult Non-fiction

Class	Holdings	Percentage of nonfiction collection	Circulation	Percentage of nonfiction circulation	Turnover rate
000	527	2	610	2	1.16
100	808	4	1,129	5	1.40
200	665	3	543	2	.82
300	3,339	15	3,361	14	1.01
400	250	1	461	2	1.84
500	1,022	5	1,105	5	1.08
600	4,956	22	7,702	32	1.55
700	3,585	16	4,881	20	1.36
800	2,204	10	1,133	5	.51
900	2,062	9	1,679	7	.81
910	950	4	646	3	.68
920	1,701	8	1,171	5	.69
Total	22,069		24,421		1.11

FIGURE 16
Collection use data from a small public library in Illinois.
Reprinted by permission of the West Chicago Public Library District

Day and Revill (1995) discuss a variant on turnover rate in which recent acquisitions only are related to circulation. While this makes sense, it would make even more sense to compare circulation with both total holdings and recent acquisitions.

Nimmer (1980) has used the measure "intensity of circulation"—number of circulations per 100 titles held. Bonn (1974) proposed a simple "use factor" (renamed as "degree of use" by Gillentine et al., 1981), which is the proportion (or percentage) of the circulation accounted for by a class divided by the proportion of the collection occupied by that class. With this type of ratio, as used by Jenks (1976), the higher the figure the greater the overuse. For example, a class accounting for 3.49% of the collection and 4.79% of the circulation receives a score of 137.25 while one that accounts for .36% of the collection but only .16% of the circulation gets a score of 44.44. Metz (1983) refers to this measure as the "proportional use statistic" and Aguilar (1986) as "percentage of expected use." Aguilar derived his use of this measure from Mills (1982).

Trochim et al. (1980) use the *difference* between holdings percentage and collection percentage for each class as an indicator of overuse or underuse. Mills (1982) is critical of this: a difference of 0.2 would apply equally to a subject occupying 0.5% of the collection and getting 0.7% of the use as it would to one occupying 2.5% of the collection and getting 2.7% of use, yet the proportional discrepancy between holdings and use is very much greater for the smaller class.

Mostyn (1974) uses the term "supply-demand equality" in referring to the relative use relationship; an overused class is one in which demand exceeds supply and vice versa for an underused class.

Mills (1982) has applied the relative use principle to the problems of collection development in a film library. In a typical film library, films have to be "booked" (i.e., reserved) in advance, so it has an advantage over most other types of library in that failure rates (i.e., "denials"—cases when particular films or films of a certain type are not available to the requester) are easy to identify and record. Mills makes use of this failure rate, as well as a measure of relative use, to make decisions relating to future acquisitions. Some of his data are shown in Figure 17. The percentage of holdings related to the percentage of bookings gives a percentage of expected use. Thus, art films account for 1% of holdings and

0.88% of bookings, so the percentage of expected use is 88. The denial to bookings ratio brings in further data. A high D/B ratio means that films in this category are unlikely to be available when needed by a user. The worst case is "stories—holidays and seasons," where 74% of the requests for films have to be denied (D/B ratio = 0.74). On the basis of relative use data (percentage of expected use), the difference between percentage of bookings and percentage of holdings, and D/B ratio, Mills is able to make recommendations relating to future acquisitions: some classes need to be strengthened by further purchases, which might be further copies of things already owned ("add prints"), some need to be weeded, and some should be strengthened and weeded.

Britten (1990) uses the "80/20" rule as the basis of a study of circulation in an academic library.* He found that, while the rule seemed to apply to the complete collection, substantial differences among the LC classes could be observed. For one subclass, 40% of the items are needed to account for 80% of the circulations. At the other extreme is a class in which only 1.5% of the items account for 80% of the use. He advocates that the classes that deviate most from the 80/20 distribution in a positive way (a higher proportion needed to account for 80% of the use) should be "rewarded" in future collection development and budget allocation. Clearly, this type of comparison of the performance of various categories of books is merely another variant of relative use or the turnover rate.

Lee and Lockway (1991) also use percentage of expected use to indicate the most deviant classes in the collection, in this case in an academic library. Figure 18 shows sample data from their analysis for selected Library of Congress classes. At one extreme, class HV5001, which accounts for 0.0809% of the collection, gets 0.5598% of the use, a use factor (UF) of 6.92 or a PEU (percentage of expected use) of 692. In contrast, class LH earns a UF of only 0.03 and a PEU of 3.

There are other ways of expressing overuse and underuse of portions of the collection. One is the proportion of items on loan (and, conversely, the proportion that should be on the shelf) at a particular time. A class in which many of the items are in use is a healthy class whereas one from

---

*The 80/20 rule refers to the fact that roughly 80% of use tends to come from roughly 20% of items, whatever these items happen to be—books, words, consumer products, and so on.

Subject	Holdings (%)	Bookings (%)	Percentage of expected use	Denial to bookings ratio	Collection development recommendations
Art	1.00	0.88	88.00	0.12	
Dance	0.06	0.05	83.33	0.45	Add prints
Drama	0.08	0.05	62.50	0.31	
Music	0.71	0.80	112.67	0.17	
Africa	0.33	0.22	66.66	0.12	
Asia	0.52	0.38	73.07	0.15	
Canada	0.14	0.11	78.57	0.18	
Europe & USSR	0.74	0.68	91.89	0.15	
Latin America	0.65	0.78	120.00	0.23	
Maps & Globes	0.24	0.17	70.83	0.33	Add prints
South Pacific	0.05	0.02	40.00	0.07	
US Geography-General	0.24	0.19	79.16	0.17	
US Geography-National Parks	0.08	0.09	112.50	0.12	
US Geography-States & Regions	0.35	0.18	51.42	0.11	Weed
World Geography-General	0.21	0.16	76.19	0.30	
Guidance	1.99	1.41	70.85	0.27	Weed
Health & Hygiene	0.44	0.27	61.36	0.22	Weed
Human Body	0.36	0.27	75.00	0.20	
Nutrition	0.22	0.27	122.72	0.17	
Physical Education	0.12	0.09	75.00	0.40	Add prints
Safety	0.56	0.35	62.50	0.18	Weed
Sex Education	0.08	0.03	37.50	0.07	
Sports	0.14	0.12	85.71	0.14	
Biography	0.12	0.12	100.00	0.24	
US Hist-General	0.34	0.30	88.23	0.22	
US Hist-Discovery & Exploration	0.10	0.09	90.00	0.12	
US Hist-Colonial & Revolutionary Periods	0.51	0.45	88.23	0.12	
US Hist-1732-1900	0.34	0.29	85.29	0.17	
US Hist-1900-Present	0.02	0.01	50.00	0.05	
World History	0.44	0.47	106.81	0.20	
Creative Motivation	0.89	0.73	82.02	0.22	
Foreign Language	0.17	0.26	152.94	0.23	
Library	0.09	0.05	55.55	0.17	
Poetry	0.17	0.12	70.58	0.09	
Reading	0.44	0.30	68.18	0.17	
Speech	0.15	0.10	66.66	0.17	
Stories-Animals	0.81	0.41	50.61	0.18	Weed
Stories-Cartoons & Comedies	0.50	0.32	64.00	0.14	Weed
Stories-General	2.01	1.65	82.08	0.22	
Stories-Holidays & Seasons	0.47	0.19	40.42	0.74	Weed & add prints
Study Skills	0.48	0.34	70.83	0.34	Add prints
Writing	0.31	0.27	87.09	0.22	
Arithmetic Operations	0.61	0.47	77.04	0.13	
Geometry	0.12	0.06	50.00	0.09	

FIGURE 17

Collection use data for a film library.

Modified from Mills (1982) by permission of the author

which few items are borrowed is not—little interest exists in this subject in the community, the library is not buying the right books, or the
class contains too much that is obsolete. On the other hand, it is not good
to have a class in which most books are always absent from the shelves;
this would indicate considerable shelf bias, and the probability that a
user would find a particular item on the shelf when needed must be very
low. Extremely active classes of this kind need strengthening, at least
through the purchase of further copies of the most used items.

Class	Items owned	Percentage of collection	Items circulated in X period	Percent of total circulation	UF	PEU
HV5001	372	0.0809%	2,925	0.5598%	6.92	692
BF866	19	0.0041%	132	0.0253%	6.17	617
HV5800	45	0.0978%	2,562	0.4903%	5.01	501
HF5801	655	0.1424%	3,413	0.6532%	4.59	459
BF1001	36	0.0800%	1,867	0.3573%	4.47	447
LH	85	0.0185%	3	0.0006%	0.03	3
Totals	460,109	100%	522,515	100%		

FIGURE 18
Circulation data used to identify most deviant classes in a collection.
Modified from Lee and Lockway (1991) by permission of Haworth Press

The monitoring of collection use by proportions of classes absent from
the shelves is not dependent on automation and, in fact, predated
automated systems (see, for example, McClellan, 1956, 1978). Nevertheless,
such monitoring is much easier when data can be drawn from an
automated circulation system. Figure 19, from Payne and Willers (1989),
is one example. Note the very wide differences between heavily used
classes, in which more than 20% of the items are on loan, and little used
classes in which less than 5% are in use. In performing analyses of this
kind, items that cannot be borrowed (i.e., reference only) should obviously be excluded.

Automated circulation records can also be used to identify items in
a collection that are receiving little use and, thus, may be candidates for
discarding or retirement to storage. Use can be expressed in several

Class no. range	Stock items (annual census) July 1985	Number of items on loan May 1986	Percent of stock on loan May 1986	Percent of stock on loan March 1986
001-009	1,029	176	17.10	(14.58)
010-099	913	2	0.22	(0.11)
100-199	690	48	6.96	(11.74)
200-299	28	2	7.14	(0.00)
300-309	1,507	79	5.24	(7.43)
310-319	5	0	0.00	(0.00)
320-329	465	48	10.32	(9.89)
330-334	9,558	940	9.83	(11.14)
335-339	7,848	716	9.12	(9.28)
340-345	4,035	571	14.15	(14.30)
346-349	3,590	777	21.64	(21.11)
350-359	713	22	3.09	(5.33)
360-369	1,232	63	5.11	(7.47)
370-379	346	5	1.45	(0.87)
380-389	3,731	113	3.03	(3.62)
390-399	8	0	0.00	(0.00)
400-499	41	1	2.44	(2.44)
500-599	1,424	231	16.22	(13.13)
600-649	433	8	1.85	(1.62)
650-656	258	17	6.59	(6.59)
657-657.9	4,616	714	15.47	(13.65)
658-658.7	6,009	691	11.50	(10.72)
658.8-659	1,793	402	22.42	(19.74)
660-699	86	0	0.00	(0.00)
700-799	426	9	2.11	(1.64)
800-899	91	6	6.59	(9.89)
900-999	537	6	1.12	(1.12)
All	51,412	5,647	10.98	(10.99)

FIGURE 19

Collection use measured by proportion of each class in circulation at a particular time.

Reprinted from Payne and Willers (1989) by kind permission of Bowker-Saur, a division of Reed Business Information, and the Institute of Information Scientists different ways, including the length of time that has elapsed since a book was last borrowed. In fact, "last circulation date" can be used to partition the monograph collection by "levels of popularity," where popularity is expressed in terms of the last circulation date, as shown in Figure 20.

It is also possible to use the circulation system to "flag" items that are now used so heavily that additional copies should be purchased or some other steps taken to improve their availability. In fact, several commercially-available systems have an alert feature to identify items for which X patrons have placed "holds."

Popularity class	Measure of popularity	Percentage of the collection
A	Borrowed in the last month	3
B	Borrowed in the last three months but not in last month	10
C	Borrowed in the last year but not in last three months	25
D	Borrowed in last five years but not last year	30
E	Not borrowed in last five years	32

FIGURE 20
Levels of "popularity" in a hypothetical monograph collection
based on the last time books were borrowed

Building of Special Databases

Analyses of circulation patterns of the type discussed in the preceding section are based on data that can be drawn from an existing database—that recording which items are borrowed, when, and by whom. But it is also possible to build other databases that can be useful in making decisions relating to collection development and management.

One such database would record in-house use of the collection. In the past, it has been notoriously difficult to get good data on in-library use (Rubin, 1986; Lancaster, 1993a). Today, however, portable data collection devices can be used to scan bar codes or OCR labels on books left on tables or in carrels in the library before they are returned to the shelves. This procedure is likely to underestimate the total volume of inhouse use, perhaps rather considerably, because not all uses will involve carrying items to seats in the library and many items may be returned to shelves by users (Lancaster, 1993a). Nevertheless, it should depict the pattern of in-house use fairly accurately: if the data show that X items are used five times more than Y items, this probably does reflect the relative use of these two sets, even though both counts may be underestimates.

Lee and Lockway (1991) have discussed the use of data gathered in this way in collection development policies. They refer to it as a "browse-use" factor for the collection. Figure 21 shows representative data for five Library of Congress classes. For example, HV5001 contains 372 items, which is 0.0809% of the total collection, and it received 1787 recorded uses in a particular period of time, which is 0.3338% of the total uses recorded. The class is used 4.13 times more than expected (.08% versus .33%), giving a "use factor" (UF) of 4.13 or a "percentage of expected use" (PEU) of 413.

Class	Items owned	Percentage of collection	Browse use	Percentage of browse use	UF	PEU
HV5001	372	0.0809%	1,787	0.3338%	4.13	413
BF	8,483	1.8437%	12,420	2.3198%	1.26	126
PN	17,690	3.8447%	19,819	3.7018%	0.96	96
PZ	14,564	3.1653%	13,735	2.5654%	0.81	81
LB	20,159	4.3814%	14,561	2.7197%	0.62	62

FIGURE 21
Representative in-house use data.
Modified from Lee and Lockway (1991) by permission of Haworth Press

Rapidly escalating costs, coupled with budgets diminishing in purchasing power, have forced many libraries to discontinue subscriptions to some periodicals or other serials. To aid decisions on which serials to discontinue, it may be valuable to build a database of information on the serials that the library now receives. Such a database has been described by Hansen (1986).

The information that Hansen records is shown in Figure 22. The most difficult data to collect, of course, are those on recorded use. If these can not be collected through use of scanning devices, as mentioned earlier, they can be obtained in various ways on a sampling basis, as described by Lancaster (1993a).

Although Hansen records binding cost, she does not calculate a total ownership cost, based on estimates of storage and handling costs as well as subscription and binding costs. The data she does record would allow an estimate to be made of cost per use (see Chrzastowski, 1991, for example) for each serial based on subscription cost and binding cost, but use related to an estimate of total ownership cost would be more accurate. In any case, the serials with highest cost per use would be prime candidates for deselection in times of budget reductions, although the other factors represented in Figure 22 (e.g., local availability, relevance to particular departments, ready accessibility through document delivery services) should also be taken into account.

1. Code for most relevant academic department
2. Subscription cost
3. Binding cost
4. Cost of microform alternative
5. Code for availability in electronic form
6. Code for availability from document delivery services
7. Availability in other local libraries
8. Coverage in printed and electronic databases
9. Recorded use

FIGURE 22
Information that might be included in a serials database.
Based on Hansen (1986)

Of course, the construction of a database of this kind, and its updating and maintenance, require an investment on the part of the library. Hansen suggests that the investment is justifiable because the database makes readily available the information needed to make deselection decisions and has value in other applications—e.g., to generate printouts of serials relevant to particular academic departments and to provide data useful to binding operations.

Although the database described by Hansen is designed for use in academia, it could obviously be modified for use by other types of libraries. All of the elements other than department-relatedness are equally relevant to other libraries, and alternative data could be substituted as appropriate. For example, a subject category could be used in place of department-relatedness in the case of a public library.

Yet another type of database can be built to record interlibrary loan transactions as described, for example, by Wessling (1989) and Chang (1990). Interlibrary loans initiated online, by staff members or library users, can be recorded automatically and others added manually. A database of this kind may be useful in a number of different ways. For example, it could be used to:

1. Identify requests made by particular constituencies (e.g., academic departments).
2. Identify monographs or journals requested more than X times.
3. Identify subject areas in which many requests are made.
4. Provide data that can be compared with other data, such as those relating to circulation and acquisitions patterns.

Data Comparisons

Decisions relating to the development and management of collections will be most firmly based when they take into account more than circulation data alone—hence the value of the specially constructed databases discussed in the previous section. Data on circulation, in-house use, interlibrary loan and current acquisition patterns can all be useful.

For example, one needs to know, for any particular subject area, what the level of current purchasing is and whether use of the class is increasing or decreasing over time. Consider the following hypothetical data that could be generated from a management information system within a library:

Class	% of collection	% of current acquisitions	% of circulation	Latest year's circulation compared with previous year (%)
y	2.8	3.5	0.2	−15

Class y is very much underused and use continues to decline. This would appear to be a class in which interest is waning and it seems hard to justify the fact that 3.5% of all acquisitions fall in an area that accounts for only 0.2% of current circulation. Similar data for other classes could lead to quite different conclusions. For example, if a class is underused and on the decline but percentage of current acquisitions is well below percentage of collection, the situation seems to have corrected itself and no further action is called for.

Class	Collection (%)	Circulation (%)	Turnover rate	Borrowings from other libraries (%)	Acquisi- tions (%)
000	1.57	1.80	1.12	3.20	2.93
100	4.00	5.10	1.26	7.40	3.90
200	3.46	2.10	0.63	5.30	2.96
300	21.80	16.40	0.738	21.30	25.94
400	0.64	0.60	0.965	1.40	0.67
500	3.75	3.40	0.89	2.60	3.30
600	14.39	25.16	1.70	21.10	27.62
700	16.09	16.69	1.01	14.60	10.98
800	12.83	5.90	0.45	8.10	3.63
900	16.30	17.20	1.03	11.90	13.37
biog.	5.05	5.47	1.06	2.57	4.60

FIGURE 23

Collection evaluation report, for the period July 1, 1989, to June 30, 1990, for a public library in Illinois

Figure 23 gives another example of complementary data useful in collection development decisions. It shows an actual collection evaluation report, for the period July 1, 1989, to June 30, 1990, from a public library in Illinois. For each of the Dewey classes, the following data are presented: percentage of collection, percentage of circulation, turnover rate, percentage of interlibrary borrowings for the past year and percentage of acquisitions for the past year. Note here some classes that seem still to need corrective action. For example, 300 is underused and has a relatively low turnover rate, but interlibrary loans are strong (proportionally more than circulation) and the current acquisition rate is very high. The low circulation and turnover, coupled with the high rate of interlibrary borrowing, suggest that what is being purchased in this class does not correspond well with the current interests of users. If better fit to user interests, acquisitions in this class might actually be reduced. The low turnover rate and discrepancy between collection and circulation percentages further suggest that the class needs some thorough weeding. In contrast, 600 is a heavily overused class; that it now accounts for almost

28% of acquisitions indicates that this fact has been recognized and appropriate corrective action taken.

The librarian should look at fine circulation data rather than coarse to avoid jumping to the wrong conclusions. The fact that Dewey class 600 is overused does not necessarily mean that the entire class is overused; it may be that only the cookbooks are overused and all other subdivisions are actually underused. Likewise, overuse of Library of Congress class QA may suggest the need for strengthening of the entire mathematics collection when, in fact, it is only the computer science books that are affecting the results.

Of course, automated circulation systems can yield data that are finer than gross use patterns; use of small subclasses or even individual titles can be examined. One example of this type of analysis can be found in Britten and Webster (1992), who analyzed MARC records for titles heavily used within an academic library in an attempt to identify common characteristics that might predict use of future additions to the collection. Common elements examined were subject heading, author, language, and imprint date.

Byrd et al. (1982) have described a method for determining strengths and weaknesses in a collection based on the difference in proportions between the subject breakdown of a library's acquisitions and the subject breakdown of the interlibrary loan requests it generates. The theory is that the classes needing greatest attention are those in which the greatest difference exists between volume of materials borrowed and volume of materials purchased. This discrepancy is expressed as a "collection balance indicator" (CBI), a relative percentage, as follows:

$$100 \times \frac{\text{New acquisitions in this class}}{\text{Total acquisitions}} - \frac{\text{Titles borrowed in this class}}{\text{Total titles borrowed}}$$

A positive value on the CBI indicates a subject area relatively strong in terms of current acquisitions while a negative value indicates one relatively weak. This can be illustrated through two simple examples:

$$1.\ 100 \times \frac{100}{400} - \frac{12}{120} = 15 \qquad 2.\ 100 \times \frac{40}{400} - \frac{30}{120} = -15$$

In the first case, 25% of the acquisitions are made in this subject field but only 10% of the titles borrowed fall in this area. The CBI is a high 15. The second case puts the proportions exactly in reverse—10% of acquisitions and 25% of titles borrowed—and the value is a low -15.

Payne and Willers (1989) have shown how circulation data can be related to acquisitions data to measure success in materials selection (expressed, for example, by the proportion of items purchased in subject X that have circulated within period Y). Success may also be related to source of selection—e.g., faculty versus librarian selection in the case of some academic libraries.

Aguilar (1984) performed a monumental study of the relationship between internal circulation and interlibrary loan requests based on about 86,000 interlibrary loan (ILL) transactions and almost two million circulation records from eighteen Illinois libraries. He found support for his hypothesis that a class that is overused (as defined earlier) in a library will be a class in which the library will borrow many items, whereas underused classes tend not to generate large numbers of ILL requests. This supports the assumption that it is overused classes rather than underused classes that are most in need of strengthening.

As a result of his research, Aguilar (1986) developed a measure "ratio of borrowings to holdings" (RBH), which is simply:

$$\frac{\% \text{ of borrowings}}{\% \text{ of holdings}}$$

Values greatly in excess of 1 would indicate a class in which the borrowing rate is very high relative to the holdings of the library. For example, a class that occupies 8% of the collection but accounts for 15% of borrowings would have an RBH of almost 1.9 (15/8). Aguilar uses the RBH data, together with relative use circulation data, to produce a collection development "model." For overused and underused classes the RBH is looked at. Decisions on the future of the class are made on the basis of relative use and RBH data. The model is shown in Figure 24.

Nutter (1987) recommends that academic libraries should study interrelations among databases representing holdings, circulation, and patron characteristics. Patron files can be coded by department/discipline to allow comparisons of usage and to study what types of materials are used by each department. In the case of academic and special libraries, the patron file could actually identify all potential users, allowing the librarian to derive a user/nonuser ratio for the community as a whole and possibly for each department.

Class	Relative use (circulation data)	Interlibrary borrowing	Decision on the class
A	Overused	High RBH	Buy more
B	Overused	No high RBH	Continue at present levels
C	Underused	High RBH	Examine class: are right items being purchased; should it be weeded?
D	Underused	Low RBH	Curtail buying in this class

FIGURE 24
Collection development model based on Aguilar (1986).
Reprinted by permission of Haworth Press

Monitoring OPAC Interactions

Another source of information of potential value in collection development is the online catalog and its actual use by library patrons. Possibly useful information can be obtained from several report generation features existing within commercially available systems. For example, the INNOPAC system will identify the names of authors most used within a particular time period (Figure 25) and the subject terms introduced by users that do not retrieve any items (Figure 26). While the latter will often be symptomatic of errors in user terminology, or search logic, they may occasionally indicate gaps in subject coverage in the collection.

In theory, interactions between library users and the catalog could be monitored to identify (1) books sought that are not in the collection, and (2) books sought and found to be in the collection but not immediately available on the shelves (which could be used to produce an estimate of availability rate). However, this presupposes that users must employ some unambiguous identifier for a book rather than a truncation algorithm that is equivocal. Monitoring is discussed further in Chapter 14.

Present System Capabilities

While all of the analyses discussed so far can be based on data obtainable from library catalogs, circulation systems, acquisitions systems or other databases, this will usually require the writing of special programs for extraction and manipulation since the commercially available systems are not likely to offer the capabilities sought as a standard feature. Features that are present in many existing systems include: (1) ability to record circulation by type of patron, (2) ability to identify the most heavily used classes, (3) ability to identify books for which many "holds" are placed, and (4) ability to identify books not borrowed within a particular period of time (Hawks, 1988).

```
                     Management Information on
                       PUBLIC CATALOG SEARCHES
           From Mon Jul 13 1992 09:47:23 to Tue Jul 21 1992 15:06:00

                     AUTHORS SEARCHES BY FREQUENCY

       SEARCH                                   TIMES SEARCHED
   walker alice                                      17
   solzhenizin                                        16
   handel g                                           15
   arnim                                              14
   baldwin james                                      14
   cortazar                                           14
   morrison toni                                      14
   reid ira                                           14
   vivaldi antonio                                    14
   black j                                            13
   bull john                                          13
   clark hugh                                         13
   cooper jane roberta                                13
   fuller margaret                                    13

    F > FORWARD one screen      B > BACK one screen    P > PRINT
    L > LAST screen             Q > QUIT
            Choose one ( F,B,L,Q,P )
```

FIGURE 25
Report on author names entered by users most frequently
within a one-week period.
From INNOPAC by permission of Innovative Interfaces, Inc.

Unfortunately, while automated systems can be used to generate better data for collection management than librarians have had before, the advantage is more theoretical than actual. Not only do commercially-produced systems fail to provide convenient access to the most useful data but many librarians seem unconvinced of the value of the data (Carrigan, 1996).

```
                    SUBJECTS SEARCHES WITH NO DIRECT HITS

    SEARCH                              TERMINAL      TIME
    age limits                            210     1:42 PM, Jul 14
    aids black women                      114     1:35 PM, Jul 20
    aids deases                           706    12:10 PM, Jul 20
    aids testing                          210     1:44 PM, Jul 14
    alanon                                702    12:19 PM, Jul 21
    alcholol                              210     2:24 PM, Jul 15
    american musicians                    116     9:41 AM, Jul 20
    amtrak railroads                      115     2:22 PM, Jul 15
    animal testing                        806     1:42 PM, Jul 14
    animals europe                        231     1:30 PM, Jul 20
    anthropology sexuality                113     1:18 PM, Jul 20
    anti censorship                       210     1:32 PM, Jul 15

    F > FORWARD one screen    B > BACK one screen    P > PRINT
    L > LAST screen           Q > QUIT
                   Choose one ( F,B,L,Q,P )
```

FIGURE 26

Report on subject terms entered by users that fail to match terms in the catalog.
From INNOPAC by permission of Innovative Interfaces, Inc.

Materials Availability in an Automated Environment

The factors that affect the availability of books owned by a library have been thoroughly discussed by Buckland (1975). The most important are level of demand (popularity), number of copies, and length of loan period. It is obvious that the more popular a particular book the less likely it is to be on the shelf at any particular time. "Popularity" is not a nebulous measure in this case, but a very practical one. As mentioned earlier, it can be expressed in terms of a last circulation date. That is, one could say that 10% of the collection circulated at least once in the last month, 25% circulated at least once in the last six months, and so on.

It seems equally obvious that buying additional copies will improve availability. But two copies are not twice as good as one copy—sometimes both are on the shelf, sometimes one, sometimes neither—and the addition of further copies may make only a marginal difference to availability. The effect of adding an additional copy varies with the popularity of the item: if a particular book is never used it will always be available and adding a second copy does not change the situation.

If a book is off the shelf for one half of the year, one can say its availability rate is 0.5. Adding a second copy will improve availability but will not double it (Leimkuhler, 1966). Buckland (1975) presents data to show the effect of varying numbers of duplicate copies on the availability of books at different levels of popularity.

Less obvious, perhaps, are the effects on availability of the length of the loan period. Suppose that every user of a library returns a book on or near the day on which it is due to be returned. There is, in fact, a strong tendency for this to occur, as reported by Newhouse and Alexander (1972), Buckland (1975), and Goehlert (1979). Then, reducing the length of the loan period from four weeks to two weeks greatly increases the probability that any book will be available on the shelf when looked for by a user. In fact, cutting the length of the period in half has roughly the same effect on availability as buying a second copy.

The librarian can improve the accessibility of books by buying more copies of popular items, reducing the length of the loan period, or both. In fact, if one wished, it would be possible to identify a desired "satisfaction level" (e.g., 0.8—a user will find a desired item to be on the shelf in eight cases out of ten) and take steps to ensure that this level would apply to every book in the library. Suppose one divided the collection into five levels of popularity on the basis of most recent circulation date. For Level 5 the probability of availability could already be 0.99 and would remain there even if the loan period for this category was extended to ten years. For Level 4 the probability of availability might already be 0.8 with a loan period of four weeks, and no further action is required. Availability for Level 3 items might be increased to 0.8 by reducing the length of the loan period from four weeks to three weeks. To reach 0.8 availability for Level 2, the length of the loan period may need to be reduced to two weeks. This leaves us with Level 1 items—the rather small number of highly popular items in the library. To ensure a probability of availability of 0.8 one might need, say, five copies of each and a loan period of one week.

Buckland (1975) has published data that show how popularity (level of demand for an item), length of loan period, and number of copies affect the probability of availability of books. His data are summarized in Figure 27. With a long loan period of ten weeks, the chance that one of the most popular books (class A) will be on the shelf, assuming a single copy, is only .37. This probability can be increased to .66 with two copies and .86 with three. On the other hand, reducing the length of the loan period, without buying further copies, also has a profound effect on the probability of availability. With a one-week loan period, even the most popular items in this hypothetical library have a high probability (.91) of being on the shelf when sought by a user. As Buckland's data show clearly, reducing the loan period or buying further copies are strategies that have most profound effects on the items in greatest demand. The data in Figure 27 should be regarded only as illustrative of the interrelationships involved among popularity, duplication rate, and length of loan period. The actual probabilities of availability within this model would be determined by the different values accorded to the levels of popularity (e.g., availability values for class A if it were defined as "last circulation date = one month or less" would be different from the values were this class defined as "LCD = two months or less").

Buckland (1975) has reported that a type of "homeostatic" effect may govern book availability. That is, if satisfaction level is pushed up from, say, 0.5 to 0.8, use of the library may increase substantially because of improved expectations of success among the community. This greatly increased demand, however, increases competition for the library's resources and forces satisfaction level down—perhaps back to 0.5. Automated circulation systems allow one to conceive of a self-regulating library with no fixed loan period. An algorithm incorporated within the system would tell the user how long a particular book could be borrowed at the time of checkout. The calculation would be made on the basis of the circulation history of the book and the number of copies held, the loan period being calculated to ensure that the desired satisfaction level (say 0.8) will be maintained. The system would probably work with a large but finite number of loan periods—in the range of, say, five to ten.

Of course, such a policy might not be popular with users, especially those who find that the several books they borrow on a particular day all have different return dates, but it would definitely make the library more efficient in terms of the probability of availability of materials sought.

Popu-larity Class	One Copy Loan Policy*				Two Copies Loan Policy				Three Copies Loan Policy			
	(i)	(ii)	(iii)	(iv)	(i)	(ii)	(iii)	(iv)	(i)	(ii)	(iii)	(iv)
A	91	79	52	37	100	98	84	66	100	100	97	86
B	94	86	62	44	100	99	91	77	100	100	99	93
C	98	94	72	56	100	100	97	87	100	100	100	98
D	99	98	82	68	100	100	99	84	100	100	100	100
E	100	100	97	85	100	100	100	100	100	100	100	100

* (i) = one week, (ii) = two weeks, (iii) = five weeks, (iv) = ten weeks

FIGURE 27
Effect on book availability of popularity level, length of loan period, and number of copies.
Reprinted from Buckland (1975) by permission of Michael Buckland

Profiles of Interest

A somewhat different approach to the monitoring of collection development practices involves the comparison of a subject profile of what is being acquired with a subject profile of community interests or probable demands. This is most appropriate to the academic world, where it is possible to express the probable interests of a department in terms of the content of its curriculum, which may be converted into class numbers from the bibliographic scheme in use, and the probable demand in terms of the size of the department (number of faculty, number of students, number of instructional units). The profile of interest for the various departments can be matched against holdings, current acquisitions, or current circulation.

Examples of use of such techniques can be found in the work of McGrath, Golden, and Jenks. McGrath (1968) showed, for each academic department, the number of circulated books relevant to the departmental profile, the percentage of the total circulation accounted for by these books, the enrollment for the department, and a circulation/enrollment ratio. Golden (1974) related the class numbers associated with a course to the number of books owned in these classes and to enrollment figures for the course in an attempt to identify strengths and weaknesses in the collection. Jenks (1976) compared circulation figures with the number of students in each department and with the number of books matching the profile of each department. He also ranked departments according to the use each made of that part of the collection matching its interest profile.

Power and Bell (1978) propose a more elaborate formula that takes into account, for each academic department, the number of faculty members, the number of students at various levels, the holdings matching the departmental profile, and circulation.

McGrath (1972) has shown that books matching the profile of institutional interests are much more likely to be borrowed than books not matching the profile, while McGrath et al. (1979) have used a subject classification approach to determine to what extent graduate and undergraduate students borrow books outside their own disciplines.

Evans and Beilby (1983) describe collection evaluation through a sophisticated management information system employed within the libraries of the State University of New York. In one database were stored student enrollment figures classified by subject field according to the Higher Education General Information Survey (HEGIS) codes. By using OCLC tapes, together with a conversion tape showing equivalencies between the HEGIS codes and Library of Congress class numbers, it was possible to relate the acquisitions data of a library to the enrollment. Thus, for each HEGIS code (e.g., 1103, German language), the system would generate a printout showing the number of titles acquired by the library, the percentage of the total acquisitions that this represents, the number of student credit hours, and the percentage of the total credit hours that this represents. Subject areas in which strong (or weak) relationships exist between student credit hours and acquisitions patterns can thus be identified, and any necessary corrections made.

More recently, Kountz (1991) has performed similar analyses. Since student credit hours or credit units in various disciplines are reported to the U.S. Department of Education in the form of HEGIS or, now, IPEDS (Integrated Postsecondary Education Data System) codes, and these codes can be converted into Library of Congress or Dewey Decimal class numbers, a profile of "constituency interests" can be matched against collection, acquisition or circulation data. Kountz uses titles per unit of student credit in the various subjects as a measure of the degree to which the collection matches interests.

Similar analyses may also be possible in the special library environment. For example, Spaulding and Stanton (1976) and Kennedy (1983) describe the use of the Dewey classification as an aid to book selection in an industrial library network. A selection profile for each member library is constructed, using DDC numbers plus verbal descriptions. Circulation data were used in the building of the profiles. Computer-generated reports allow a manager to determine to what extent materials purchased in a particular time period match a library's profile.

While such analyses are not completely dependent on automated systems, it is obvious that they become more practical when the figures needed can be extracted from databases representing holdings, circulation or current acquisitions.

Allocation Formulae

A significant collection management problem in the academic world is that associated with the equitable distribution of the materials budget over the interests of the various departments: how much should be spent on the acquisition of chemistry materials, how much on history, how much on education, and so on? The types of analyses discussed in the previous section can be useful in suggesting criteria for such allocation—e.g., dollars allocated in proportion to student credit units. An allocation formula may be more easily justified if it takes into account a number of different criteria. Again, the development of allocation formulae is not dependent on automation. Nevertheless, many of the figures needed to develop a formula may be available from various databases, and it is much easier to develop a multi-component formula when the component data can be manipulated by computer.

Figure 28 shows sample data that have been considered for use as components in a materials allocation formula for a large university in the United States. While some justification can be made for any and all of these components, a formula that takes into account so many components may be too complex to apply in practice. The major problem involved is that of getting agreement on how much weight each component should receive in the calculation of the allocation. The list of possible components in Figure 28 is a long one, but it is by no means complete. In general, it is based more on inputs to a department than on outputs. While instructional outputs can be considered to be reflected in number of students graduating, research outputs (e.g., in publications produced) are not considered at all.

For each department:
        Size of faculty (in full time equivalents—FTE)
        Percentage of total university faculty
        Masters degrees awarded
        Percentage of total masters degrees awarded
        Doctoral degrees awarded
        Percentage of total doctoral degrees awarded
        Instructional units
        Percentage of total instructional units
        Departmental budget
        Percentage of total university budget
        Grants and contracts received
        Percentage of total grants and contracts
        Items borrowed from the library
        Percentage of total library circulation
        Size of departmental collection (in titles)
        Percentage of total library collection
        Average cost of a monograph in this subject area
        Average cost of a serial subscription in this subject area

FIGURE 28

Possible components in a materials allocation formula
for a large university library

Brownson (1991) discusses the limitations of allocation formulae of the type that have been used in the past. He proposes a somewhat different approach based primarily on (1) the collection strength desired in a particular subject, (2) an estimate of the present strength in that subject, (3) the number of items owned in that class, (4) the circulation in that class, and (5) extent of faculty research in the subject as reflected in number of research projects.

Ottensmann and Gleeson (1993) and Gleeson and Ottensmann (1993) have described an approach to the development of a budget allocation formula for a public library, based on data derived from a computerized circulation system. The objective is to allocate the budget in such a way as to optimize circulation "within the constraints of other objectives established by librarians."

Expert System Approaches

Various investigators have attempted to apply expert system techniques to the selection of materials for library collections.

Rada et al. (1987) have described an expert system approach to the selection of journals. While their objectives were somewhat different—the decision on whether or not a journal should be included in the MEDLARS database—the criteria built into their system (type of publisher, language, type of article, type of author, publication standards) would be among those relevant to a knowledge base designed to aid a librarian in journal selection decisions.

Meador and Cline (1992) describe a workstation designed to make readily accessible all of the information that a librarian might need in selection decisions—collection development guidelines, holdings and circulation data, financial data, and so on. While not an expert system per se, this approach can be considered as a first step toward the development of such a system.

Sowell (1989) describes a rudimentary expert system to aid in monograph selection, but he deals only in a very narrow subject area and the prototype developed was tested with very few cases.

This chapter has dealt with computer-based systems as sources of information or assistance in collection development and management. However, it relates primarily to collections in print-on-paper form. Collection development and management of resources in electronic form is the subject of the next chapter.

CHAPTER 7

Collection Management and Electronic Resources

IOIOIOIOIOIOIOIOIOIOIOIOIOIOIOIOIOIOIOIOIOIOIOIOIOIOIOIOIOIOIOIOIOIOIOIOIOIOIOIOIOIOIOI

"ACCESS RATHER THAN OWNERSHIP" has become virtually the motto of the library profession. Dougherty and Hughes (1991) refer to the "transition from the physical library to the logical library" and Michalko (1991) stresses that the research library "must move with minimal disruption from a library model directed primarily at ownership of materials to one in which access and delivery play a more central role."

This message has been presented, in one form or another, by others prominent in the library field. For example, Penniman (1993) argues that libraries must be active, not passive, emphasizing the delivery of information rather than its storage. Line (1993) agrees that libraries should be evaluated in terms of the services they provide rather than the collections they own, and Dowlin (1993) refers to the need to transform the library from a "fortress" to an information "pipeline." Hitchingham (1996) sees the transition as one from the library as place to the library "as many places."

This chapter will look at the changes that have occurred in libraries in the last few years, in terms of the collecting and accessing of information sources, and will speculate on what "collection development" may mean at some future date.

It is obvious that electronic technologies have already had considerable impact. Virtually all libraries, at least in the most-developed countries, are now members of networks that greatly facilitate the location of sources of information and the gaining of access to them. Card catalogs have largely been replaced by online catalogs and these are being expanded through the addition of materials not previously included. The whole idea of what a catalog should be is changing; it is no longer seen as a tool bounded by the collections of a single library but one that reveals the availability of resources in a network of libraries or even one that is essentially a gateway to a universe of information resources in printed, electronic or other forms. Use of terminals or workstations to access databases of various kinds is now routine for many libraries, and most now add electronic resources to their collections in CD-ROM or other forms.

These developments have occurred with surprising speed, suggesting that the changes of the next decade will be more dramatic and rapid than those of the past decade, a point made clearly by Govan (1991):

> It is startling to realize that in 1983, as I recently read, no library owned a CD-ROM. . . . When one thinks of the widespread use of them today, one wonders about the future proliferation of other forms of digitized information: intelligent workstations, optical scanners and optical discs, expert systems, artificial intelligence, hypertext, broadbands and satellites, and local area networks (LANs) and other kinds of networks, as well as devices yet unknown . . . (Page 24)

That this electronic revolution in libraries has occurred, of course, is due to developments over which the library profession has had little direct control, most obviously the growth of electronic publishing and of networks that facilitate scholarly communication.

Of course, some libraries have been much faster than others in turning the technology to their advantage and thus offering innovative services to their users. One that has been at the forefront is the Butler Library at Columbia University. Its Electronic Text Service (ETS), established in the 1980s, integrates electronic primary research materials into the library's collections and services. The ETS includes several thousand texts and hypermedia research tools in many languages (Lowry, 1990, 1992). Similar in scope is the Electronic Text Center at the University of Virginia Library, which has also assumed the responsibility for the SGML-tagging of certain texts that lack such encoding (Seaman, 1993). Several other major universities now have centers of the same type. Gaunt (1995) has discussed their organization and functions. Other libraries or consortia have taken the lead in archiving or providing access to electronic journals (Duranceau et al., 1996; Cochenour, 1996).

Electronic Publishing and Scholarly Communication

What happens to the library in the future will depend to a very large extent on developments in related sectors, most obviously the publishing industry. One must assume that the proportion of the world's publications issued in some electronic form will increase and, thus, the proportion issued as print on paper will decline. Less clear is the form that the electronic publishing will take. How much will consist of resources that can be accessed only through networks and how much will actually be distributed, for purchase or lease, as CD-ROM, videotape, videodisk, electronic book or formats yet to be devised?

Of course, what happens to the format depends on what occurs in the creative process itself. Electronic publishing is still in a largely "simulation" stage of development in that most authors tend to think in terms of the static printed page and the static illustration. Hypertext and hypermedia capabilities free the author from static representation, allowing publications that are dynamic and interactive. It seems likely that future authors, whether research scientists or poets, will increasingly exploit the full capabilities of the electronic media (sound, movement, animation, simulation, color, and so on), thus changing the nature of many publications and determining the format in which they are best issued (Lancaster, 1995). The truly dynamic and interactive publication brings with it other important implications, not least of which is the fact that it cannot be printed out on paper.

The subject of electronic publishing cannot be divorced from the broader issues of scholarly research and communication. Scholarly endeavors are being profoundly affected by technology. As Shreeves (1992) points out, "The emergence of machine-readable texts, of computer-based networks, and of all the attendant technological apparatus, has provided the means to alter radically scholarly communication and scholarly method." He was speaking specifically of the humanities, but the observations are also true of the other disciplines, perhaps even more so.

The influence of technology on scholarly research extends much further than the obvious effects of word processing capabilities. Scholars now use a variety of networks to access sources needed in their research, to exchange information with colleagues, and to collaborate with them in research and publishing activities. Some more subtle changes are also taking place. The scholarly journal in paper form has not yet been replaced by electronic journals, although more and more journals are beginning to appear only in network-accessible form (Clement, 1994;

Woodward, 1995) and electronics obviously offers the potential for more effective dissemination of information—for example, journals tailored to individual interests. Network resources have also caused a significant increase in informal communication—informal "journals" now exist within electronic mail and computer conferencing facilities. Such resources diminish the role of the conventional printed journal as a vehicle for the dissemination of research results; increasingly it exists solely to satisfy social (publish-or-perish) and archival requirements. One obvious sign of the increasing importance of the informal electronic sources is the fact that they are now frequently cited in the conventional printed journals.

The existence of text in electronic form even alters the nature of scholarship. For example, Shreeves (1992) has mentioned how the ability to manipulate text by computer has changed the types of research that can be undertaken and the types of research questions that can be asked. This point has also been made strongly by Gaunt (1990):

> The potential research activities using the electronic version of a text are limited only by the interest and ingenuity of the individual researcher. As social science data in machine-readable form is valuable to the researcher for analysis of trends, for hypotheses and conclusions, so too is the literary text in machine-readable form for similar ends, and for particular work perhaps even more valuable. (Page 89)

The changes in scholarship that have occurred so far may be merely cosmetic compared with changes that could take place in the future. Most radical is the possibility that networked scholarly publication could become the direct responsibility of the universities and other research institutions (Lancaster, 1995).

Role of the Library

The library profession does seem to be fairly unanimous in the belief that libraries and librarians will continue to have important functions to perform vis-à-vis electronic resources. Indeed, several writers have warned that, unless the library takes a lead in this, its role will be usurped by other bodies—other departments on a campus or other organizations entirely. For example, Johnson (1990a) has said:

> Libraries, in their central role as providers and organizers of information, cannot afford to ignore computer files or to approach them in a piecemeal fashion. To do either places the library at risk of becoming less valuable to and less

supportive of the academic community. Libraries will no longer be regarded as the focal point for information as more of it slips outside their purview. Researchers will no longer think of the library as the first resort because they will be unable to depend on its catalogs, collections, and directional tools to provide access to the universe of information resources. The library's significance to the administration will diminish as well. (Page 12)

A similar message has been delivered by Alberico (1991):

If we don't become involved at all levels, there is a very real possibility that resources will shift to other segments of the economy that can deliver the electronic services that academic and post-industrial organizations will need to survive. It is already happening in some places. (Page 154)

Lewis (1988) has also pointed out that users will demand more from the library than they have in the past:

Students may expect the library to be as powerful and easy to use as electronic teaching tools. Unfortunately, libraries are rarely easy to use. If analysis with new computer tools becomes easier and more productive than library research, students can be expected to use the new tools rather than the library. If libraries do not improve their services so that they remain an essential teaching tool, they risk becoming irrelevant to the teaching process. If this is allowed to happen, it is easy to predict a decline in library funding. (Page 293)

The compilers of one influential report seem to feel that it is almost inevitable that the academic library will decline. Martyn et al. (1990) suggest that individual academic departments will provide their own electronic resources and the library will decay into little more than a study hall.

Collection Development and Management

Given that the library *must* continue to take a lead in the exploitation of information sources in electronic form, what exactly does this imply for collection development? Obviously, electronic resources, particularly those that can only be accessed when the need for them arises, present a set of problems that have not been encountered by librarians in the past. As Alberico (1991) points out: "'Collecting' electronic information is more problematic than collecting printed texts. And, as we all know, collecting printed texts is not without its own problems." Welsch (1991) warns that the entire approach and philosophy of collection development must change: "Simply duplicating the collection practices we evolved for print materials in the network environment does not seem responsive to current needs or capabilities." Nevertheless, collection development, whatever form it takes, still requires policies, as Summerhill (1991) has noted: "The advent of networked resources does not eliminate the need for a formal policy governing the acquisition of electronic resources."

An obvious challenge is the problem of how to integrate electronic resources with more traditional forms. The need for complete integration seems taken for granted by librarians and library users alike, at least in the scholarly community; as Dougherty and Hughes (1991) report: "Provosts and librarians ... prefer a future in which there is universal access by faculty and students to multiple information sources in all possible media via a single multifunctional workstation."

Ghikas (1989) points out that the future library must be a combination of "actual" and "virtual" materials:

> The twenty-first century collection will, I believe, be an accumulation of information-bearing objects—printed, aural, graphic, digital—housed within the physical library, *and also* indices, abstracts and catalogs through which, using electronic channels, the library user has access to *pre-identified* resources held by other libraries and information providers. The twenty-first century "collection" thus combines the actual and "virtual" collection. The "virtual collection" is an *electronically browsable* collection. In contrast, tomorrow's library, like today's, will go beyond the limits of its own collection—*both* actual *and* virtual—in response to specific information requests. In this case, neither location nor delivery time and channel will be preidentified. (Page 123)

The integration issue is also dealt with by Welsch (1991):

> Technology and technological resources need to be integrated as closely as possible with traditional resources within a unified approach to information founded on principles derived from studies of information seeking and use. Users want to be able to identify information through one access point and not through a series of separate catalogs or information utilities with varying search strategies and command structures that complicate as much as they help. Until a search device, a dynamically updated online guide, or satisfactory resource guides are created, we will have to continue to depend on that hypermedia, intelligent (but not artificial), semi-robotic system that is known as a "librarian." (Page 172)

An obvious problem in collection development is that of the costs involved in acquisition or access. Haar (1988) has pointed out that reference sources in optical disk form are very popular with library users, yet they tend to be more expensive than their print counterparts. The addition of several optical disk systems might well mean that monograph purchases would have to be further reduced, perhaps drastically, in many libraries. Moreover, one must recognize the fact that different formats actually interact with each other. For example, an index to periodicals in CD-ROM form may increase demand for periodicals in printed form.

It is true, of course, that electronic resources, particularly network-accessible resources, are economical in space. However, the saving in space is unlikely to compensate for cost increases elsewhere. Moreover, while the costs of computer/telecommunications technologies have obviously declined dramatically, and are likely to continue to do so, such cost reductions do not apply to all the technologies of concern to libraries.

Another consideration is that, in the electronic world, libraries have much less to show for their expenditures. Some resources are leased rather than owned, and others do not exist within the library at all. The bodies that fund libraries must recognize and accept this fact.

It is undeniable that access to electronic resources reduces the funds available to acquire other formats. As Shreeves (1992) indicates: "Taking the cost of electronic information from current resources is not a pleasant prospect, but it may be the only strategy available for many."

It is Govan (1991), however, who has been most forceful in warning of the economic dangers facing the library in a research setting:

> If any transformation of our present intricate system of acquiring materials should come about, it would change drastically both the practices and the structure of academic libraries. The larger point is that the present system is not working economically for those libraries. The combined costs of assimilating electronic technology, recent printed materials, and preservation, have eaten deeply into their infrastructures. For all the professed recognition of information as a commodity, legislators and university administrators have offered little relief, and much of the new funding seems to have gone to computing services elsewhere on campus. Any prognostication about libraries' future would be irresponsible if it did not lay heavy emphasis on their perilous fiscal state today and the economic problems that lie ahead. All that we have discussed carries a large price tag, and the parent institutions must face the question squarely as to the very considerable costs of supporting a contemporary academic library in a world awash with information. (Page 37)

He goes on to suggest that libraries will become vastly more expensive or they will become useless.

Van Gils (1995), speaking of the Library of the Royal Netherlands Academy of Arts and Sciences (KNAW), is another who has recognized the need for substantial additional funding and for the recovery of costs through sale of services:

> For the library it is a matter of a radically changing situation, both in terms of expenditure as well as receipts. Looking at the budget and the operating turnover of the Library KNAW I come to the conclusion that for the past two years, and also in the next two years, substantial extra budgets are needed in order to keep up at all with the developments in the field of digital information supply. Achieving a leading position in this, which is one of the objectives of our organisation for the biomedical disciplines, demands even more money.
>
> All this together entails an enormous increase of our annual expenditure, roughly estimated at 15% to 20%. We will have to work hard to recover these costs via existing services. (Page 536)

But costs are not the only issues facing the collection development librarian. Gaunt (1990) identifies other significant problems:

1. Finding out what is available,
2. Evaluating the sources available, and
3. Acquiring and servicing the sources required.

As she explains, electronic resources are not adequately controlled bibliographically, they are not easy to identify, and they are not well reviewed. The problem has also been recognized by Shreeves (1992):

> ... a major obstacle for the selector of electronic texts is the difficulty of defining the available universe. The usual selection tools (reviews in scholarly journals, national bibliographies, publishers' catalogs, etc.) do not cover such resources effectively, nor is there a developed system of publication and distribution. Finding out about electronic texts requires attention to a number of specialized sources of information. (Pages 587-588)

The critical problem, of course, is access and what collection development really means in an electronic environment. Reed-Scott (1989), for example, sees the role of the collection developer as altering dramatically:

> Because electronic texts are fluid and interactive and are changed frequently, it will be difficult to capture information. Building collections will move from a static process of acquiring library resources to a more fluid position of providing access to information. (Page 49)

Creth (1991) claims that the collection development librarian will continue to do many of the things he or she is now doing, at least in the foreseeable future, but will also take on new responsibilities:

> The context for the future library suggests that rather than relinquishing functions that are currently an integral part of university library activities (e.g., selecting and organizing materials, assisting and educating users in locating information) these will continue, although in different ways, along with new activities that will emerge. (Page 48)

In dealing with electronic sources that are distributed, of course, the collection development role is little different from the situation in the print-on-paper world, even though some of the sources acquired may not really be "owned" by the library. It is in dealing with the remote sources, those that can be accessed only through telecommunications, that the collection development function becomes ambiguous. Atkinson (1990), for example, raises the important question: "What role does the research library play, if most research consists primarily in the searching and downloading of information from a distant database by a scholar at a personal workstation?"

He hopes that libraries will restructure their operations around three basic functions: mediation, primary record definition, and secondary record definition. *Mediation* involves helping users to identify needed information and to download this to local storage facilities. In a sense, this can be considered as a kind of deferred collection development operation—locating information sources as they are needed rather than trying to predict the needs in advance. Nevertheless, some prediction will be required, according to Atkinson. The *primary record definition* role he identifies would consist of identifying resources that are likely to be of greatest interest locally and downloading these to a local database. His *secondary record definition* function is the most unconventional; it is an uploading rather than a downloading activity.* In essence, the library becomes the publisher and disseminator of scholarly information:

> When a scholar at an institution has written something which is deemed by a select group of peers to be worth communicating broadly to other scholars, that communication should take place by the library's uploading that publication into the library database, thus disseminating it to other libraries, and thereby to other scholars, throughout the nation and the world. The ultimate purpose of the academic library is to provide bibliographic support for

---

*In a more recent paper (Atkinson, 1996), he distinguishes between an "open zone" of resources accessible through the network and a "control zone" of resources selected from the network and "controlled" by the library community. The control zone would include, among other things, scholarly articles published by the academic community itself.

education and to serve as a basis for communication among scholars—in short, to disseminate significant information. In the predominantly paper era, we rely heavily upon commercial publishing for that purpose, but such commercial publishing is merely a means to achieving that ultimate end—and already that particular means is becoming economically prohibitive and technically unnecessary . . . The library—in conjunction with the computer center and the academic press—must assume direct responsibility for disseminating information among scholars. Providing scholars with the channels through which to communicate, working with scholars to establish the technical and bibliographical standards and procedures for online publication in this fashion—these are responsibilities which should therefore also be assumed by the library in the online era. (Page 357)

The mediation role, in one form or another, is one that seems to be fairly widely accepted. Welsch (1991) describes it in these terms:

This is where librarians should find their niche: identifying resources regardless of format and encouraging suppliers of network information to make their products readily and easily available. Focusing their future role not on being a warehouse of electronic or printed information, but on becoming an information utility that locates data in diverse sources seems more appropriate. (Page 187)

The view that libraries should build local databases from network resources elsewhere, however, is not one that appears to be widely held. More commonly, the library is seen as more of a switching center, possibly also having such value-added responsibilities as user education. For example, Britten (1991) has said: "Libraries should not think primarily in terms of collecting information stored on networks, but should instead pursue strategies for teaching users how to locate and retrieve this information." This agrees with several prominent librarians who see the library of the future as primarily a node in a vast information network. Kilgour (1993), for example, believes that a major function of such a library node will be to build local indexes to aid users in accessing remote sources. Atkinson (1990), on the other hand, claims that the view of the library as a switching center is a shortsighted one:

What we have perhaps failed to recognize, however, is that the library must also continue to maintain its responsibility for record definition—for collecting, i.e., for moving a carefully selected assembly of graphic utterances from the environment into a library database, and thereby stabilizing that information for future reference. The most serious error the library could make at this time would be to assume that its role in a predominantly online environment will be mainly that of a switching point. That role as switching point belongs not to the library side, but rather to the computer center side of information service. The library's function has always been—and will remain regardless of changes in technology—to select, stabilize, protect, and provide access to significant or representative graphic texts. (Page 356)

Atkinson is supported in this by Summerhill (1991):

Clearly, groups of local users will have an ongoing need for the proximate location of heavily used data. Thus, achieving a balance between local "collections" of heavily used electronic resources and the provision of network access to less frequently used resources should be the goal of the library acquisition process in a networked environment. (Page 184)

A few other writers agree with Atkinson's view that the library, in association with other segments of the research community, should become publisher and disseminator of information. Welsch (1991) has said:

Yet, the concept of individuals and organizations, including libraries, as self-publishers of new information, who would then make it available through networks, is so tantalizing that I am reluctant, despite obstacles, to surrender it. (Page 196)

Alberico (1991) is more specific:

The "electronic book" of the future is as likely to be a composite as it is to be a single coherent entity. Scholars will compile their own electronic books by gathering separate pieces of information from different parts of the network. Libraries may become publishers simply by using the network to build customized multimedia documents for clients or by providing the technology, training, and facilities to allow clients to build their own composite documents. (Pages 190-191)

Quinn (1995), a professor of mathematics, also makes a good case for why the research library is to be preferred as the publisher of electronic journals.

To become an effective creator and disseminator of new information composites, the library must be more active than it is now. In the words of Welsch (1991): "Unfortunately, the image that emerges for me when I think of scholarly societies, universities, and libraries and their roles in the creation of information systems of all kinds is, with rare exception, one of passivity."

One specific problem to be faced in the future is how to deal with electronic journals, assuming that these journals are accessible through networks. Stoller (1992) identifies three options:

In simple terms, those options are: first, to print the journal either directly from the online file or with the intermediate step of a download and manipulation by word processing software; second, to download the online file to an electronic medium, usually a diskette, manipulate the file with word processing software, and provide access through personal computers; third, to maintain the file on a mainframe computer and provide access through a local area network. (Page 659)

He goes on to discuss the pros and cons of each of these options. Unfortunately, he seems to assume that electronic journals will be little more than print on paper displayed electronically. If, as seems likely, completely new forms emerge—e.g., with analog models or other forms of animation—certain options, such as printing out on paper, remove themselves from consideration.

The University of Pennsylvania Libraries (1990) concluded, perhaps not surprisingly, that there is no one best method of providing access to electronic resources. All forms of access—remote time-sharing, CD-ROM, and locally mounted files—are needed. Factors influencing the choice for a particular set of data include timeliness, expected volume of use, the probable number of simultaneous users, and whether remote access (from offices, laboratories, classrooms, and so on) is required.

One library that has already gone a long way toward the adoption of collection development policies for electronic resources is the Mann Library at Cornell University, as discussed by Demas et al. (1995). They identify various levels or "tiers" of access, illustrated in Figure 29. Note that some high-demand items may be downloaded from the national network to the campus network while others are merely accessible from the national network on demand (possibly through the aid of "pointers" provided locally).

Policies of other academic libraries, vis-à-vis electronic journals, can be found in Parang and Saunders (1994a, 1994b). Approaches to access will be discussed further in Chapter 10.

Archiving and Preservation

Preservation of materials is an important facet of collection management. What are the library's responsibilities for preservation in an electronic environment? Summerhill (1991) seems to believe that libraries collectively should strive to preserve almost everything communicated: "Computer conference logs, electronic serials, even archived exchanges of electronic mail transmissions may all be appropriate for a library to acquire and preserve, given sufficient interest on the part of the user community."

Tier 1
Delivered over the campus network via the Mann Library Gateway. Anticipated high demand and need for quick response and manipulation time dictate the use of media and software, which will provide very fast response time.

Tier 2
Delivered over the campus network via the Mann Library Gateway. Must be interactively available, but a relatively low number of simultaneous uses is expected and slower retrieval time acceptable. Therefore a slower storage medium, such as optical platter, may be acceptable.

Tier 3
Resources that can be delivered online via the Gateway on demand, but are not continuously available online. Tier 3 resources may be mounted on request for Gateway access or may be used in the library at any time.

Tier 4
Resources that are available in the library only (i.e., not delivered over the campus network), but that are available from many public access workstations within the library over a local area network.

Tier 5
Resources that are available in the library only, at single user stations

---

FIGURE 29
Levels of access to electronic resources identified at
the Mann Library, Cornell University.
From Demas et al. (1995) by permission of the American Library Association

He goes on to defend the position that even "ephemeral" communications need preservation:

> Those who doubt the suitability of personal exchanges of electronic mail might consider what value such materials would be to a historian of the twenty-first or twenty-second century faced with the task of reconstructing the correspondence of an individual (or organization) who ceased writing letters on paper late in the twentieth century. (Page 185)

A very similar claim has been made by Stoller (1992), but not everyone holds such a view. For example, Shreeves (1992), quoting a speaker at a Symposium on Scholarly Communication held at the University of Iowa in 1991, introduces the argument that not all communication among scholars is scholarly communication and that much of what is transmitted by electronic mail or computer conferencing is nothing more than "high level, high-tech cocktail party conversation"; only peer-reviewed communication can be considered scholarly and thus worth preserving.

Brichford and Maher (1995) suggest that the library and archive professions may be too preoccupied with techniques and standards for the preservation of physical media. Preservation should be more a matter of access to information than the survival of any particular storage media. It is the information and the access points that need to be protected and preserved. They identify three options for ensuring the ongoing accessibility of electronic resources:

1. Printing onto hard copy once use has tapered off and interactive access is no longer essential.
2. Retaining the original storage media, software, and hardware.
3. Continual conversion of the data, with appropriate verification, to newly developed hardware and software.

While the last option is preferred, it is obviously the most expensive and could only be justified if the information involved continues to have high value and to be of interest to a large community of users. In the case of the second option, the library would become a cross between a modern information center (embracing the newest technologies) and a museum (preserving the old).

Graham (1995) is one of the writers who has stressed that libraries must continue to take a major responsibility in the preservation of resources:

> It will be important to establish standards for the number of repository locations necessary to assure long-term existence of specific electronic information and access to it. (Page 334)

> Nothing makes clearer that a library is an organization, rather than a building or a collection, than the requirement for institutional commitment if electronic information is to have more than a fleeting existence. (Page 335)

The policies of several major research libraries regarding electronic journals (Parang and Saunders, 1994a, 1994b) also suggest that these institutions recognize the need to preserve and archive these resources and not just to provide remote access to them.

While Europe appears to favor the idea of a central depository for the preservation and archiving of electronic materials, the U.S. approach is more decentralized, with the responsibility shared among a variety of national, public and university centers (CEU addresses . . . 1996).

Luijendijk (1996) and Nisonger (1996) have both discussed responsibilities in the archiving of electronic journals. The former considers that this could be undertaken by libraries, publishers or vendors; the latter mentions libraries, publishers or cooperatives as alternatives. Participants in the recently completed TULIP Project (Hunter, 1996; TULIP, 1996) have pointed out why the library community, rather than the publishing industry, should take on the task.

Costs and problems associated with the archiving of electronic journals by individual research libraries are discussed in some detail by Duranceau et al. (1996). They recommend that their institution, MIT Libraries, should store locally ("archive") only the electronic journals published there. Access to others would be provided by "pointing" to them, perhaps through some other library-maintained system such as CIC-Net. Neavill and Sheblé (1995) provide another useful discussion on several related issues relevant to electronic journals: archiving, preservation, storage, and "authentication of content."

The JSTOR project, supported by the Mellon Foundation, is making significant progress in preserving back issues of important journals by creating high quality bit-mapped images (DeGennaro, 1997).

Conway (1996) has dramatically highlighted the "dilemma of modern media," which refers to information density versus life expectancy—the more efficient the medium in terms of storage capacity, the shorter its life expectancy. He points out that:

> Understanding how to adapt preservation concepts to manage risk in the midst of rapid technological ferment is what preservation in the digital world is all about. (Page 1)

Resource Sharing

Technology has already had a profound beneficial effect on resource sharing activities. What form will this take in the future? Few doubt its importance. Dougherty and Hughes (1991) report: "It was also observed that libraries and library services were no longer individual university problems and that a collective approach is now absolutely essential." In a similar vein, Cline (1994) has pointed out that "Alliances will be increasingly important to libraries in the networked environment."

Summerhill (1991) has given some specifics:

Striking the delicate balance between local ownership and network access will be aided by, if not achieved by, a formal acquisition process that accounts for network access. Librarians must shift the focus of their acquisition policies from the collection of materials by and for an individual library to policies that weigh the merit of acquiring the same resource by consortia of local libraries, regional library cooperatives, and/or state library networks. The funding agencies that back libraries must come to accept this type of cooperative venture. At the same time, vendors of commercial data products must understand the imperative facing libraries to enter cooperative collection development agreements. Accordingly, they must develop fee structures that accommodate such ventures. (Page 184)

To what extent will what we now think of as "interlibrary loan" (though most of it is not) continue in the future? The topic is dealt with by Stoller (1992):

Finally, on the access level, interlibrary loan must be considered as a potential method for ensuring reasonably universal availability of electronic journals. This seems, on its face, to be a preposterous notion. Electronic text, by its nature, does not seem "loanable." But bibliographic control will invariably result in requests by individuals who either do not realize the title they have discovered is a computer file or who harbor the hope that the host library will consider printing out that file's contents on their behalf. For libraries that approach local access by printing out the journals, of course, such requests would be easily met. For others, the level of service they are willing to provide over interlibrary loan will need to be determined, much as has been the case with CD-ROM products. In a world where online computer access is still not universally available to students and scholars, such determinations will have important implications for access to a scholarship in a format that is likely to become increasingly common. (Page 663)

Even since 1992, when these remarks were published, the situation has changed considerably and it is probably no longer true that "online computer access is still not universally available to students and scholars," at least in the most developed countries. Moreover, Stoller is making the assumption that future journals will still be "printable." In fact, it seems likely that the electronic journals of the future will incorporate dynamics and hypermedia features that precludes their reproduction on paper. Ra (1990) was more realistic when she pointed out that, while technology at first increased resource sharing, "it will probably make interlibrary loan obsolete within a generation."

Of course, resource sharing involves more than interlibrary lending. The major research institutions that are members of the Committee for

Institutional Cooperation (CIC) have taken a lead in exploring the possibilities for resource sharing in a network environment (Dannelly, 1995; MacEwan and Geffner, 1996). Cochenour (1996) reports that the CIC-Net Web server, which makes over 800 titles available, is now accessed about 35,000 times each day through the Internet. Cataloging, bibliographic control and the provision of a user-friendly interface are other services provided by the CIC libraries. CICNet does not "archive" all 800 titles (most are accessed by pointing to their location at publisher or other sites) but has established a smaller "managed" electronic journal collection (50 titles in 1996) for which "consistent archiving" is provided. Thus, at present at least, CICNet is more a provider of access than an archiving center.

One possible model for resource sharing in a virtual library environment is exemplified in the initiatives of the Virginia Academic Library Consortium (Hurt, 1995), of which a key element is the recognition of several major academic institutions as regional electronic resource centers. Libraries will participate in building the statewide virtual library in the following way:

> All participating colleges and universities in the state will be encouraged to contribute online materials to the virtual library, either by providing them electronically to the appropriate electronic resource center or by linking their online resources directly to the system. Thus we have a system of networked resources using distributed client-server architecture and exploiting the enormous potential of the Virginia Research Network to link libraries and educational institutions together. Because the information is cooperatively acquired and maintained by the regional resource centers and patrons are assured easy access, libraries will no longer need to duplicate holdings of materials. (Page 51)

Hurt claims that the consortium will provide "a common system of easy-to-understand menus" and a "powerful search mechanism," the objective being an access system that is "seamless."

Another obvious facet of resource sharing is the development of joint licensing agreements that permit consortia of libraries to share responsibilities and costs of providing access to electronic resources (Gosling et al., 1995).

More than a decade ago, Lancaster (1982) stated that:

> Electronic sources, at least those remotely accessible, do not need to be acquired, nor do they need selection. Rather, the selection activity is of a

> different kind: Librarians select what to access to satisfy a known demand
> rather than what to purchase in anticipation of future demands.*

To a very large extent, he still agrees with this. However, in the last ten years, and particularly in the last two or three, the profession has given much more thought to what collection development and collection management really mean when electronic communication is the focus of attention. As we have seen in this chapter, views range from the librarian as primarily mediator between users and network resources to the librarian as creator and publisher of new information resources.

One does not really know what the world will look like even a decade from now. It is possible that the whole system of scholarly communication will be very much different from the situation today. Shreeves (1992) considers the collection development librarian as primarily a gatekeeper—one who identifies that portion of the universe of information resources that is likely to be of greatest value to a particular user or group of users. Whatever happens to scholarly communication, and whatever happens to the library as an institution, it is clear that gatekeepers of this type will still be needed in the future. Indeed, they will be even more important than they are today.

---

*Hitchingham (1996) makes the distinction rather nicely as, on the one hand, a "collection function" and, on the other, a "connection function."

CHAPTER 8

Library-Vendor Relationships

IOIOIOIOIOIOIOIOIOIOIOIOIOIOIOIOIOIOIOIOIOIOIOIOIOIOIOIOIOIOIOIOIOIOIOIOIOIOIOIOIOIOIOIOIOI

TECHNOLOGY and shrinking acquisitions budgets have had an important effect on the relationship between vendors and libraries. In the 1980s, the advent of online systems for ordering, receiving, and tracking the acquisitions process introduced a crucial service component into what was once a simple transaction between libraries and vendors. Today, vendors are no longer judged solely on their ability to supply books, but also on the added electronic services that libraries believe will make the work of ordering and obtaining books more efficient and cost-effective. Further, vendors, publishers, and academic institutions are grappling with the challenge of providing access to electronic publications, and developing adequate and reasonable pricing and delivery structures to support their production and maintenance. This chapter examines the impact of technology on the relationship between libraries and vendors.

Relationships and Roles: Publishers, Vendors, and Libraries

Vendors play an intermediary role between libraries and publishers. Put simply, they perform the function of buying books and other materials from publishers, and selling them to libraries. In doing so, they supply services such as ordering, claiming, and tracking book and journal orders that help libraries buy books from one or several places without having to establish labor-intensive relationships with individual publishers. They help libraries to keep track of their orders, to profile their acquisition needs and, when possible, they pass on publishers' discounts. Prior to the introduction of automation in libraries, the relationship between libraries, vendors, and publishers was fairly simple and straightforward. Fisher (1993) cites three major factors that have had a significant impact on the relationship between libraries, publishers, and vendors, two of which are associated directly with technology:

... libraries (as well as other organizations) have been transformed through automation ... Libraries, publishers, and vendors have all had to deal with this change, sometimes because they wanted to, sometimes because they simply had to in order to remain competitive.

This technology has also had two other effects on libraries that changed their relationship with publishers and vendors. First, we have seen the creation of a whole new brand of vendor, the automation vendor. Second, as funding leveled off or even decreased for libraries, much of this technology had to be acquired at the sacrifice of book/journal funds. The question is quickly becoming one of allocating funds by type of information format (print, CD, online) regardless of the product, by type of product (book, journal, map) regardless of the format, or some other method. Publishers will not only have to compete with their print counterparts, but they will also need to be aware of what is happening electronically and how that is impacting their market share. Vendors will have to *carry* more lines and have personnel that can help their customers select the right format for their clientele. (Pages 63-64)

As Fisher suggests, numerous vendors have adapted automation within their own organizations, and are now giving libraries access gateways to electronically published resources. Vendors have also begun to use technology to expand their services. They are becoming increasingly involved in the outsourcing of activities that libraries traditionally perform, such as pre-order searching and verification, the creation of order records, and the provision of cataloging records. Concurrently, libraries have begun to allocate increased portions of their acquisitions budgets to fund the purchase of electronic resources. All of these activities suggest a subtle shift in the relationship between libraries and vendors, with vendors providing an increased amount of service for libraries and libraries working with them to determine where, in the technical services chain, economies can best be achieved.

Effects of Change on Vendors

Since vendors have occupied an intermediary role in the information publishing and procurement chain, they, as Presley (1993) notes:

... became as much of a victim of the changing times as the libraries. Not only were publishers increasing their prices but they were also not giving the vendors as much of a discount, and in many cases, as with Bowker and UMI, they deliberately refused to deal with vendors and forced the library to order direct. In other cases, publishers undercut the vendors and encouraged libraries to order directly by offering a better price than they could possibly get through a vendor ... Of course, the overhead of dealing with orders, claiming, and following up on address changes, etc., is a tremendous cost, but it is an indirect cost that does not show up in the cost of subscriptions on a materials budget line. (Pages 55-56)

Through budget cuts and dramatically rising costs for serial subscriptions, Presley notes that libraries grew to expect vendors to develop a "unified front" with them to fight publisher price increases and to provide libraries with automated systems that enable the tracking of expenditures to optimize the use of shrinking acquisitions budgets. The expectations of libraries for automated acquisitions systems were complex indeed:

> There were several needs for automation services. One was that as the cost of library materials continued to escalate, libraries needed information and measuring tools to determine exactly which materials were increasing in price, in what areas, and by how much. From vendors, we needed more sophisticated management reports that not only gave us information on specific accounts and expenditures, but also information on the holdings of area institutions, and information on how the economic situation was being projected for publishers and the economy as a whole. This need included current and dependable analyses of the national economic forecasts. Also, because of the fluctuating dollar and the high price of foreign publications, libraries needed predictions and services based on global and international monetary exchanges. This was particularly important for libraries that did not have sophisticated in-house automation resources and systems. (Presley, 1993, pp. 56-57).

In order to exploit this information effectively, libraries needed to receive it in an online format that would enable them to incorporate it into their growing OPAC and accounting systems. In the 1980s, vendors faced the inevitable challenge of automating their own operations, providing automated acquisitions systems for libraries, developing the telecommunications that would enable them to link their ordering systems to those of libraries, and attempting to cut their general operating expenditures in spite of declining publisher discounts (Secor, 1987). These demands changed the company organizational fabric, necessitating that vendors move from a primarily sales orientation to one of service. They began to hire professionals with library and systems experience in order to create systems that support acquisitions and serial check-in as well as to provide the required changes in specialized services to libraries. This trend in automated system development also fostered intense competition between "library materials vendors and library hardware and software vendors." (Presley, 1993).

Presley notes that rising serial prices and flat-to-decreasing library acquisitions budgets further fueled a "painful ethical battle for the library: should it continue its subscriptions with a long-time vendor with impeccable service or switch to one who would supply online ordering and check-in?" In the end, Presley notes, the vendor who supplied the most efficient and technologically-advanced service was awarded his library's subscription service. He reflects on the point that libraries are responsible for communicating directly to vendors their overall needs and expectations for acquisitions service and support, so that vendors can develop a position of partnership and reasonable performance to meet library needs.

Impact of the Internet
on Communication and Vendor Services

It appears that Presley's perspective has been rapidly adopted by numerous libraries, with the most convenient and effective communication tool being the Internet. Libraries, publishers, and vendors now participate in Internet conversations through listservs and the Web, providing one another with up-to-the-minute information on their services and their needs.* Several listservs, including the ACQNET-L listserv, enable discussion of operational and philosophical acquisitions issues among libraries, publishers, and vendors. Using the Web, vendors now provide a convenient gateway for access to their own services. Libraries use the Web to share information about acquisitions policy, procedures, and vendor services, and performance. One such example is the Web page maintained by Peter Stevens at the University of Washington both for internal consultation, and for public access (Stevens, 1996a). The University of Washington Acquisitions home page contains information on their acquisitions policies, procedures, and operations, as well as links to similar pages for a number of academic libraries.

An excerpt from the University of Washington Libraries' vendor selection policy reflects that institution's requirements and needs, and indicates that the library monitors the efficiency and cost margin of their vendor services:

> Whether a vendor becomes a source for Acquisitions depends on many factors: the type of order, the vendor's speed of supply, the discount the vendor

---

*The World Wide Web is discussed in Chapter 13.

provides, the vendor's service and responsiveness, whether the vendor can accept electronic orders, and communicate via electronic mail. While Acquisitions is always interested in learning of vendors in its fields of interest, the choice of whether to use a vendor or try them out is an individual decision.

Once Acquisitions adds a vendor to its vendor list, that vendor is subject to regular monitoring of its speed of supply and, for U.S. vendors, its discount levels. Vendors who fail to remain competitive among Acquisitions' sources may be relegated to inactive status, whether they are high-discount but slow vendors or fast vendors with poor discounts. (Stevens, 1996b)

Stevens provides annual reviews of the speed of supply from various vendors, including U.S. and international vendors. This information is generated in reports from the online acquisitions and serials subsystems of Innovative Interfaces Inc. (Figure 30).

Whenever possible, the University of Washington encourages the use of vendors that accommodate electronic ordering; it provides a list of recommended vendors that supply this service and maintains current information on those vendors on the staff web page. A cursory review of the average delivery time for various vendors suggests that electronic ordering capability is not necessarily an indicator of faster delivery.

The University of Washington's acquisitions Web page also tracks the percentage of vendor discounts on materials. Figures 31 and 32 from the University of Washington Web site show the discount rates for a number of U.S. vendors, for a two-month time frame in 1994, and for the time period July 1995 through April, 1996. The format of the two figures varies slightly, although the discount rate is displayed consistently.

It would be difficult to make specific comparisons between the discount amounts in these two figures because the information is presented differently for each year. However, it can be concluded that Blackwell's discount rate of 16% for approval plan books has remained consistent since April, 1994, and that other major vendor discount rates (such as those of Midwest Library Services and Baker & Taylor) may have declined slightly within the same time frame. This information could become more valuable as a comparison tool over time as more annual pricing and discount rates are added. The review of studies of vendor performance by Reid (1990) highlights several reasons to perform evaluation of vendor services, including: confirming or refuting informal staff assumptions; communicating needs to a vendor; determining where and

U.S. RUSH ORDERS
    1. University Book Store   1.3 weeks
  *2. Academic Book Center   3.8 weeks
  *3. Midwest Library Service   6.3 weeks
  *4. Blackwell North America   6.7 weeks

U.S. REGULAR ORDERS
  *1. Matthews Medical Books   3.1 weeks
  *2. Academic Book Center   4.7 weeks
  *3. The Book House   4.8 weeks
  *4. Yankee Book Peddler   5.6 weeks
  *5. University Park Media   6.5 weeks
  *6. Midwest Library Service   6.7 weeks
  *7. Blackwell North America   6.8 weeks
  *8. Coutts Library Service   7.1 weeks
  *9. Login Brothers   9.3 weeks

OTHER U.S. VENDORS
MEDIA
    1. Facets Video   2.8 weeks
    2. Ambassador Media   4.4 weeks
MUSIC SCORES
    1. Pepper   3.7 weeks
    2. Eble   5.3 weeks
    3. Theodore Front   8.4 weeks
DOCUMENTS
    1. Unipub   2.5 weeks
    2. Accents Publications   5.0 weeks

OTHER MATERIALS
    1. World Bank   2.4 weeks
    2. University Microforms   4.0 weeks
    3. Worldwide   4.9 weeks

FOREIGN ORDERS
All vendors (US, foreign)   4.0 weeks
16,255 orders received

CANADA:
    1. MacNeill   6.9 weeks
  *2. Coutts   7.6 weeks

FIGURE 30
Vendor speed of supply, July 1995–April 1996.
Source: University of Washington Libraries,
URL: http://weber.u.washington.edu/~acqdiv/vendorspeedapr96.html

This speed of supply information is obtained from the vendor performance module in an Innovative Interfaces acquisitions system and reflects local vendor selection decisions. Other libraries' experience may differ from the experience of the University of Washington.

ENGLAND:
- *1. W. H. Everett — 7.5 weeks
- *2. B. H. Blackwell — 7.9 weeks

FRANCE:
- *1. Aux Amateurs — 5.9 weeks

GERMANY:
- *1. Harrassowitz — 6.4 weeks
- 2. Brockhaus — 7.7 weeks

ITALY:
- 1. Casalini — 10.0 weeks

SPAIN:
- 1. RJ Books — 5.0 weeks
- 2. Passim — 8.7 weeks

GENERAL EUROPEAN:
- 1. European Book Centre — 7.8 weeks
- *2. Nijhoff — 8.2 weeks

SCANDINAVIAN:
- 1. Hemlins — 4.0 weeks
- 2. Norli — 4.5 weeks
- *3. Munksgaard — 8.7 weeks

MEXICO:
- 1. Mexican Academic Clrhse — 7.0 weeks

BRAZIL:
- 1. Susan Bach — 7.3 weeks

SOUTH AMERICA:
- 1. Cambeiro — 17.0 weeks

VENEZUELA:
- 1. Inca — 6.0 weeks

ISRAEL:
- 1. Jerusalem Books — 14.0 weeks

INDIA:
- 1. Vedams — 11.0 weeks

PHILIPPINES:
- 1. Heritage — 22.7 weeks

* = orders sent electronically

FIGURE 30 *Continued*

how current practices ought to change; determining when to use a vendor; exploring approaches to reducing the number of vendors used or even to select a vendor to use exclusively.

Firm Orders:

Vendor	No. of Books	Total List	Amount Saved	Net Discount
1. Baker and Taylor	170	$5,562	$1,462	26.28%
2. Ambassador Book	65	2,299	405	17.60%
3. Midwest	112	3,294	536	16.27%
4. Conant & Conant	226	12,272	1,803	14.69%
5. Academic Book Center	94	4,604	639	13.87%
6. Blackwell	243	9,201	981	10.66%
7. Majors	25	3,042	316	10.40%
8. Yankee Book	21	1,122	935	8.43%
9. Book House	28	1,213	53	4.31%

Approval Programs:
Approval program net discounts are negotiated at flat rates as follows:

1. Blackwell--books	16%
Blackwell--forms	13%
2. Majors--books, forms	12%

FIGURE 31
U.S. vendor discounts, April 1994-June, 1994 (24 June 1994).
Source: University of Washington Libraries,
URL: http://weber.u.washington.edu/~acqdiv/vendordiscjun94.html

Invoices for firm orders to U.S. major book vendors have been surveyed during the months of April, May, and June 1994. Orders to Academic, Ambassador, Baker and Taylor, Conant & Conant, Majors and Midwest are based on a list of publishers negotiated with the vendors, with publishers assigned to the vendors who offer the best discount for each publisher. Orders to Blackwell, the Book House and Yankee are not based on this list. Orders to Blackwell are generally for publishers not offered by the publisher-list vendors above. The Book House and Yankee have been tested on a range of publishers. Total list prices cover the volume of orders invoiced during the survey period, but have been limited for the vendors used the most. Discounts are net, after shipping. The totals do not reflect the actual fiscal year average discount of 18% since they do not mirror the volume of actual vendor use throughout the fiscal year.

Vendors themselves have quickly adopted the Internet as a convenient and viable communications method that provides them with a platform from which they can offer efficient and expanded services such as ordering and links to related information resources. The Web enables vendors to provide both services and information about themselves to the general public. With this point of presence, vendors, many of which are privately held, can publish non-sensitive business information to familiarize the general public with their mission.* Baker & Taylor's home page, for example, provides historical information on the development of the firm. It also provides the information on how many titles the company routinely stocks, and describes an online paid subscription database (B & T Link) that covers over three million book titles that can be searched through the Internet (http://www.baker-taylor.com).

Orders:		Discount	Average List Price
1.	Baker & Taylor	23%	$ 40.73
2.	University Park Media	22%	62.76
3.	The Book House	17%	22.17
3.	Midwest Library Services	17%	31.18
5.	Academic Book Center	16%	50.56
6.	Matthews Medical Books	15%	123.81
	Average	14%	
7.	Blackwell North America	13%	43.36
8.	Coutts Library Services	13%	28.47
9.	Login Brothers	10%	59.96
10.	Yankee Book Peddler	7%	33.73
Approvals:			
	Blackwell North America books	16%	
	Blackwell North America forms	13%	
	Majors Scientific Books	12%	

FIGURE 32

U.S. vendor discounts, July 1995-April 1996 (1 July 1995-30 April 1996).
Source: University of Washington Libraries,
URL: http://weber.u.washington.edu/~acqdiv/vendordiscapr96.html

Outsourcing

Perhaps the highest potential for change and for merging of library and vendor roles is in the area of outsourcing as applied, for example, to acquisitions, collection development, and cataloging. Bush et al. (1994)

---

*Fisher 1993) notes that it is difficult to gather specific information on library vendors because they are usually privately held, and are fairly young companies. His research revealed that only four major firms that serve libraries were initiated before 1959: Baker & Taylor (1928), Majors (1909), Ingram (1933), and Brodart (1939).

performed an extensive survey of book jobbers, cataloging services, and library consortia to determine what services for collection development, acquisitions, and cataloging are currently offered or in process of development. The survey focused its questions on what the authors felt were areas of potential development of vendor services in acquisitions—contract acquisitions, distributed acquisitions using gateways to external systems, and a model relying directly on vendor systems. Of interest here are the numerous electronic services that vendors have developed to meet the needs of acquisitions functions in libraries. Summarized in Figure 33 are the results of the acquisitions portion of the Bush et al. survey of fourteen vendors or library consortia who responded.

Clearly, vendors have traditionally offered a number of these services to libraries. However, each of these services can be performed more quickly and reliably using technology, and vendors have quickly adopted electronic methods for doing so. For example, Bush et al. report that one vendor loads the holdings of the client library into its own database to check for duplicates, and that they have even accessed library online catalogs through the Internet to check a library's holdings on an item-by-item basis for small projects. It has been suggested that perhaps OCLC might in future provide such a search service for book records that are sent to them by vendors. Bush et al. suggest that the area of pre-order verification is one in which there is "considerable opportunity for expansion of vendor services capability." Vendors normally use a combination of Books in Print, their internal databases, and LC MARC tapes to verify prices. They create electronic order records which can be transmitted into a library's local acquisition system. Claiming is another area in which technology has enabled a significant number of the vendors surveyed to develop interfaces between their own online systems and those of library customers (Bush et al., 1994). Further, six vendors reported that they "either have or are working on a centralized interface for firm ordering with OCLC." Others reported that they are working with regional consortia to implement similar centralized ordering interfaces. This type of service would simplify the ordering process considerably, because it would enable the simultaneous searching of titles against several vendor databases. Presumably the ordering process could also be initiated from that point with the individual vendor.

Function	Vendor/consortium offering service (N=14)
X12 used for electronic data interchange	7/14
BISAC standard used	14/14
New orders checked against firm orders	9/14
Firm orders checked against library holdings	4/14
Price verification	14/14
Electronic order record	13/14
Electronic interface for fund accounting	5/14
Electronic claiming interface	8/14
Customized management reports	13/14
Centralized ordering interface (e.g., OCLC)	6/14

FIGURE 33
Survey of acquisitions services provided by vendors.
Based on data from Bush et al. (1994) by permission of Elsevier Science Inc.

The survey also addressed collection development services provided by vendors and consortia to libraries. The results indicated that,
in the area of approval plans, most vendors surveyed now use automated
profiles or some variation of such a format to assist in identifying the
areas in which a library is interested in collecting (Bush et al., 1994). These
automated profiles contain a considerable amount of information,
including subject, classification, format of material, publisher, author,
series, price, audience, and foreign imprint. Reports can be generated
flexibly in most cases from these profiles. Other types of plans related
to the approval plan model are available, with the automated profiles serving as a common basis for determining the collecting interests of the
library. Nine of the fourteen vendors surveyed offer libraries access to
online databases of titles of in-stock and forthcoming titles, and nearly
all can supply files of new book titles that libraries purchase. Several vendors provide table of contents services, and seven can supply specialized
lists of purchased titles in electronic form. Vendors also supply other services that are facilitated by access to ancillary databases, including
checking new titles against retrospective holdings, creating special catalogs, and automatic shipment of titles that appear in standard book review
sources such as Choice or New York Times Book Review (Bush et al., 1994).

Technology has enabled both vendors and libraries to develop a perspective on book selection and acquisition that does not require a centralized and rigid paper record-keeping activity. Bush et al. suggest that vendors and libraries may in fact be moving toward a more user-centered acquisitions model:

> ... these models could entail authorizing library users to access library or jobber systems for ordering titles directly. The librarians could place price limits and designate the acquisition accounts. This would contribute to a user-centered selection and acquisitions system. In the distributed model, the library's system would track to preapproved accounts and send to preapproved vendors. Applications of artificial intelligence embedded within the library's system could add sophistication to this process ... The vendor system model implies that the vendor would maintain records of the order and track library accounts, although an alternative might be to download the vendor record to the library's system to show what is on order. (Pages 406-407)

The authors of the survey also examined cataloging outsourcing services, noting that collection development, acquisitions, and cataloging are the areas in which the activities have developed increasing overlap. Bush et al. further note that OCLC is poised to play a potentially important role in the area of firm ordering and approval plan processing. In 1995 OCLC introduced the PromptCat service, which provides libraries with cataloging copy for books that are ordered through approval plans with vendors. The vendors who participated in the PromptCat project from its inception included Academic Book Center, Blackwell North America, Yankee Book Peddler, and Baker & Taylor. The PromptCat service batch processes approval plan order information from vendors in electronic format (in the X12 EDI standard), searches these titles against the OCLC Online Union Catalog for copy, sets the library's holding symbol on OCLC, and transmits the matching record to the library (Kircher, 1994).

Several libraries participated in the test phase for the PromptCat service in 1993. Michigan State University Libraries, one of the test phase participants, found that 99% of the records received from OCLC exactly matched the book in hand; however, when OCLC supplied records based on CIP data, 51% required the addition of collation information (Campbell, 1994). Additionally, the PromptCat project served as a catalyst for the technical services unit at Michigan State University Libraries to rethink the work flow that had previously existed between acquisitions and cataloging:

> This experiment gave us the opportunity to implement an intellectual shift in the way we view and process approval plan titles . . . We call this process monograph check-in rather than copy cataloging, allowing us to move these titles through technical services very quickly, with little handling, and with entry-level staff. (Campbell, 1994)

In sum, the Bush et al. survey suggests that vendors are currently offering or developing an increasing number of electronic and specialized services to libraries that appear to fulfill a number of aspects of the selection, ordering, and cataloging processes that libraries formerly carried out or tracked internally. Bush et al. also feel that decisions about whether libraries will move further toward contract acquisitions depend both on technological development and individual library acquisitions practices:

> Ready to speed the interchange among systems are the EDI standards for communicating business information now being developed and implemented. Whether full contracting for acquisitions becomes commonplace rests with technology, communication standards, and the collection development practices of libraries. (Page 407)

The EDI (Electronic Data Interchange) standard enables vendors and libraries to exchange order information in a consistent format. The upgrading of fund accounting and ordering software to accommodate this standard promises to simplify the exchange of order information.

Combined Effects of Technology and Role Changes

In February, 1996, the authors informally posed the question on the ACQNET-L listserv of how technology had affected the acquisitions process and the relationship between libraries and vendors. The several responses received indicated an overall positive effect, although one respondent noted that technology had decreased vendor ability to tend to important details. Harsin (1996) indicates that technology has enabled Loyola University of Chicago to "reengineer our entire Technical Services operation," with an emphasis on using automation to improve efficiency. This change also brought about a consolidation of a considerable portion of that institution's acquisitions business, and transferred to the vendor some of the processing operations that the library had previously performed internally:

> As a result we: adopted PromptCat as the means for obtaining cataloging for our approval materials; consolidated all our North American business with a single vendor including standing orders, approval and firm, so our vendor could catch duplicate items for us before they were shipped; began having the vendor do some processing of the books for us such as applying barcodes before shipment; began activating forms in the approval plan via telnet rather than mailing the forms in; and numerous other innovations.
>
> There has been no area of our operation that has not been affected and changed. There has been no aspect of our relationship with our vendor that has not been impacted by the increased use of technology. (Harsin, 1996)

A report of a recent discussion at an American Library Association conference on the acquisition, access, and retention of electronic journals (Coulter, 1996) indicated that most librarians felt that the Web was the most logical place for publishers to provide access to electronic journals. The participants in the discussion indicated that they use the same procedures for ordering electronic journals as they do for print journals. However, the group noted that ambiguous licensing issues made the purchase process more complicated. Most participants in the discussion were still grappling with the issues of archiving and storage as well as monitoring the use of the electronic journals.

One respondent felt that, with automated matching programs, vendors rarely used additional search methods beyond an ISBN match or human intervention to locate titles. The respondent suggested that author or title searches may turn up an alternative edition of a work that the library might in fact purchase if the edition they request is unavailable (McAbee, 1996):

> As an Acquisitions Librarian I am disturbed by the lack of personal attention given to our orders. These days if a book with a particular isbn is not in a vendor's system they report it as unavailable, OP, etc. They do not pursue an alternative edition by searching by title or author. e.g. Tom Sawyer or Grapes of Wrath are all available in paperback but the printings may change and as a result a new isbn is issued. The vendors report that these are out of print when in fact if they searched by author or title they would locate another printing. They are so dependent on automation that only an isbn hit is worth pursuing.

The Future

Technology, combined with other forces, has caused the roles and responsibilities of acquisitions departments in libraries and vendors to blur. The information examined in this chapter suggests that technology has enabled vendors to simplify the ordering, accounting, and claiming process for libraries, and to supply access to increasingly complete electronic files of their materials. In turn, acquisitions vendors are able to team up with cataloging vendors to simplify the searching and cataloging process, especially in the cases of approval plan materials. Secor (1996) believes that four values will help to determine whether some vendors survive in the short term. These values include competitive pricing, technology leadership, a clear understanding of customer needs, and operating excellence. He suggests that both libraries and vendors are driving the technological changes that are occurring in the area of materials ordering and processing. He emphasizes that the most mutually beneficial relationships can be established by libraries and vendors teaming up to develop and test new products and services, as opposed to operating on the assumption that "cutting edge" technology ought always to be superior to current practice and support. Secor predicts that the current market cannot continue to support the number of vendors currently in business, and that the field will see an increase in "strategic alliances" with companies collaborating to develop both technology and marketing approaches.

Distinctions between types of vendor are becoming less precise also. For example, firms that were once considered as primarily subscription agents are now taking on other roles such as providing access to the full text of certain journals.

Atkinson's (1992) approach to analyzing future scenarios for acquisitions within the electronic library posits an active role for acquisitions librarians in the procurement and delivery of information. He advocates that acquisitions departments ought to assume significant responsibility for delivering scholarly publications and that they ought to develop increased expertise in the technical aspects of networked information delivery. Atkinson suggests that traditional operations that are currently not linked, such as acquisitions, interlibrary loan, publishing, and networking, should all be linked within an electronic library environment, with the primary focus on the acquisition, creation, delivery, and mediation of use for electronic texts and other bibliographic information. He argues that the library is in the best position to assume responsibility for scholarly publishing in the electronic library environment:

> If the library is truly to serve the interests of scholarly communication, it must appropriate increased economic responsibility for scholarly publishing. The economics of scholarly communication cannot be left solely in the hands either of the information technicians or the commercial publishers, although both of those groups—one in the interests of expediency, the other for purposes of profit—have been and will continue to be quite prepared to assume that control. Rather, it is the library that is in the best position to assume responsibility, as it has always sought to do, for ensuring that scholarly information is available to all who need it for educational and research purposes. (Page 17)

The extent to which libraries will assume responsibility for electronic publishing is not yet known. It is also not yet clear how library and vendor relationships with respect to traditional print materials will evolve, but evidence examined in this chapter suggests that the technology has enabled significant changes to occur in ordering, cataloging, and making print materials accessible in libraries.

CHAPTER 9

The Impact of CD-ROM

IOIOIOIOIOIOIOIOIOIOIOIOIOIOIOIOIOIOIOIOIOIOIOIOIOIOIOIOIOIOIOIOIOIOIOIOIOIOIOIOI

CHAPTERS 9-12 deal with various aspects of technology that directly affect users of library and information services, although organizational issues are dealt with in addition to impact on users. CD-ROM is discussed first because it is a technology that has become reasonably pervasive and it seems logical to cover this topic before the related but broader issues that follow.* This chapter reviews the effects on staff, services, and users. CD-ROM is compared with other forms of database access, particularly from the aspect of cost-effectiveness, in Chapter 10.

Effect on Staff

The obvious appeal of CD-ROM is that it can be used to put bibliographic databases and other reference tools directly into the hands of users, giving them a more sophisticated searching capability than they have with comparable printed tools, and reducing the need for online searches performed for users by members of the library staff.

But CD-ROM technology does not necessarily offer major savings in staff time. Time that was formerly spent in conducting searches for users may now be spent in teaching them how to search the CD-ROM databases for themselves, and in offering assistance to these users when they need it. Where many different CD-ROM databases are made available, a considerable amount of time may be spent by the staff in learning how to use them since each vendor's software will have somewhat different commands and search capabilities. Moreover, while not

---

*Nevertheless, fewer libraries have been affected than one might suppose. A survey undertaken in 1990 by Hauptman and Anderson (1994), involving 238 libraries of all types, revealed that 47% had no CD-ROM workstations and 51% no CD-ROM subscriptions. Batterbee and Nicholas (1995) report that CD-ROM was used in only 62% of British public libraries in 1994 (up marginally from 60% in 1992) and only 12% of public libraries made these sources directly accessible to library users. Kirby (1994) discusses some of the issues involved in introducing CD-ROM into a large public library in England.

all members of a reference staff needed to perform remote online searches, they all may need to be able to search CD-ROM in order to help patrons when necessary.

CD-ROM installations also require supervision and maintenance: disks may have to be changed, printers serviced, and so on. These activities need not involve professionals—they may be performed by clerical staff, perhaps by students in certain settings—but they represent a cost to the library nonetheless.

In the majority of libraries, the introduction of CD-ROM databases drastically reduced the number of online searches performed for users by librarians (*delegated* or *mediated* searches). To take one example, the Education/Psychology/Teaching Materials Center (E/P/TMC) of the Milner Library, Illinois State University (ISU), performed approximately 700 online searches in 1986. The availability of appropriate databases in CD-ROM form in the library brought a decline in online searches (i.e., online to the ERIC or other databases via some telecommunications network) to 200 in 1987 and about 100 in 1988.

Other librarians have also reported a decline in online searching as a result of the introduction of CD-ROM products. For example, Reese (1990), referring to the situation at Vanderbilt University, reports:

> The amount of online searching we do has been cut dramatically with the introduction of optical products. Librarian-mediated online searching has decreased at least 58 percent during a two year period. From July 1985-June 1986 there were 493 online searches; from July 1986-June 1987, 203; and from July 1987-June 1988 there were only 85. (Page 49)

On the other hand, Brahmi (1988), at the Indiana University School of Medicine Library, reports that CD-ROM has caused a dramatic reduction in online end user searching but has had little effect on mediated searching.

Stratton (1994) suggests that CD-ROM may eventually create a demand among users for more online access to remote databases, and Huang (1991) reports that this has occurred in libraries that provided little or no online searching prior to the introduction of CD-ROM.

Use of CD-ROM products continues to increase dramatically in many libraries. Geldenhuys (1995), for example, reports a 700% increase in use of the CD-ROM network at the University of Pretoria from 1993 to 1994.

User enthusiasm for CD-ROM seems to have taken some libraries by surprise. For example, Cox (1991), writing of a school of medicine library, found that the MEDLINE database generated so much demand so rapidly that users were having to wait as much as a week to get a scheduled search session; it was obvious that the single workstation available was completely inadequate. Dyer (1990) has reported a wait of as long as two weeks to access MEDLINE in one British academic library.

The migration from mediated online searching to nonmediated searching of CD-ROM databases by library users may also have some undesirable consequences on the professional staff of the library. Some libraries have reported a decline in the morale of staff members who were formerly heavily involved in database searching as they begin to feel their searching skills deteriorating, contributing to the fear of deprofessionalization alluded to in Chapter 3 (Butcher and Scott, 1990).

Effect on Other Library Services

Besides causing a decline in mediated online searching in most libraries, CD-ROM installations can have other effects on the policies and services of the library. Perhaps most obvious is the decline in use of printed tools for which CD-ROM equivalents exist. For example, Massey-Burzio (1990), writing of an academic library, has said that:

> Our paper index and abstract area is becoming deserted because of the CD-ROM products. Even when all of our workstations are occupied, our library users would rather wait than use the paper indexes. (Page 24)

This decline in use, coupled with the fact that CD-ROM materials compete for funds with other forms, has led to the cancellation of various printed tools in some libraries.

The adoption of CD-ROM also has implications for the use of library space. Installations close to a reference desk are convenient in terms of database use by staff and the provision of search assistance when needed by users, but this is "prime" space in many libraries; moreover, some library users prefer to work in a less public atmosphere especially if they are unsure of what they are doing. Setting a room or rooms aside for CD-ROM tools offers more privacy but makes supervision more difficult and may reduce the accessibility of the databases to members of the reference staff.

The enthusiastic adoption of CD-ROM technology by library users has also had less obvious impacts. Users are likely to want to borrow more or obtain more photocopies from other libraries, and this will increase the workload of certain members of the staff and overall costs to the library (Siddiqui, 1995). Increase in interlibrary loan has been so great in some libraries that they have had to consider some way of limiting the demand (Fairman, 1991), Also, the use of CD-ROM databases may create greater use of other materials within the library, so more time must be spent on reshelving and the overall maintenance of the collection.*

CD-ROM technology has other effects in libraries that are heavily involved in bibliographic instruction since much greater emphasis must now be placed on instruction in the use of electronic resources. In research environments, too, it may create a demand for other types of software, such as software for building and manipulating personal databases (Cox, 1991; Stratton, 1994).

CD-ROM has also had impacts on resource sharing beyond the increase in interlibrary lending. Moody (1990) has discussed several aspects, including union catalogs on CD-ROM and the sharing of databases within a group of libraries. Marks (1994) has described the production of a public-access catalog on CD-ROM, mentioning some of the problems involved.

In general, libraries have simply absorbed the costs of adding CD-ROM databases to their collections, frequently at the expense of other types of materials. However, in some situations, particularly in special library environments, it may be possible to find some creative approaches to cost recovery or partial cost recovery. For example, Cox (1991) describes how an academic medical library was able to generate income for the expansion of its CD-ROM service by establishing a fee-based current awareness service.

Fairman (1991) suggests that CD-ROM databases could actually improve the economics of collection management in some libraries, with the library subscribing to only the high use journals and relying on the CD-ROM databases, coupled with interlibrary loan or commercial document delivery services, to provide access to the contents of others.

---

*Chrzastowski (1995) reports that easy access to database searching facilities in an academic chemistry library led to increased use of the nucleus of key chemistry journals rather than a demand for more obscure sources.

Cox (1994) has identified other problems associated with the acquisition of CD-ROM databases, besides the cost aspects, including relatively poor characteristics compared with remote access to the same source: less current, slower access time, and usually covering a much shorter time span. He, along with Abbott and Smith (1994), also mention as a significant disadvantage the fact that most CD-ROM databases are leased by the library, rather than owned outright, and that the licensing agreements imposed by publishers may be very unfavorable to the library. Some of these issues are touched upon further in the next chapter. A very thorough treatment of criteria for the evaluation of CD-ROM databases, covering all aspects, can be found in a book by Jacsó (1992).

In a large library system, such as that of a major university, a decision on mode of management of CD-ROM resources may need to be made. While most libraries treat CD-ROM in the same way as other resources—with acquisition, control, and use decisions made by branch or departmental libraries—the possibility of centralized management also exists. O'Donovan (1994) has summarized the pros and cons of each approach (Figure 34).

Effect on Library Users

Most library users, especially student users, much prefer to use a reference source on CD-ROM than an equivalent printed tool. In general, their use of the electronic source is said to give them greater personal satisfaction and to improve their attitudes towards the library. They may also demand more help from the staff than they did in the past, and their overall expectations relating to other library services may be raised. Some users may express annoyance when they discover that their library does not own many of the sources indexed in a particular database.

While CD-ROM offered limited access when first introduced, libraries are increasingly adding CD-ROM resources to their local area networks (LANs).* Besides the technology required for this application, it is necessary to take into account the added load placed on the LAN. Also, the library must maintain a menu gateway for access to multiple

---

*An up-to-date guide to networking of CD-ROMS is Bradley (1996); the perspective is British.

resources, each of which has a different user interface. The diversity of resources available from a single workstation poses challenges for the librarian as instructor or intermediary, as well as for the user—who needs to negotiate each system separately.

CD-ROM as a separate responsibility	CD-ROM integrated within departments
Complete overview should lead to service responsive to user needs	Fragmented management may lead to less coherent service to users
Complex issues running across the library, e.g., relationship to inter-library loans, may not receive adequate attention	The place of the service within the range of library services will be discussed throughout the library
Straightforward decision making	Decision-making process may be complex, as differing viewpoints are reconciled
Expertise and skills may be lacking if relatively few staff involved	Wide range of expertise and skills can be called on throughout the system
Isolation may lead to conflict within the library	Integration should enable all staff to have a stake in CD-ROM

FIGURE 34
Centralized versus decentralized management of CD-ROM resources in large libraries.
Reprinted from O'Donovan (1994) by kind permission of Bowker-Saur, a division of Reed Business Information

It is now feasible and economical to offer access well beyond the scope of a local area network. Barbour and Rubinyi (1992), Onsi et al. (1992), and Sylvia (1994) are among the authors who have described dial-in access to CD-ROM databases, and Cutright and Girrard (1991) have put this in the context of support to the distant learner. Technology is now available that will allow several libraries to collaborate in running a server over the Internet using CD-ROM products copied onto large hard drives (Meyer, 1996).

A very substantial body of literature has already accumulated on user acceptance of CD-ROM databases and user satisfaction with the results of searches in these databases. Almost all of this is purely subjective, based on user impressions rather than objective evaluative data. Even the extensive studies of MEDLINE on CD-ROM do not include any true evaluations (Woodsmall et al. 1989) . User response to CD-ROM databases has been overwhelmingly enthusiastic. For example, Steffey and Meyer (1989) report that the majority of the comments of their users were of the "Wow! This is fantastic!" type. Nevertheless, some evidence exists to indicate that the initial enthusiasm of some users does decline with increased use of the medium (e.g., Allen, 1989a; Miller, 1987).

It is rather disturbing that so many library users seem completely uncritical in their evaluation of CD-ROM. Many express satisfaction even when they achieve very poor results. For example, Nash and Wilson (1991) found that undergraduate students were generally satisfied with their search results even when very few of the citations retrieved were useful to them.

An extreme example of this misplaced enthusiasm is cited by Dalrymple (1989):

> As we got further into the study, we became more and more concerned about the reliability of using the idea of satisfaction and what it really meant when somebody said that they were satisfied. Most everybody loved the system. They liked using it. It's fun. They get in and they get something out, but we can tell from our observations that a lot of them are not using the system terribly well and perhaps not getting what they think that they're getting. This is a real concern for us. I had an extreme example of a woman who never got the hang of combining terms. So she would go in with a couple of search terms and she would print out her citations and then she would put in the next term and print out her citations. Then she would walk out with her two printouts, really happy, really satisfied. She loved the system. She was there a couple of times a week. (Page 30)

People exposed to CD-ROM databases overwhelmingly prefer these to printed indexes even when there is rather little difference in the search results achieved (Stewart and Olsen, 1988). Moreover, CD-ROM may be used by some people who would not use the equivalent printed source. For example, Fairman (1991) has said:

> . . . students who would not go within a bargepole's length of a print abstracting service are queuing up to use CD-ROMs (Page 362).

Putting electronic databases into the hands of large numbers of library users is an exciting development but it has its dangers. As Charles and Clark (1990) report, "In our enthusiasm to embrace CD-ROM technology, librarians have neglected to make patrons aware of its drawbacks." They were specifically referring to the fact that CD-ROM databases tend not to be very current, but a greater danger lies in the fact that they give some library users a false sense of security—the feeling that, because the source is "technological," they are finding everything or, at least, finding the best materials. This even extends to the fact that some users feel they can do better than experienced searchers: "Using the disc," said one Columbia student, "is much better than having someone else search and give you useless information." (Miller, 1987)

The dangers have also been highlighted by Kirby and Miller (1986):

> It is well known that user-friendly online search systems are enthusiastically received. End users are well satisfied because they enjoy being able to find relevant references with simple techniques, with little expenditure of time, perhaps in the convenient location of their own offices. They are in danger, however, from "unquestioned answers." At demonstrations of user-friendly systems, when a simple search has retrieved only a few references, the comment may be heard: "Well, that's all there is in the computer!" End users sometimes do not realize that the computer finds only what they specify, not necessarily what they want. (Page 27)

Perhaps the most disturbing aspect of this false confidence syndrome is the fact that most CD-ROM users find these products to be so easy to search that they feel no need for instruction in their use (Lynn and Bacsanyi, 1989; Schultz and Salomon, 1990).

Some investigators have come closer to true evaluation. For example, they have at least asked users to indicate the proportion of the retrieved references they consider useful (one such study is LePoer and Mularski, 1989). But these indications of search precision give an incomplete picture of the success of a search. Some estimation of recall is needed. Also, it is necessary to make some distinctions among items retrieved (or not retrieved) in terms of their relative value to the user. For example, a user may find five or six "useful" items but may miss one so much more valuable that it makes the retrieved items almost redundant.

Kirby and Miller (1986) performed a rare evaluation in which the search results achieved by end users were compared with results for searches on the same topics performed by experienced intermediaries. The searches were performed online, using the BRS/Saunders Colleague system, rather than on CD-ROM, but this is not really significant. It was found that users were generally satisfied with their results even when they were very incomplete relative to the intermediary's search.

Lancaster et al. (1994) conducted a study to determine how success-ful library users are in performing CD-ROM searches on their own behalf. The investigation involved use of the ERIC database by faculty and graduate students at Illinois State University. For each of 35 searches, the results achieved by the user were compared with those achieved on the same topics and in the same database by (a) a highly experienced searcher and (b) a team of experienced searchers. It was discovered that, on the average, the library users found only about a third of the items in the database that they judged useful in relation to their information needs and, more significantly, only about a third of the really important items.

The results of this study provide some hard data to support the con-clusions of other writers. For example, Ankeny (1991), reviewing end-user searching in general, concludes: "Evidence is accumulating that actual suc-cess rates of end-user searches are quite low." The user search results in the Lancaster et al. study are quite compatible with the sparse evaluation results reported previously (e.g., by LePoer and Mularski (1989) and by Kirby and Miller (1986)).

The enthusiasm for CD-ROM among library users, their largely uncritical attitude toward the technology, and the fact that they may get rather unsatisfactory results from its use, suggest that libraries need to do much more than make the databases available. Indeed, they may convey the impression that these sources can be used satisfactorily with little or no training. Schultz and Salomon (1990) claim that CD-ROM, as presently used, may be fine for the student who needs to find two or three references for a paper, but is inadequate to support more serious research.

The provision of CD-ROM databases carries with it the obligation not to overglamourize these sources but to convey to potential users their lim-itations as well as their advantages. The library should also assume responsibility for attempting to improve the results achieved by users through adequate user instruction in some form or through the use of effective search interfaces.*

Many interfaces for CD-ROM systems have already been developed, and they have been described and discussed in the literature (Kahn, 1988;

---

*The results of some studies suggest that instruction in use of CD-ROM databases may not have as much positive effect on results as one might expect (Stewart and Olsen, 1988). How-ever, a lot more evidence is needed before one can generalize on this. Clearly, a lot depends on the quality of the instruction.

Puttapithakporn, 1990; Rosen, 1990; Beheshti, 1991; Zink, 1991). User interfaces for online catalogs in CD-ROM form have also been developed (Bills and Helgerson, 1988) and work towards a standard CD-ROM interface has been performed (CD-ROM Consistent Interface Committee, 1992). Bosch and Hancock-Beaulieu (1995) have evaluated the appropriateness of Windows-based interfaces for CD-ROM applications.

Existing interfaces are designed primarily to help the user with the mechanics of the system, such as identification of appropriate commands and the combining of terms into logical relationships. Some do offer users limited help in the selection of terms. For example, given an appropriately structured database vocabulary, Wilsondisc and Dialog OnDisc can display terms "related to" a term input by a user.

While interfaces designed to help users with system mechanics, or to enable them to browse in database vocabularies, are certainly useful, they will not in themselves lead library users into effective search strategies. Even highly experienced searchers are unable to come up with all useful search terms, or even the most appropriate ones, without considerable effort in using the thesaurus and, most importantly, studying the terms associated with items judged to be relevant. Unless users are willing to go through this type of effort, and are able to do so, they are unlikely to achieve very satisfactory results. Moreover, they will still need additional searching aids.

If library users are unwilling to undergo some level of search training, and if the producers/vendors of databases are unwilling to develop the searching aids needed by the inexperienced user, less conventional search approaches will be needed. An existing example of a CD-ROM interface designed for the unconventional approach is Knowledge Finder, which will allow users to enter a request as a narrative statement, will truncate words automatically, and will present records in a ranked order based on the degree to which they match the request statement.

The results of the Lancaster et al. (1994) study suggest that even the more sophisticated of library users (faculty and graduate students in this case) may achieve rather poor results when searching CD-ROM databases. They tend to find some pertinent items, but not all of them, and not necessarily the best of them. Librarians must be careful not to give the impression to users that CD-ROM products will satisfy their information needs completely and with a minimum of effort. The development of new instructional materials and searching aids should be a high priority for libraries and database producers/vendors.

CHAPTER 10

Alternative Access Modes

IOIOIOIOIOIOIOIOIOIOIOIOIOIOIOIOIOIOIOIOIOIOIOIOIOIOIOIOIOIOIOIOIOIOIOIOIOIOIOIOI

THIRTY YEARS AGO there were few decisions to be made in giving library users access to materials. Publications existed in only one format except for a rather small proportion that could be obtained either as print on paper or as a microreproduction of print on paper.

This situation is changing rapidly and some sources of information can now be acquired as print on paper, acquired as CD-ROM, or accessed online. For some sources, and for some libraries, online access can be provided either through telecommunications connection to a remote site or by loading the source on the institution's own computer facilities. While such choices apply most obviously to databases representing indexing and abstracting services, choices of this kind now exist for other types of information source, such as encyclopedias and directories, and access alternatives are likely to be increasingly common in the future. For example, it is now becoming possible to purchase certain scholarly periodicals in paper or in electronic form or to access them through some network. Indeed, several thousand titles are already accessible in electronic form. Access alternatives of these kinds are the focus of discussion in this chapter.

Decision Criteria

Cost is the most obvious criterion governing the choice of one access alternative over another. Clearly, it is important that no costs be overlooked in such comparisons. For example, the cost of providing access to an indexing/abstracting service in printed form extends beyond the cost of subscription to include cost of the space occupied, cost of checking-in and other handling activities, and (possibly) binding costs.

But cost should be balanced against some measure of return on investment. Put differently, if access decisions are to be made on the basis of cost-effectiveness, a measure of effectiveness is needed. Unfortunately, a rather extensive and expensive evaluation would be required to compare the effectiveness of two or more access modes. For example, to compare the effectiveness of a search in a printed index with one in an equivalent CD-ROM product, one must evaluate the *results* of these searches (e.g., in terms of overall user satisfaction or, more concretely, the number of useful items retrieved). Similarly, some measure of the amount of useful information found would be needed to compare the effectiveness of a search in a printed encyclopedia with one in an encyclopedia in electronic form.

Since true effectiveness is difficult to assess, one must usually be satisfied with a cruder measure—volume of use. Presumably, the more a source is used, the more likely it is to be valuable to the community even if "value" is not being determined in any precise way. When "use" is accepted as the measure of effectiveness, the cost-effectiveness measure becomes "cost per use."

While cost-effectiveness should be the paramount criterion in choosing among access modes, there will always be secondary factors to be taken into account—for example, implications for user instruction and potential effects on other library services.

Electronic Alternatives

In the academic world, certain electronic databases can now be made available in one of three ways: (a) by acquisition as CD-ROM (with the possibility of networked CD-ROM access), (b) by loading onto the university's own computer network, (c) and by accessing from a remote location as the need arises.* These alternatives have been discussed by Meyer (1990, 1993), Halperin and Renfro (1988), and Hanson (1994a,b).

Given that the ultimate criterion governing the choice among alternatives is a cost-effectiveness one of cost per use, it is necessary to look at the cost components on the one hand and the factors affecting volume of use on the other, as shown in Figure 35

---

*Although these alternatives relate most obviously to the academic situation, they could possibly apply elsewhere—e.g., in a large corporation, a school district or a consortium of libraries.

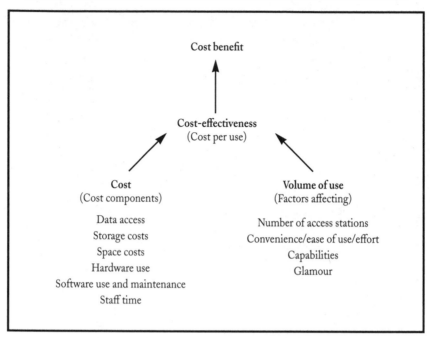

FIGURE 35
Factors affecting choice among access alternatives

Meyer (1990, 1993) has discussed the cost aspects in some detail, and some of the cost-pricing factors for commercial databases are dealt with by Tyckoson (1989a). Clearly, some of the cost components shown in Figure 35 will not apply to all alternatives. "Data access" refers to the cost of obtaining access to the database: of leasing it for use inhouse, of subscribing to it in CD-ROM (or printed) form, or of accessing it via telecommunications when the need arises. Storage cost applies most obviously to the cost of storing a database on the institution's own computers—a major element in the total cost of this mode according to Meyer. In the case of a database present in the library in physical form, the equivalent cost would be the cost of the space occupied—probably trivial for CD-ROM but less so for a large indexing/abstracting service in printed form. But "space costs" apply to more than the database per se. They apply also to the space occupied by equipment—terminals and workstations for CD-ROM or online access to institutional or remote sources.

IOI

"Hardware use" refers to the cost to the library of using the institution's computer resources or the cost of owning its own resources—computers, terminals, workstations, networks—amortized over the life expectancy of the equipment. "Software use and maintenance," again, is associated most obviously with a database loaded on the institution's own computers but might also apply to the CD-ROM situation, especially if the library has developed its own interface programs.

"Staff time" applies to all personnel costs that come out of the library's budget: for supervising and maintaining equipment and database use, for instruction of users, for assisting users, for preparation of software, or for purchase of staff time (e.g., programming time) from the parent institution or elsewhere.

Two factors must be kept in mind in relation to Figure 35 and the preceding discussion:

1. Only costs to the library have been considered. Costs to the parent institution, not borne by the library, and user costs have not been taken into account.
2. In the case of remote database access via telecommunications, the "data access" costs reflect many of the other components (storage, hardware use, software use, staff time, space costs) listed in Figure 35, as well as others, such as database royalties, that are charged to the library by the vendor.

Figure 36 summarizes the major cost components associated with the various electronic access modes as well as for access in printed form. Such minor cost elements as cost of paper for printers are ignored.

Figure 37 presents some hypothetical relative costs for the various alternatives. No attempt has been made to deal in actual monetary values because of the great variations in costs associated with different databases and with different institutions, as well as the fact that these costs may change rapidly. Nevertheless, if we accept x as a unit of cost, the relative values are probably realistic.

The cost of remote access is not volume-dependent or, at least, is affected little by number of searches performed.* The table does show

---

*Indeed, some vendors allow unlimited access to library users at a flat subscription rate.

some effect of reduced costs associated with high-volume discount. On the other hand, cost of the three alternatives that require a capital investment in database purchase or leasing is very sensitive to volume of searches performed. In the hypothetical example of Figure 37, the cost per search for the locally mounted database option only drops below the remote access search cost when the volume of searches performed per year approaches five thousand.

Access alternative	Cost Components					
	Data access	Storage	Space	Hardware	Software	Staff
Print	Cost of subscription	Cost of space occupied				Checking-in Reshelving User aid and instruction
CD-ROM	Cost of subscription	Cost of space occupied		Equipment amortized over x years	Software development (if any) amortized over x years	Supervision User aid and instruction Maintenance of facilities
Locally mounted	Cost of leasing	Date storage	Space occupied in library by terminals, workstations, computers	Cost of equipment in library amortized over x years	Software purchase or development amortized over x years	User aid and instruction Maintenance of hardware and software
Remote access (a) unmediated	Vendor charge per minute of access		Space occupied in library by terminals, workstations	Cost of equipment in library amortized over x years		User aid and instruction
(b) mediated	As above		As above	As above		Librarian searching time

FIGURE 36

Major cost components for various access alternatives.

In the hypothetical example, the cost per search is still lower for the print and CD-ROM alternatives, even at the level of five thousand searches per year. However, this is misleading for it assumes that the print or CD-ROM alternatives will attract as much use as the locally mounted database, which is unlikely.*The locally mounted database option is competitive with the CD-ROM option if it attracts five times more searches per year. It is competitive with the print option if it attracts around twenty times more searches per year. Based on his experience at two universities, Meyer (1996) believes that the comparison is more like several hundred searches in the electronic version versus "a handful" in the printed tool. Since cost per search is so dependent on volume of use, it is necessary to look further at factors affecting the number of searches performed.

| Access alternative | Cost per search for indicated number of searches per year | | | | |
	One	10	100	1,000	5,000
Print	1,000x	100x	10x	1x	0.2x
CD-ROM	3,000x	300x	30x	3x	0.6x
Locally mounted	17,000x	1,700x	170x	17x	3.4x
Remote access					
(a) unmediated	8x	8x	8x	7x	5x
(b) mediated	12x	12x	12x	10x	8x

FIGURE 37
**Hypothetical relative costs for alternative access modes
where x is a single unit of cost**

Factors Affecting Volume of Use

Mooers' Law (Mooers, 1960), the principle of least effort (Zipf, 1949) and pain avoidance theory (Poole, 1985) all lead us to conclude that the extent to which any information service is used will be determined primarily by the cost to the user, where cost may be in monetary

*Most writers have reported that ease and economy of access to databases through OPAC interfaces, or other institutional facilities, promotes greater use as well as a migration from printed or less accessible electronic forms. However, Fiscella and Proctor (1995) report that, in the case of the University of Illinois at Chicago, improved availability "has not necessarily promoted frequent end-user searching by faculty." Many faculty, they found, continue to use print sources. They wonder how long academic libraries will be able to support access to both print and electronic forms.

terms or in less tangible human terms—convenience, effort, and general ease of use.

Monetary costs to the user will deter use, except in the case of the more critical information needs, and will discriminate against the less affluent.

Given no monetary cost to the user, there are several other factors that will influence the extent to which a database is used. The most obvious is accessibility. Because a network can be established, a database in CD-ROM form will usually be more accessible than one in printed form. Although a CD-ROM network can be designed for dial-in access, it still may be limited in accessibility compared with a network based on an institution's mainframe computer, which may put terminals in every office and allow access from homes, dormitory rooms and other external locations, including Internet access. All other things considered, then, the locally mounted database option is likely to attract a greater volume of use and thus a lower cost per use.

The effect of number of stations on annual costs of operating a database searching service is illustrated by Halperin and Renfro (1988) in Figure 38. Note how the CD-ROM installation is much cheaper than the mainframe network for small numbers of access stations and competitive in the 25-35 station range. Beyond that, the mainframe network becomes cheaper. It is important to recognize that this comparison assumes stations dedicated to library use (e.g., making the catalog and other resources available). The obvious advantage of the locally loaded database situation is that it offers an economical way of extending access well beyond the walls of the library (e.g., through a multipurpose, campus-wide network) and of making resources accessible at times when the library is closed. However, dial-in access to CD-ROM facilities is also becoming more common.

Figure 35 identifies some further factors that are likely to influence volume of use of a database. Both search capabilities and "glamour" factors will favor any electronic alternative over print on paper. Not only will the electronic alternative offer improved searching (ability to combine terms, to truncate and so on) but it will frequently offer more access points per record. The locally loaded and remote search alternatives both offer some convenience advantages over CD-ROM: databases will be updated more frequently and retrieval time may be considerably faster. Display speed will favor the locally mounted database and CD-ROM situations over remote access. Dyer (1990) points out that printed databases still offer certain advantages over other forms, including the fact that single copies or volumes are easily transportable to tables or carrels for use with other materials.* On the other hand, for certain types of materials, such as newspapers, use of a CD-ROM version may be much more convenient. Batterbee and Nicholas (1995) point to the fact that newspaper access is the major application of CD-ROM in British public libraries.

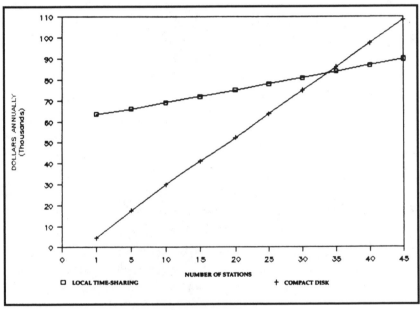

FIGURE 38
Cost of locally mounted database versus CD-ROM
related to number of stations.
Reprinted from Halperin and Renfro (1988) by permission of Online, Inc., publishers of *Online*

The comparison on the basis of ease of use is more difficult. The software available to search the locally mounted databases can be user-friendly or not and some versions of some CD-ROM databases employ

---

*Chrzastowski (1995) asks if libraries, in promoting electronic access, are "luring patrons away from other, possibly more appropriate, print indexes"?

tutorials that make them easy to use. Nevertheless, the locally mounted situation offers the obvious advantage that the same software can be used to search multiple databases so users need to learn only one approach. Moreover, there is an obvious attraction in being able to search many resources, including the library catalog and a variety of other databases, from a single workstation and using the same or similar approaches. Peterson (1995), however, points out that the separation of OPAC from other databases means that one resource is still usable if the other is down. Moreover, as Meyer (1996) has pointed out, the single interface will confuse some users who will not recognize the distinction between locally owned items and those not owned locally or between databases of books and of journal articles. Databases in printed form may or may not be more difficult to use than an electronic equivalent. The fact remains, however, that most patrons, particularly the younger ones, seem to feel that the printed version is more complicated.

CD-ROM is at an obvious disadvantage in the case of searches that must be truly retrospective since it may be necessary to search several disks to go back in time even as little as five years.* Moreover, there may not be any possibility of creating a true retrospective search capability because the CD-ROM producer may require the return of an earlier disk for each new one received.

It is clear that the use of information resources will increase as cost to the user declines and as accessibility, search capabilities and ease of use all improve. As volume of use increases, cost per use is reduced. Halperin and Renfro (1988) report that, in one academic library, use of resources in electronic form went from less than 100 hours annually to over 8,000 hours annually in a four-year period, and that costs per hour of use declined from an average of $105 per hour to $10 per hour between 1983 and 1988. These dramatic increases in use and reduction in costs were due to three successive developments: free or subsidized end-user searching of remote databases, the introduction of CD-ROM facilities, and the introduction of locally mounted databases.

In general, then, the greater the investment made by the library in making resources more accessible, the greater the convenience to users,

---

*However, the use of CD-ROM towers with multiple disks and disk changers, as well as LAN access, can alleviate the disk changing burden.

the savings in their time, and their use of the resources. Meyer (1996) suggests that use and convenience go up by several orders of magnitude when electronic access is used in lieu of print. He believes that user costs must be the paramount consideration in selecting access alternatives. Indeed the subsidization of access may be one of the major justifications for the existence of libraries in a largely electronic world.

Other Factors

There are factors other than those already discussed that can influence access choices (see Machovec et al. (1991) and Cibbarelli et al. (1993) for a rather complete list), including:

- Pricing policies of database producer.

  If the database producer charges on the basis of hours of use, or number of records retrieved, local mounting is not an attractive option since costs are not under control.
- Space available.

  The electronic alternatives may be especially attractive to those libraries that face critical shortage of space.
- Completeness.

  Machovec et al. point out that the printed version of a tool may sometimes be more complete than the electronic equivalent (e.g., the electronic version of an encyclopedia or journal article may not include all graphics.)
- Resource sharing

  A locally mounted database may allow greater possibilities for resource sharing with other libraries.
- Additional capabilities

  With databases in electronic form, libraries can offer new services to users—e.g., downloading to personal databases and more sophisticated current awareness services (see Chapter 12). Also, locally loaded databases can be linked with OPACs to show local holdings, although this is not necessarily problem-free (Caswell et al., 1995).
- Effect on other services

  As discussed in another chapter, use of electronic databases may increase demands on other library services: photocopying facilities, document delivery and, perhaps most significant, user instruction.

Some print versus online versus CD-ROM issues for school libraries, including issues relating to encyclopedias and magazine indexes, are presented by Dickinson (1994).

Welsh (1989) gives an example of the remote online search versus CD-ROM comparison based on use of the NTIS database—estimated at 162 searches or sixty four hours per year in his library. Welsh estimates the CD-ROM cost per hour to be $35.17 (annual subscription cost to the database, $2250, divided by sixty four) as opposed to per hour costs of $80 for DIA-LOG/Dialnet access. At the rate of sixty four hours of searching per year, annual savings from CD-ROM acquisition are estimated to be $5120-$2250, or $2870. As Welsh himself recognizes, this is a rather simplistic cost comparison. Not considered for the online access mode are the costs of printing bibliographic records ($.30 online, $.45 offline), which can be a substantial component in the overall cost of a comprehensive search. On the CD-ROM side, however, some allowance must be made for the cost of paper and other supplies consumed. More importantly, some part of the cost of acquisition of the CD-ROM equipment must be allocated to each hour of CD-ROM use. Assume equipment purchase costs (workstation and CD-ROM drive) of $2195, that the lifetime of this equipment is estimated to be five years, and that it is used for 1600 hours of searching in the five-year period (this estimate is based on five CD-ROM databases, each one used an average of sixty four hours per year). Then, one must add about $1.40 ($2195/1600) to the cost of each hour of CD-ROM searching for equipment use, plus a little more for paper consumed and for the space occupied in the library by the equipment (which would be more or less comparable for CD-ROM workstation and online terminal). So, the actual cost of an hour of CD-ROM searching may be closer to $37 than the $35 that Welsh estimates, although this is still considerably less than the cost for online searching.

But this analysis is obviously based only on database access costs and ignores the extremely important element of human costs. From the library's own point of view, the CD-ROM database has the obvious advantage that most library users will perform their own searches, whereas online searches in Welsh's library (in a government agency) are performed by professional librarians. From the agency's viewpoint, however, the situation may be quite different: users searching the CD-ROM database may be paid more, on the average, than the librarians and they will probably spend more time on a search than the more experienced librarians (indeed Welsh himself points out that users of CD-ROM tend to spend more time on a search because they know they are not paying for connect time), so the actual cost per search to the agency, taking salaries and overheads into account, could be very much greater for the CD-ROM situation.

Of course, this comparison takes into account only the cost side of the cost-effectiveness equation or, at least, it considers cost per search as the unit of cost-effectiveness rather than cost per useful item retrieved. If the librarians can find many more useful items, through the online facilities, than the library users can from the CD-ROM databases, the cost per useful item retrieved (the true cost-effectiveness measure in this situation) may well be less for the online access alternative. On the other hand, the most cost-effective alternative, from the agency's point of view, might well be the one in which the librarians perform CD-ROM searches for library users. It is clear that this comparison is quite complicated. The decision on which is the better alternative cannot be made solely on the basis of costs, but must take search results (the effectiveness) into account. Moreover, a different decision would probably be made if total agency costs are considered instead of only the library's costs.

Print Versus Electronic Access

So far in this chapter, major emphasis has been placed on choice among electronic alternatives. It is also necessary to give more direct attention to the electronic versus print situation and to the decision on whether or not to retain the printed version if the electronic source is acquired.

Machovec et al. (1991) identify several factors affecting this latter decision, including:

- Cost differentials.
    If a publisher offers a significant discount for the CD-ROM product when the printed version is also received, discontinuation of print may not be worthwhile.

- Accessibility.

  The printed product may still be needed if there are not enough CD-ROM workstations available to satisfy demand or if CD-ROM access is not available during all the hours that the library is open.
- Space available.

  Discontinuation of the printed version will be especially attractive if the library is critically short of space.
- Continuity.

  If a CD-ROM product needs to be dropped for some reason, it may be necessary to return all disks to the publisher (in a leasing arrangement), and backfiles of the printed version may no longer be available. More significantly, print on paper is a technology that lasts (leaving aside the important issues of physical preservation) in that a book printed, say, a century ago is quite usable today. On the other hand, more modern technologies become obsolete rather quickly* and electronic products purchased now, perhaps at considerable expense, may not be usable a decade hence.

Huang and McHale (1990) have put forward a "cost-effectiveness" model to aid the decision on when to discontinue a printed source and to rely entirely on online access to that source. They develop an "online/print threshold" which relates the cost of making the printed source available in the library to the average cost of an online search in that database. The "average yearly cost" of a printed source (yearly subscription rate) is used to derive an "average daily cost," which is the subscription cost divided by the number of days the library is open (estimated at 260 in this corporate library setting). If the average cost of the online search is equal to or less than this daily cost, it is assumed to be desirable that the print source be discontinued. While this is an original approach to the analysis, it is rather simplistic. It is difficult to see why average daily cost is used in place of cost per use of the printed source, other than the fact that some survey must be performed to estimate annual use whereas average daily cost is easily derived (except that cost of ownership exceeds subscription cost). The "model," in fact, is not

---

*For example, some people still have 78 rpm phonograph records but no equipment on which to play them and LP turntables may be impossible to obtain in the near future.

a true cost-effectiveness model since search effectiveness is not considered (i.e., it is assumed that searches in print or online databases are equally effective).

For the time being, access alternatives may not apply to all databases, at least in certain libraries. That is, some libraries may want or need to continue to provide access to a source in several forms. Potter (1989), for example, has referred to the possibility of different "tiers of access":

> While several libraries have loaded indexes to periodical articles, no library has been able to abandon online searching of commercial databases, and each library is continuing to purchase CD-ROM-based indexes. Emily Fayen, writing about Penn, points out that they have found that they actually need MEDLINE in all three forms—online as part of their local system, on CD-ROM, and through commercial services. The local system only contains up to three years of data but is free to readers. The commercial, remote version of MEDLINE meets the need of the serious researcher who needs to cover the entire file and needs the assistance of an experienced searcher. The CD-ROM version is an excellent teaching tool.
>
> Penn's experience with three tiers of access suggests a pattern for other libraries. There are some databases, usually the more general ones or the ones that match an institution's strengths, that should be incorporated into the local online system. The wide use these databases receive will justify the expense. Other databases may be used less often but frequently enough to justify their purchase on CD-ROM. Still other databases will be used infrequently and may be so difficult to use that mediated searching of an online commercial database is justified.
>
> There is a fourth tier that should be addressed, and that is printed indexes. Some indexes are simply not available in machine readable form. Others cover only the past few years in an online or CD-ROM version. There are also readers who do not want to go near a computer. So, printed indexes should be with us for some time to come. (Page 104)

It must also be remembered that the type of resource influences the formats available. For example, certain electronic forms are preferable to print for encyclopedias and training materials because of their multimedia capabilities.

The results of several studies suggest that paper sources have advantages over equivalent electronic sources in some applications and that the electronic sources outperform the paper sources in others. For example, Wu et al. (1995), perhaps not surprisingly, found that students could access an electronic book more rapidly than they could retrieve the physical item from library shelves. However, once the book was in hand, answers to questions could be found more rapidly in the paper source.* Horner and Michaud-Oystryk (1995) compared the performance of librarians in answering reference questions when using paper sources and online databases. In general, "bibliographic" questions (those requiring the location of journal articles on a particular topic) were answered more efficiently online, while factual answers were found more efficiently in the paper tools.

Global Considerations

Figure 35 includes an important element that was not addressed directly in the preceding discussion, namely "cost-benefit." This is because the true benefit of a library service to its users tends to be very intangible and thus extremely difficult to assess. Nevertheless, volume of use can be considered to be a predictor of benefit, albeit an imprecise one, in the sense that the more a community uses some service the more likely it is to benefit from it. Also, the fact that members of the community use a service, perhaps repeatedly, reflects their perceptions that they are receiving benefits from it.**

As mentioned earlier, the discussion in this chapter has looked at the issues—especially the costs—from the library's point of view. Somewhat different conclusions might be arrived at if one took a more global perspective—that of a parent institution or of "society" as a whole. Since the time spent *using* the resources would be the major cost of library service if a monetary value were placed on the time of users, alternatives that minimize this cost are particularly attractive. It is especially important to minimize user time, even if this means greater library expenditures, where the institution is paying for time spent using the library (the corporate setting and perhaps academic and other research settings too) and the cost of the user's time is considerably greater than the cost of the time of the library staff.

Based largely on work performed at the Mann Library, Cornell University (Demas et al., 1995), as mentioned in Chapter 7, one can now

---

*The sample on which these conclusions were reached, unfortunately, was embarrassingly small.

**One advantage of electronic access that is frequently overlooked is the fact that, for some forms at least, it is easy to determine volume of use so cost-benefit analysis becomes much more feasible. In-library use of printed resources is more difficult to determine.

visualize a library providing various levels of access to electronic resources, as illustrated in Figure 39. Electronic resources in great demand (level A) are made permanently accessible through a campus network, while others (level B) can be accessed remotely via the campus network when needed (e.g., through the Internet). These are strongly linked to the library because the library may have been responsible for selecting the level A resources from the international network and downloading them to the campus network. It may also have been responsible for building the indexes or providing the pointers that draw attention to the level B resources. Alternatively, the level B resources may be brought personally to the attention of individual users by reference librarians consulted face-to-face, by telephone or through electronic mail. The level C and D resources are not available through the campus network but must be used within the library through a local area network or a single dedicated workstation.

The entire situation of electronic access is changing with great rapidity. Indeed, significant changes have occurred in the short interval between the time we began work on this chapter and the time the text was ready to go to press. For example, various commercially available gateways now offer access to many databases on a flat subscription basis that makes this option cheaper than mounting locally. Also, it is now possible to combine the benefits of local loading with networked multi-location access. For example, several libraries can jointly run a server over the Internet using CD-ROM products copied onto large hard drives. As Meyer (1996) claims, this is somewhat like loading your own database but with "much reduced labor and better potential for economies of scale."

Of course, no access mode can be considered completely permanent. For example, many writers have discussed the likelihood that CD-ROM may be only a transient technology (see, for example, Stratton, 1994) and it is quite possible that new modes for the distribution of resources in electronic form will emerge in the future—although it is now difficult to envision what these might be.

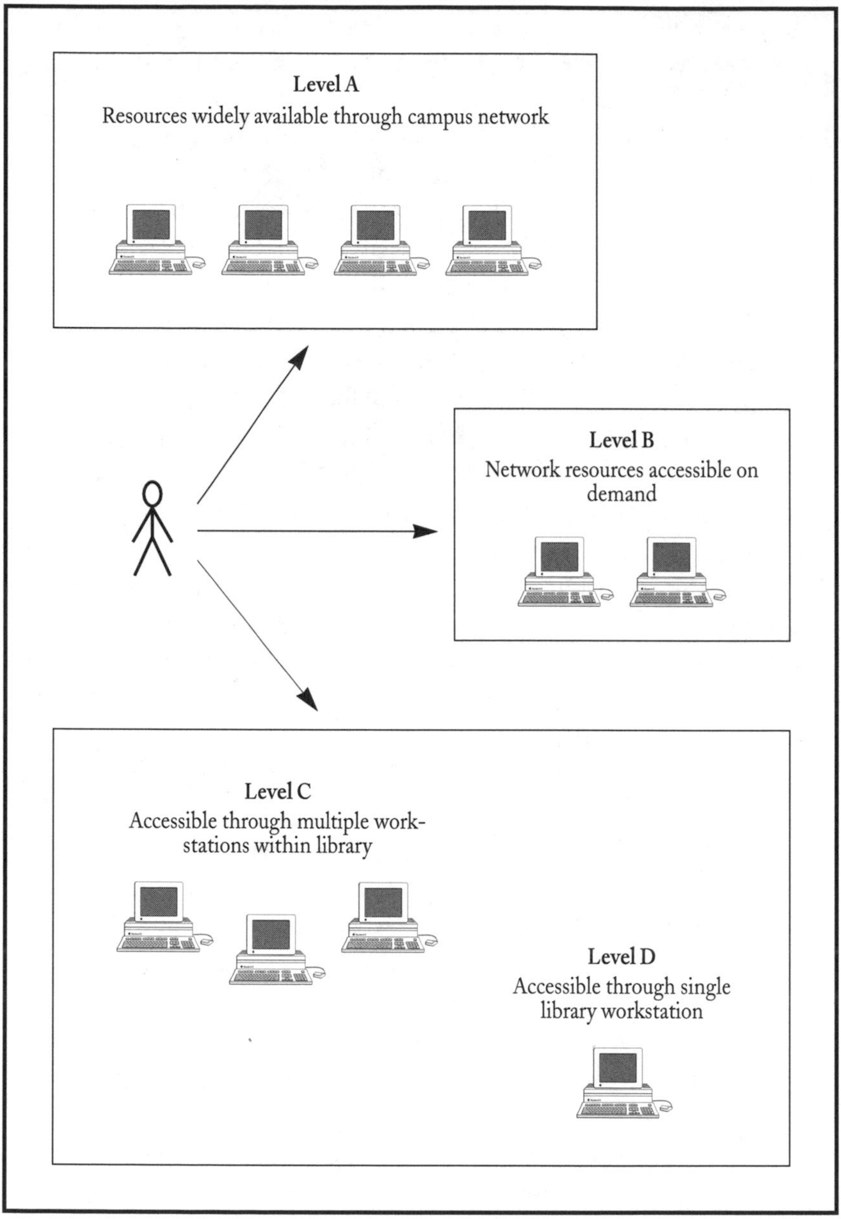

FIGURE 39
Possible levels of access to electronic resources provided by the library
in an academic setting

CHAPTER 11

Document Access and Delivery

IOIOIOIOIOIOIOIOIOIOIOIOIOIOIOIOIOIOIOIOIOIOIOIOIOIOIOIOIOIOIOIOIOIOIOIOIOIOIOIOI

THE TERM "DOCUMENT DELIVERY" refers to a service in which a library (or other agency) makes some form of publication available when needed and requested by a library user. Forty years ago this almost invariably meant the delivery to a user of an original publication (e.g., monograph, journal issue, bound volume of journal) from the library's own collection or borrowed from another library. As photographic methods of reproduction became more efficient and economical, the delivery of an original item began to be replaced by the delivery of a photocopy, especially for individual journal articles, and the term "interlibrary loan" (although still in common use) was soon rendered meaningless by the fact that many of the items supplied by one library to another were not actually on loan.

The supply to a user of an original item, or a photocopy of it, from the library's own resources or obtained from another library, was the norm in document delivery until fairly recent times. Today, however, the delivery of a publication, or part of it, to a library user can be achieved by a wide variety of methods and sources, and these possibilities are multiplying rapidly. While document delivery does not *per se* imply technology, its inclusion in this book seems fully justified by the fact that electronic methods are being used increasingly to provide access and delivery of materials.

The major access/delivery options available today are summarized in Figure 40. This is based on the journal article situation but it could also apply, with certain modifications, to other publication forms. Even this macrolevel depiction gives some idea of the variety of options available to libraries or their users, and the situation is changing rapidly, with new possibilities emerging on almost a daily basis. Higginbotham and Bowdoin (1993) state that "The variety of services is just short of mind-boggling" and they refer only to the commercial document suppliers. Their book is a thorough survey of this complex area as of 1993.

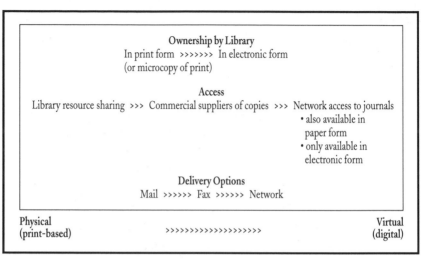

FIGURE 40
Access/delivery options for journal articles

One way of looking at the possibilities shown in Figure 40 is as a continuum ranging from the most "physical" to the most "virtual." The most physical form can be considered as the delivery to a user of an original item from the library's collection or from that of another institution. Only somewhat less "physical" would be the delivery of a photocopy of the item. The most "virtual" document delivery is the provision of access to journals that exist only in network-accessible form. This is most virtual because, while text from such journals could be printed out onto paper, the full features (e.g., hypertext linking and windowing capabilities) cannot be adequately represented in any non-electronic medium, and other features (most obviously motion) cannot be captured at all on paper.

Note that the figure treats delivery as "making available" and does not distinguish between physical delivery of an artifact, or part of it, and the delivery of text or illustration to a terminal, workstation, or other electronic device. In discussing the options depicted, the more exotic will be dealt with first.

"True" Electronic Journals

A "true" electronic journal is one that has been designed *ab initio* for the electronic medium and that exists solely, or at least primarily, in this medium. If one adopts a rather loose definition of "journal," to include more informal and newsletter-type publications, there are already several hundred of these accessible through the Internet (Mogge, 1996). Some librarians may be surprised by the number of more scholarly journals that are available primarily in network-accessible form. Clement (1994) lists 25 such journals, in implementation or planning stages, in the sciences alone, and the number is increasing on a regular basis. Woodward (1995a) claims about 100 true electronic journals that are refereed. While some are also made available as paper copy, the majority are only network-accessible. van Brakel (1995) gives a good explanation of why electronic journals are likely to proliferate in the future.

OCLC Inc. has been a pioneer in true electronic publishing of scholarly journals. As of 1996, it offers access to nine such publications (Noble, 1996) and has plans to expand in this area.* Many of the other true electronic journals have been established and made network-accessible by various academic departments in major universities.

All of these scholarly journals are similar in that they exist only (or, at least, primarily) in electronic form, can be accessed online, and editors and/or referees impose certain standards on the contents of the database. There are also differences among them. Some group papers into "issues," in much the same way that a paper journal does, while others merely add new papers to the database as they are accepted. Some accept graphics as well as text, while others do not. Some journals offer contents pages and abstracts, requiring users to request the full text if wanted, while others initially disseminate the full text to users. Several are offered free** to users but others are available only on a subscription

---

*The Electronic Journals Online program of OCLC actually includes some journals that exist in printed form as well as electronic form, besides those that exist only in network-accessible electronic form. The electronic versions of the printed journals, of course, provide enhanced capabilities, such as hypertext linkages to bibliographic databases and e-mail connections to editors and publishers, as well as greater currency (Noble, 1996).

**This is a little misleading. While free online access is allowed, other options—e.g., to receive in paper, microfiche, or diskette, form—will involve a cost to recipients.

basis. Some of the online journals are merely "delivered" to users via a file server or e-mail system while others allow true interaction between user and journal. Of the existing electronic journals, OCLC's *Online Journal of Current Clinical Trials* is one of the most sophisticated, offering elaborate windowing facilities, hypertext linking (including the ability to view an abstract of an item cited in an article), and graphics.

A scholarly journal in electronic form can potentially offer several advantages over one printed on paper, including:

1. More rapid publishing of research results through electronic submission of articles, and network communication among authors, editors, and referees, and by the fact that contributions can be added to a database as accepted rather than held to form the next "issue".
2. More efficient dissemination of information through the matching of articles newly accepted into databases with the interest profiles of potential readers.
3. Innovative ways of presenting research results and other forms of data and information—analog models, motion, sound, hypertext, and hypermedia linkages (including linkages between journals and other electronic resources).
4. Public peer review facilitated through the ability to link reader comments and evaluations to published articles.
5. Lower cost per successful match between article and reader.*
6. Speed of publication, and ease of communication, lead to a more interactive journal in which one contribution may spawn rapid responses from other researchers.

Carried further, an electronic journal established within a network can assume a scholarly role that is more comprehensive than the role played by the typical journal in paper form. As Harrison and Stephen (1995) point out, it can become the central component in an electronic center of expertise and a key element in an online intellectual community.**

Electronic journals accessible through the networks are now receiving considerable attention from academic libraries. Duranceau et al. (1996)

---

*For costs of publishing a scholarly journal in electronic form see Rowland et al. (1995).

**For other perspectives on the advantages of electronic journals see Gaines (1996) and Malinconico (1996).

discuss the approaches taken by one major academic library and Cochenour (1996) describes the consortium approach to archiving and provision of access, as mention earlier in Chapter 7.

Duranceau et al. (1996) make a distinction between first- and second-generation electronic journals. The first-generation journals are "simpler" in several ways: ASCII text files, simple file structure, produced by groups of scholars (e.g., the faculty of a single department) rather than established publishers, distributed primarily through electronic mail, and little concerned with copyright issues. In contrast, the second-generation journals are more formal and complex, and present greater challenges for libraries: may be HTML-based or make use of specially formatted files; may incorporate graphics, multimedia features and/or links to other network resources; likely to comprise much larger files; usually need to be "fetched" from servers by subscribers rather than delivered to them automatically; present much greater diversity in formats, file structures, and other features; and, finally, they are more likely to be produced by traditional publishers having profit motives and copyright concerns.

Electronic journals are still in their infancy. Consequently, they are far from completely free of problems. Harter and Kim (1996), for example, have pointed out that present versions tend to have relatively poor usability and accessibility.

The emergence of network-accessible scholarly journals, many at the initiative of academic faculties, has led many to speculate that the present system of paper-based scholarly publishing, controlled mostly by commercial interests, will eventually be replaced by a new scholarly communication system, network-based and under the control of academia. Clearly, such a development would have a profound effect on libraries in general and academic libraries in particular. The characteristics of such a system, and many of its implications, are discussed in detail in Lancaster (1995) and in Peek and Newby (1996).

Paper Journals Accessible Electronically

A clear distinction must be made between the new scholarly journals, designed for network access, and those that have long existed in paper form but have more recently been made electronically accessible as well.

Everett (1993) refers to the several thousand journals that can now be accessed in full text form through various vendors of online service, and points to the advantages of using such databases for article delivery, as follows:

> Full-text databases as a document delivery system appear to offer several clear advantages—the speed and ready access of the databanks, prices competitive with commercial document delivery services and traditional interlibrary loan, and the payment of copyright royalties as part of the price, thus eliminating copyright concerns. The most serious drawbacks are the lack of any graphics and the fact that the online version of a periodical may be less complete than the print equivalent, rendering minor articles inaccessible. (Page 22).

It is clear that full-text databases accessible online cannot meet all of the document delivery needs of a library of any significant size because too few titles are now accessible, and those that are accessible are not necessarily complete in terms of timespan of coverage and inclusiveness (some types of articles, as well as some graphics, may be omitted). Nevertheless, full text access is a viable alternative document delivery system for some articles for some libraries, especially for articles that are needed very quickly. Full text databases have the additional advantage that they are fully searchable online, using index terms, text words, or both. Moreover, text can be delivered to a user's workstation in some libraries, avoiding use of paper copy. Hawley (1992) quotes $3 to $3.50 as the average cost of an item taken from a DIALOG full text database.

In fact, full text access is becoming increasingly competitive with periodical ownership in at least some applications. The Article First component of OCLC's FirstSearch covers around 5000 journals but provides full text access to only the more recent issues. Hawbaker and Wagner (1996) claim that their academic library can offer access to twice as many business journals by moving from ownership to full text access at an additional cost of only 15%.

Another option available to some libraries, but still with very limited coverage, is the ability to acquire journal text and illustrations as a database in CD-ROM form. In the oldest example of this approach, ADONIS (Stern and Compier, 1990), several hundred journals are made available as CD-ROMs distributed to libraries or other customers. The customer pays an annual subscription plus royalties for articles printed out. Journals acquired in this way can be made widely accessible (e.g., throughout a campus) by means of a local area network.

Several commercial journal publishers are experimenting with the distribution of journals in electronic form and are using various academic libraries as test sites to gauge acceptability and to identify potential problems.

In the case of projects that make existing journals available on CD-ROM, the text is stored as "bit-mapped" images of the printed journal pages, achieved through optical character recognition. Bit-mapped images require rather large amounts of storage, allow terminal display that is of low quality compared with the display of computer-readable text (e.g., in ASCII format), and cannot be searched or otherwise manipulated by computer (although ancillary databases, such as indexes to and abstracts of the page images, can be). Nevertheless, the bit-mapping approach has the obvious advantage that it allows older materials to be made available in electronic form without the need for rekeying and can also provide some level of access to illustrations. Of course, a particular implementation can incorporate both page images (to give the reader "the feel" of the familiar journal format) and computer-readable text; this is true, for example, in the Red Sage project, which makes use of the RightPages system devised at AT&T Bell Laboratories (Story, et al, 1992; Hoffman, et al, 1993), the CORE project (*Annual Review*, 1992; Entlich, 1994), and in TULIP.

TULIP (The University LIcensing Program) made the text of forty-two Elsevier and Pergamon journals available in both bit-mapped and ASCII full text formats. A participating university could receive these databases, and mount them locally, or could access through the Internet. The objective was to deliver the electronic journals to the desktops of users. This experiment, recently completed, showed that there still exist some technological impediments to the completely digital, network-based library. Moreover, most users still see electronic journals as a supplement to paper journals, rather than a replacement, especially at the present time when a "critical mass" of journals is far from being reached (Hunter, 1996; TULIP, 1996).

Commercial document delivery services, such as UMI, have developed systems that combine network access to ASCII text with the ability to access bit-mapped images of journals on CD-ROM (Orchard, 1997) and the JSTOR project, funded by the Andrew W. Mellon Foundation, is also noteworthy as an extensive effort to provide access to retrospective journal issues in the form of bit-mapped images of high quality (DeGennaro, 1997).

When the complete text of print-on-paper journals is made accessible through online networks, the text is in ASCII format and fully searchable. Nevertheless, such journals are merely examples of print on paper made accessible electronically. The "true" electronic journals referred to earlier were designed *ab initio* as journals in electronic form and can be given capabilities not present in the electronic manifestations of printed journals. For example, the text can be encoded with SGML tags to improve its functionality (e.g., in the implementation of such features as windowing, hypertext, and the integration of text with graphics).

At present, it is clear that libraries cannot fully dispense with paper journals in favor of electronic alternatives—the coverage is not yet extensive enough and other barriers to the replacement of print on paper may exist (e.g., a publisher may supply a full electronic version only to libraries that already subscribe to a paper version). Nevertheless, library managers must continue to monitor developments in this entire area. Moreover, use of databases of full text available online may already be a viable option for obtaining rapid access to articles from journals to which a library does not subscribe.

Interlibrary Loan

Technological advances have brought about significant improvements in document delivery through conventional resource sharing among libraries. Online union catalogs greatly facilitate item location, and network messaging systems make the transmission of a request from one library to another a virtually instantaneous process. In some library consortia, some users can bypass the local library,at least for monographic materials, using the network to make their requests directly to another library and having the item delivered to their campus offices (in the case of academic consortia) or local library.

The supply and return of the item can still be very slow when regular mail service is used, but some consortia improve this situation through use of vehicles and drivers dedicated to interlibrary delivery. Urgently needed items can be moved by express mail or, depending on their length and type, by fax transmission. Of course, fax can also be used for the transmission of a request.

The transmission of a journal article by fax will usually incur long distance telephone charges but may still be cost-effective when compared with the making of a photocopy, addressing envelopes, packaging, and other activities associated with the physical movement of items. The obvious disadvantage of fax is that it produces copy of an inferior quality, especially for illustrations, and involves the use of thermal paper in most institutions.

The resources of the Internet now give libraries an alternative to fax for the rapid transmission of text and illustrations. The Ariel system, developed by the Research Libraries Group, offers many advantages over fax. The supplying library uses an Ariel workstation, comprising a PC and a scanner, to create a bit-mapped image of an item, compress it, and transmit it over the Internet to a receiving workstation consisting of a PC and laser printer. High-resolution scanning, digital transmission, and use of a high-resolution laser printer result in quality of copy that is much superior to fax. Other advantages are the fact that scanning can be done directly from bound volumes and that transmission costs are absorbed through the Internet and not charged directly to the library. The main disadvantage at the present time is that an Ariel workstation can only transmit to another Ariel workstation so the capabilities are limited by equipment availability within libraries. However, the workstation incorporates commercially available equipment, the PC involved can also be used for other purposes if necessary, and cost of the Ariel software is modest (Jackson, 1993a; Bennett and Palmer, 1994).

Jackson (1993a) has described other experiments that have been conducted in the area of network transmission, including the interfacing of Internet capabilities with regular fax machines. While these particular experiments are no longer active, it seems entirely probable that, in the future, the library community will routinely use network resources to exchange items, both those already in electronic form and those scanned from paper copy for subsequent transmission. Tuck and Moulton (1995) discuss the advantages of using electronic mail protocols for the transmission of scanned page images, a method being used experimentally by the British Library Document Supply Centre.

Commercial Suppliers

Commercial document delivery services, which emerged in the late 1960s as a logical extension of online searching services, have experienced tremendous growth and are now a significant alternative to conventional library resource sharing. The major suppliers in the United States offer delivery from several thousand journals (in the ten to fifteen thousand range in 1995) and the British Library Document Supply Centre has access to more than 200,000 journal titles. Many suppliers will accept orders in a variety of modes—online, telephone, mail or fax—and delivery can be by fax, mail, express mail, or (in some cases) Internet.

Libraries, particularly academic and special libraries, have adopted these services because they can be faster than interlibrary delivery* and, if all costs are considered, are economically competitive with it. Consequently, some libraries see the commercial services as offering an alternative to ownership of expensive journals that are less frequently in demand. Another advantage of the commercial services is that they automatically take care of copyright requirements. Kohl (1995) claims impressive gains in one academic library: for an annual cost of $20,000 (to provide free article delivery to faculty and graduate students), journal subscriptions were reduced by $180,000 a year and the 350 cancelled titles were replaced by ready access to 10,000 titles formerly unavailable.

The ability to use commercial suppliers, in addition to interlibrary resource sharing, has greatly encouraged the use of table of contents (TOC) services to allow access to the contents of a much wider range of journals and also, possibly, to permit the cancellation of subscriptions for some less used titles. Databases of journal contents pages can now be accessed online, acquired on CD-ROM, or obtained in a form suitable for loading on local computer facilities. TOC services also permit personalized current awareness since some will automatically transmit the contents pages for each issue of journal titles selected by a user to that user's e-mail address. The commercial TOC services also provide document delivery and, in some cases, allow online access to complete text. TOC databases can be searched on keywords in titles, possibly supplemented by use of index terms.

---

*A survey of faculty at two universities, reported by Roberts (1992), indicated that delays, rather than cost, were the most significant barriers to the use of ILL.

A number of evaluations of the performance of commercial suppliers have been undertaken, and some have compared the commercial suppliers with interlibrary delivery. Unfortunately, these studies, many of which have been summarized by Higginbotham and Bowdoin (1993), Truesdell (1994), and Mitchell and Walters (1995), have produced conflicting results. While some claim that the commercial services are efficient and economical, others report no advantages over interlibrary loan in fill rate or delivery time, and that costs are greater. However, Cain (1995) reports data from an Association of Research Libraries/Research Libraries Group study (Roche, 1993) that indicates that ILL now costs $29.55 on the average (borrower and lender costs) and that commercial services are certainly competitive with this. Getz (1991-2) has prepared an analysis of costs of ownership of a journal versus cost of use of a delivery service, but some of the newer delivery options are not included in his analysis.

In one of the more recent studies, Mancini (1996) evaluated four commercial suppliers. Based on a sample of 175 requests, she reports a fill rate of 135/175, about 76%, but this varied from a low of 35% for one supplier to a high of 96% for another. Average arrival times of articles using fax was in the 2-3 day range, while average arrival time for items mailed (two suppliers only) was in the 5-6 day range, still a considerable improvement on interlibrary lending, which she reports at around 14 days on the average. Total cost per article for fax delivery was in the $14-20 range; for mail delivery it was in the $10-20 range. She concludes that, while commercial suppliers cannot completely replace ILL (most obviously because of the continuing need for access to older materials), "they can enhance the productivity and flexibility of current services and increase user access to many necessary titles."

A survey performed by the Association of Research Libraries (Jackson and Croneis, 1994) indicates that the great majority of the research libraries surveyed (78/90) do use commercial suppliers and that delivery speed and copyright/royalty handling are the reasons most often cited for use of these services.

Jackson (1993b) and Mitchell and Walters (1995) have produced useful lists of criteria for evaluating document delivery services. These are summarized in Figure 41. Data on turnaround time and fill rate would be obtained by collecting relevant statistics based on actual use of these services over a significant period of time or, alternatively, through use of a test in which the same set of orders is submitted to various vendors, although some data might be extracted from studies performed in other libraries. In comparing vendors, it is important to seek the data that are most meaningful. For example, average (mean) turnaround time can be very misleading. Much more valuable would be data on the number of requests filled in x days, in x+1, in x+2, and so on.

---

1. Turnaround time
2. Delivery options
3. Ordering options
4. Coverage (by journal titles, dates, and/or subject areas)
5. Fill rate
6. Costs for different service options
7. Billing options
8. Library access only or direct patron access possible?
9. Currency (how soon after publication an article is available for delivery)

FIGURE 41
Criteria for evaluating document delivery services.
Many of these are presented and discussed by Jackson (1993b)
and by Mitchell and Walters (1995)

Just as network-based union catalogs and circulation systems permit library users to generate their own interlibrary loan requests, and databases accessible online or as CD-ROM allow them to perform their own subject searches, so document delivery and TOC services put document ordering into the hands of the individual library user. Clearly, this raises the significant issue of how such orders are paid for. This issue will occur again in Chapter 12.

Integration of Document Delivery Services

Jackson (1993c) mentions five possible models for the integration of commercial delivery services with conventional interlibrary resource sharing. These can be summarized as follows:

1. Commercial services used only after interlibrary resources have failed.

2. Commercial services are the first source a library goes to for any item not available locally.
3. Library patrons use commercial services directly.
4. Some patrons (e.g., faculty with generous research grants) use commercial services directly; others must go to the library to request service (interlibrary or commercial).
5. Patrons access full text in electronic form, either online or via CD-ROM.

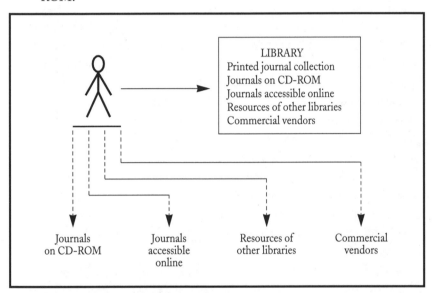

FIGURE 42
Journal article access options for library user

Figure 42 shows the possible ways in which a library user might now be able to access the contents of journals. Of course, some of these options are available only on a very limited scale at the present time: there are still relatively few journals accessible in electronic form, either as CD-ROM or as full text online, although the number thus available is increasing rapidly and some journals can only be accessed online. As the diagram shows, the user may be required to go through the library for all forms of access. However, apart from visiting the library to use the printed journal collection, it is now possible for users of some libraries to bypass the library for virtually all of these access modes. Haricombe and Lusher (1995) believe that library services will go through three phases: (1) library users dependent on the library for all services, (2) users and libraries sharing the tasks and responsibilities, and (3) users bypassing the library for virtually all services.

Where libraries allow users to place document orders directly (e.g., following their own online searches), they still may require the orders to be channelled electronically through an interlibrary loan office, although at least one has experimented with subsidizing direct, unmediated ordering (Sellers and Beam, 1995).

Clearly, libraries cannot yet discontinue en masse their subscriptions to journals in print-on-paper form, not only because an electronic alternative does not exist for most titles but because at present the printed journal still has many advantages to offer, including quality of illustration and better (conventional) browsability. Nevertheless, the commercial document delivery and electronic access alternatives make it increasingly possible for libraries to discontinue subscriptions to the less used titles, relying on the access alternatives to satisfy demands for these as they arise.* Access becomes a viable alternative to ownership for all titles in which the total cost of obtaining an article rapidly (by fax, express mail, or network access) is less than the total annual cost of owning the journal (subscription, handling, and storage costs) divided by the expected number of uses in a year.

The options of Figure 42 are not mutually exclusive. Some vendors are now implementing systems that combine network access to full text in ASCII format with the ability to access text and illustrations in bit-mapped form on CD-ROM (Orchard, 1997).

Institutional Databases

The Internet facilitates the building of specialized databases by a particular institution, or consortium, and the making of these widely accessible for use by other organizations. For example, the Museum Educational Site Licensing Project, initiated by the J. Paul Getty Trust, is making art images and information from six museums (including the National Gallery of Art) available to seven universities. The databases

---

*Some libraries have already virtually eliminated periodical subscriptions in favor of access approaches (see, for example, Widdicombe, 1993).

thus created combine text and digital images and are designed for use in teaching in art and related disciplines. Academic libraries are participating in the project as test sites, performing research on access modes and evaluating use.

Projects of this type suggest that one significant role for the research library of the future will be to participate in the building of databases of resources in which the local institution is unusually strong (in text, image, sound, analog model, or other form) and in the design and implementation of interfaces to maximize the accessibility and utility of these resources.

However, the building of network-accessible databases is as important to the future of the public library as it is to the academic. Holt (1993) refers to one library's achievements in this area (e.g., databases of local artists and of genealogical resources) and its plans for the future, and Doman (1994) describes the databases compiled and made accessible by the Pikes Peak Library District, which has long been a leader in this area.

The Future of Access and Delivery

The trends discernible today strongly suggest that more and more journals (and, indeed, other types of publications) will become available in electronic form and that, increasingly, these will be accessed directly by the public without the intervention of the library. In the short-term, this will mean electronic access to existing sources. There are strong forces pushing in this direction, most notably the massive Digital Library Initiative funded by the National Science Foundation and other agencies (Fox et al., 1995; Jeapes, 1995, 1996; Berry, 1996), the establishment of the National Digital Library Federation (Lamolinara, 1996), and the fact that some libraries have reached their own agreement with publishers to acquire sources in electronic rather than paper form.* ELINOR and successor projects at De Montfort University already make many thousands of pages from textbooks, journals, and other sources accessible through an online, full text retrieval system (Zhao, 1994; Collier, 1997).** Other libraries have implemented electronic access to materials previously made available in conventional printed form, including "reserve" materials

---

*See McClung (1996) for a current inventory of digitizing projects.

**The licensing aspects are dealt with by Collier (1996) and Arnold (1996).

needed in support of university coursework (Enssle, 1994; Butler, 1996; Goodram, 1996), and some publishers are making it possible for faculty to build their own customized teaching materials from digital text drawn from books, journals, and other sources (Borman, 1993; Hunter, 1994b). In the Digital Library Initiative, many major publishers, including professional societies and commercial enterprises, are making textbooks, journals, and popular magazines available to research libraries in dig-ital form to allow studies of use factors and problems of implementa-tion. The JSTOR project, funded by the Mellon Foundation, is working with publishers to get the full text of back issues of leading journals into digital form (DeGennaro, 1997).

Commercial document delivery services are now putting great emphasis on providing network access to the full text of journals, and other materials, through Web interfaces designed for direct access by end users (Orchard, 1977).

In the longer term, it seems very likely that print-on-paper publi-cations will very largely be replaced by completely new electronic forms, publications that cannot exist as paper by virtue of their char-acteristics—incorporating motion, sound, and hypertext/hypermedia fea-tures, and allowing the user to interact or participate with the publication. Very likely this will eliminate distinctions now made among monographs, journals, and certain other publication forms (Arnold, 1995). For a realistic vision of the electronic publications of the future one must go beyond the literature of library science and read such authors as Lan-ham (1994) and Negroponte (1995) as well as writers in the area of vir-tual reality—Rheingold (1991), Helsel and Roth (1991), Pimentel and Teixeira (1995), and especially Krueger (1983). Barden (1995) emphasizes how important it is today for libraries to develop capabilities for mul-timedia document delivery.

CHAPTER 12

General Trends in User Services

IOIOIOIOIOIOIOIOIOIOIOIOIOIOIOIOIOIOIOIOIOIOIOIOIOIOIOIOIOIOIOIOIOIOIOIOIOIOIOI

As MENTIONED throughout this book, technology has had major effects on the services that libraries provide and on the way these services are used. These effects can be categorized as (1) modification of traditional services, (2) introduction of new services, (3) disintermediation of services, and (4), perhaps most significant, the extension of services to remote users. This grouping seems a useful one even though the categories are not mutually exclusive.

Modification of Traditional Services

The modification of traditional library services, hopefully their improvement, has been illustrated in many of the other chapters. Perhaps the most obvious example is the gradual substitution of electronic access for more conventional tools—the OPAC for the card catalog and electronic databases for much use of printed indexes and other reference tools. Such developments are generally considered to have improved the quality of services although, as implied elsewhere in the book, some libraries may be inclined to exaggerate the improvement. At the very least, surveys of library users tend to show that the great majority prefer the new tools to the old. Furthermore, the new tools have expanded the horizons of library users—e.g., by replacing the catalog of a single library by one covering the holdings of many—and have made possible significant improvements elsewhere—e.g., online union catalogs, coupled with fax, have greatly increased the probability that an urgently needed item can be delivered expeditiously to a user.

New Services

Computer and telecommunications technologies have allowed libraries to develop services that would have been almost impossible to offer earlier. Some of these have developed logically as extensions of traditional services or tools. Most obvious is the expansion of the catalog from a single-library finding tool to one that may now be a doorway to a universe of information resources:

1. The holdings of other libraries
2. Databases providing access to millions of journal articles
3. Databases constructed by the library itself (e.g., of community resources, of local history, of carpooling information)
4. Via the Internet, the holdings of even more libraries and an almost limitless variety of formal and informal sources of information.

Tyckoson (1989b) gives a dramatic illustration of the importance of the expansion/enhancement of the catalog, especially by its inclusion of references to the journal literature, when he points out that the "traditional" catalog provides access to only about two percent of the collection in a typical academic library.

The enhancement of the catalog is likely to continue in a number of directions in the future. For example, the PALINET consortium in the Philadelphia area is experimenting with the augmentation of the catalog through the inclusion of tables of contents of monographic publications (PALINET announces, 1995).

The ability to access databases in electronic form has allowed libraries to offer a number of nontraditional services to their users. Hanson (1994a), for example, provides a useful discussion on aiding users to build their own electronic resources by downloading from CD-ROM or other databases, In this context, he believes that the library can play an important role in (1) alerting users to software that can be applied to build and manipulate their own databases of downloaded records, (2) making such software available, perhaps through some form of central site license, (3) training of users, and (4) offering assistance or troubleshooting where necessary. Hanson (1995) presents a useful survey of bibliographic software that library users can apply to their own databases.

A related development is the improvement of library-provided current awareness services. Libraries have long offered various current awareness facilities or services to their users. The most obvious, and least sophisticated, is simply the placing of current issues of journals on a special and prominent display. Another obvious example is the preparation of booklists representing items recently added to the collection. The circulation of current issues of journals on a routing list was very common in special libraries in the 1950s and 1960s, and continues in some today, while a few special libraries have prepared and distributed their own bulletins of abstracts. Major improvements in photocopying technologies, leading to greatly reduced costs, led many special libraries to distribute multiple copies of journal contents pages instead of routing the journals themselves. As discussed in Chapter 11, table-of-contents (TOC) services have become increasingly common in libraries of all types and many such services are offered online by publishers and other vendors. Mountifield (1995) gives a useful survey of these.

In the late 1950s, Hans Peter Luhn of IBM first discussed the possibility of a more sophisticated level of current awareness in which computers are used to match subject terms associated with newly published items against subject terms in "interest profiles" of users. He later referred to this as "selective dissemination of information" (SDI). SDI services became popular in the 1960s because they were very cheap compared with the cost of using computers to search databases retrospectively on demand. Based on databases made commercially available by major publishers, and occasionally on in-house databases, SDI services were offered by many special libraries and, later, by dissemination centers selling such services on a fee basis.

Services of this type, involving the searching of magnetic tape and the distribution of printed lists of retrieved references, were rendered somewhat obsolete by the emergence of online systems that allow a library user (or a librarian on his/her behalf) to access a database periodically to achieve a continuing current awareness service.

The increasing availability and diversity of CD-ROM databases in libraries has made it even easier for a library user to keep somewhat up-to-date in an area of interest through a search of one or more sources on a regular basis as they are updated. The intelligent user, presumably, would develop an effective search strategy (interest profile) and retain it for continued use.

Nevertheless, some believe that a better level of service would result if librarians involved themselves in the process. For example, Hanson (1994a) describes a librarian-mediated "electronic current awareness service" offered at the University of Portsmouth. Subject specialist librarians help users to develop their interest profiles and to select the CD-ROM databases that will be searched regularly on their behalf. The actual searches are run by clerical personnel on the library staff and the retrieved references are supplied to users in an electronic form that allows their input into personal databases.

Cox and Hanson (1992) have discussed similar current awareness services, in special and academic libraries, based on CD-ROM, floppy disk, online databases, and library catalogs. Again, output is delivered to users in electronic form. In one of the services, offered by a hospital library, an annual fee is charged. The authors believe that the "image of the library can undoubtedly be enhanced by the introduction of an electronic current awareness service" and they report that such a service can be expected to increase demand for document delivery and may even affect journal subscriptions (indicating titles that should be added to the collection but also, possibly, some that could be discontinued).*

Herala et al. (1995) describe the use of software that can process SDI profiles on CD-ROM databases automatically (most software packages supplied with CD-ROMs do not support automatic processing of saved search strategies). They emphasize the value of CD-ROM in providing SDI services in the less developed and less affluent countries.

Modern technologies also allow libraries to offer current awareness services of a completely different type. For example, Webb (1995) refers to a video news service of Kapiolani Community College at the University of Hawaii:

> It is delivered by a large-screen television that broadcasts continuous cable news in a special alcove adjacent to the library's current periodicals and reference areas. This arrangement permits students to follow a topic of interest from its most current stages, through recent treatments in periodical format, and then to perform further research into historical and other background aspects of the topic by using the library's reference, general, and special collections. (Page 25)

It is quite possible that libraries, especially those in industry, might use technology to offer completely new services to their communities. In particular, commercially-available databases could be applied to

---

*On the other hand, Brudvig (1991) has argued for the desirability of restricting outputs from database searches to items locally available.

several activities beyond the more conventional bibliographic searching and current awareness. For example, Lancaster and Loescher (1994)
have discussed how databases might be applied in corporate intelligence
and in various forms of technological or social forecasting, as well as in
historical analyses (tracing the movement of "ideas" through the published literature).

Disintermediation

As mentioned several times elsewhere, new technologies now allow
library users to undertake for themselves various activities previously provided for them by members of the library staff. Examples include
charging items for later pickup or delivery, the searching of union catalogs, the initiation of interlibrary borrowing and ordering from commercial suppliers, and the unmediated searching of remote or CD-ROM
databases.

One obvious effect of such disintermediation is that it should free
some time for librarians and support staff to spend on other activities,
perhaps in providing some of the new services alluded to earlier.

Disintermediation can also have less obvious effects. For example, Ison
(1995) has pointed out that it can have a rather profound effect in changing interlibrary lending patterns, perhaps making the whole service more
equitable:

> A somewhat surprising outgrowth of patron-initiated interlibrary loan is the
> shifting of the lending away from the larger libraries to a reliance on smaller,
> more rural, libraries. According to statistics, rural libraries were better able
> to rely on each other and, in several instances, smaller libraries loaned more
> than they borrowed from the largest libraries in the consortium. (Page 146)

Not unexpectedly, she also reports dramatic increases (fivefold) in
overall interlending.

On the other hand, Farber (1995) has pointed out that disintermediation may have undesirable consequences because it makes it increasingly difficult for librarians to instruct users at the moment of need (the
"teachable moment"):

> An undergraduate's request for many interlibrary loans, for example, can pro-
> vide a perfect teachable moment: explaining to the student at the moment
> of need which items are appropriate and which are not—and why. Several
> institutions have automated that process, and others are in the process of doing
> the same. In this case, such automation precludes the possibility of a poten-

tially valuable educational experience. That is why the move toward "disintermediation"—removing the librarian from a procedure that was once performed by individuals and substituting an automated procedure—should be examined carefully to ensure the gain in efficiency is worth the loss of educational benefits. (Page 437)

The aspect of disintermediation that is causing most problems for libraries is that related to document delivery. Haricombe and Lusher (1995) recognize three phases in this activity:

1. The user asks the library to acquire a particular item from another library or commercial vendor.
2. The user interacts with a librarian to select a source for an item and the user then places the order directly.
3. The user handles the entire process, bypassing the library.

Clearly, the third phase (and, to some extent, the second) creates problems if the library continues to bear the cost of providing access and delivery to users. If some users have the ability to charge items to a library account, some obvious dangers emerge—including the possibility that costs will be incurred for items readily available locally, that many items purchased will turn out not to be useful (the librarian may have prevented some of this), and that the library staff loses control of its own budgeting. Issues such as these have been raised by a number of writers, including Jackson (1992), Leach and Tribble (1993) and Higginbotham and Bowdoin (1993). Jackson implies that these are problems that libraries must face squarely because users who have network access to a myriad of information sources, perhaps from their offices or homes, will expect to be able to order documents directly as references to them are located. She suggests the need for some routine that would automatically check outgoing document orders against local holdings. The automatic blocking of orders for things held locally is now possible with at least one vendor interface (Sellers and Beam, 1995).

Jackson and Croneis (1994) point out that traditional interlibrary resource sharing is expensive and that "patron ordering may be more cost-effective and more staff-efficient . . . in the long run." In their survey of ARL libraries, they determined that 49 (out of 89) do allow direct patron ordering but none now absorbs the costs. Of the 40 that do not allow patron ordering, eleven claim to be exploring it. Since the ARL survey, at least one library has experimented with subsidized unmediated document delivery using a single vendor (Sellers and Beam, 1995).

In actual fact, while a definite move toward disintermediation can be observed in the services referred to earlier, with certain other activities the reverse situation (i.e., mediation where it did not exist before) has occurred, at least to some extent. One example of this has to do with referral of users to other libraries or institutions. In the past, the user of a research or special library may have been informed that another institution might be an appropriate source of information but contact with that institution was frequently left to the user. Today, the referring librarian may use electronic mail to contact the target institution on behalf of the user and may even use Internet resources to search that institution's catalogs. Kovacs et al. (1994) have discussed the role of librarians in using Internet resources in the provision of reference service.

While Ewing and Hauptman (1995) cast doubt on the need for reference librarians in an electronic environment, others have taken the opposing position:

> Contrary to the arguments put forth by Ewing and Hauptman, reference librarians and the services they provide are needed more now than at any other time in the past due to the increasingly [sic] popularity and complexity of such resources as the Internet in the automated reference environment. (Kong, 1995, page 14)

Service to Remote Users

The disintermediation trend, discussed in the previous section, leads logically to a more profound matter that libraries now must contend with—the fact that electronic networks allow people to use certain of the library's resources, and to obtain services traditionally provided by the library, without visiting the library or consulting a member of the library staff. Service to "remote users," then, has emerged as a major issue facing libraries, particularly academic and special libraries.

Not surprisingly, remote access to at least some of the library's resources is becoming increasingly common, as demonstrated in the results of surveys undertaken by the Association of Research Libraries in 1986 and in 1993. In 1986, some 57 libraries (48% of those responding) provided remote access; by 1993, the coverage had increased to 67% (Haynes, 1993). The 1993 survey showed that access to the online catalog was the remote service offered most often (71 of the 75 libraries responding), followed by reference service—typically through electronic mail (46 libraries), circulation services (40 libraries), and interlibrary loan (38 libraries). In addition, 59 libraries (82% of those responding) claim to offer "technical assistance" to remote users, including helping users with computer-related and bibliographic-related questions. Only twelve of the libraries claimed to have a formal policy on service to remote users and these appear to be of only a very general nature (e.g., remote users should have the same capabilities and level of service as in-library users).

Remote users of library services are difficult to identify and may include many individuals who have not been regular visitors to the library. Such users may encounter problems that would be more easily solved if they *were* physically present in the library and had ready access to staff members. Kalin (1991) mentions the need to provide various support services to such users. She discusses various forms of support, including help with the technology itself and with the more intellectual aspects such as search strategy, as well as such longer-term support as the instruction of users and the development of improved tools (interfaces or gateways).* As Kalin points out, the big problem is the fact that remote users, while they may have less immediate access to assistance from library staff, may also have higher expectations regarding quality and speed of service.

At the present time, a remote user may be able to perform the following activities that would previously require a visit to the library: (a) search the library's catalog, (b) search the catalogs of other libraries, (c) search other databases, (d) charge out an item owned by the library for subsequent pickup or delivery, (e) charge out a book from another library for subsequent pickup or delivery, (f) initiate an order for a photocopy from another library or a commercial supplier, (g) communicate with members of the library staff for reference service or other assistance, (h) have the results of searches or current awareness services delivered electronically, perhaps in a form suitable for incorporation into personal data-

---

*DiMattia (1991) suggests the need for a hardware/software "troubleshooter" on the library staff "to assist offsite users with the transition stage of system access."

bases, and (i), in some cases, have the full text of required items delivered to a personal workstation.

It is clear that this last capability represents the ultimate in remote use since search, retrieval, and delivery need not involve the library at all. In the case of academic and public libraries, of course, it will still be a long time before most of the items that users need will exist *in toto* in electronic form. In the case of certain special libraries, however, the completely or nearly-completely virtual collection may already exist. This might be true, for instance, in an industrial setting in which the library is concerned primarily with the company's internal information resources. Norbie (1994), for example, describes a library of this type: "The library sits on employees' desktops throughout 14 western states. It does not matter where the librarian is located." In this environment, she sees the following as important roles for the "electronic librarian":

- The focus is on identifying which employees are not yet customers and turning them into users and gathering statistics on users by divisions within the company to determine where the library needs to be marketed;
- The librarian function focuses on making partnerships and designing user-friendly interfaces; users do their own research or reference work;
- Space planning has become screen planning;
- Instead of helpful, smiling people, friendly customer service is now the friendliness of computer menu screens;
- The pieces of data that become metrics for the success of the service are different. Circulation statistics become statistics on how frequently document groups are accessed by users and how users are realizing a savings of time and increasing productivity; and
- New measurement models for the cost of information must be developed, because users now perform research themselves. (Page 275)

Some of the problems involved in remote reference service have been discussed by Abels and Liebscher (1994). While it may be convenient for a user to transmit some form of reference request by electronic mail, and to receive certain results electronically, asynchronous communication does not permit the traditional "reference interview." Nevertheless, because writing out a request is likely to help many people in clarifying their own needs, a question submitted electronically may often be relatively precise. Abels and Liebscher suggest the need to develop electronic "templates" to guide users into formulating more precise questions. Horwitz (1989) points out that remote reference service removes geographic and certain physical barriers (e.g., service to some handicapped groups) to information access.

A debate held at the annual meeting of the Medical Library Association in 1995 posed some questions to library administrators that reflect real concerns regarding the problems of remote reference service:

- Is electronic access to reference the most effective way to answer reference questions? Isn't a reference interview important? Does effectiveness of electronic reference depend on the type of library (i.e., hospital versus academic)?
- How do you communicate with users you never see; how do you know what they need? (Nagle, 1996, page 662)

Remote use of library resources is likely to increase and, in fact, significant increases have already been reported.* For example, Lewontin (1991), referring to use of business-related databases made available by an academic library, reports that use of these resources was greater within the library in August 1988 but that remote use exceeded in-library use one month later; by 1990, remote access exceeded in-library access "overwhelmingly". Bristow (1992), in a larger academic library, reports approximately 330 reference questions answered through electronic mail for 51 different users in a three month period. Users were enthusiastic about the service and some suggested that the library "train everyone to use e-mail and abandon the phone."

Heller (1992) also claims significant increases in library use as remote access to resources became more feasible:

At Norwich University, delivering services beyond the physical confines of the library has had the result of increased performance in every category by which the library measures its success. Marked growth in these statistical yardsticks comes at a time when the student population has significantly decreased, further underscoring the importance of greater access to the delivery of service. (Page 287)

He claims that remote access can bring the library more directly into the teaching process because faculty members now often use office terminals to refer to library resources during conferences with students.

Remote use has the obvious advantage that it can make some, at least, of the library's services accessible twenty four hours a day. Bellamy et al. (1991) point out that it can also save money—e.g., avoiding the need

---

*Projects focusing specifically on services to remote users obviously tend to promote this trend. For example, the BIBDEL Project funded by the Libraries Programme of the European Commission has stimulated several relevant experiments (see Wynne, 1996, for one example)

for individual academic departments to acquire database searching capabilities. Remote use will also have impact on other library services, perhaps reducing the demand for interlibrary and commercial document delivery.

Davis (1988) discusses the training needs of remote users and describes a number of approaches within a university environment, including an electronic instructional module that can be used in classroom and other settings.

Bobay et al. (1990) mention some other effects on the library: the instruction of users changes rather dramatically (designing interfaces and offering electronic mail assistance rather than face-to-face instruction); collection development policies may need to be re-examined if the remote user community includes groups that were not previous users of the library; and resource sharing among libraries grows in importance as increased use puts greater demands on document delivery services.

DiMattia (1993) has discussed the importance of maintaining the quality of remote services—by ensuring system reliability, upgrading capabilities where necessary, and offering various forms of help to users. Speaking from the viewpoint of the public library, he implies that reaching the "information poor" should be one of the priorities in developing remote access to library services. Sloan (1991) emphasizes the need for good communication with remote users and suggests that some form of newsletter would be valuable.

Clearly, remote library use also implies that members of the library staff need somewhat different skills than they did previously, such as the ability to offer various levels of technical support (deKock, 1993) and to have the facility to communicate with users in an asynchronous electronic mode rather than through direct face-to-face interaction or even telephone contact.* Weller (1985), however, reports that the interpretation of the requests of remote users is not as difficult as one might expect.

Sloan (1991) suggests that remote users of OPACs may be significantly different from those who visit the library: more sophisticated users of computers, more likely to use online help facilities, and more likely to

---

*For an alternative approach to remote reference service, incorporating videoconferencing, see Pagell (1996)

be searching for known items than to be performing subject searches. He also points out that they can be at a serious disadvantage as information seekers because they do not have the full resources of the library readily available. One result of this is that they are more likely to request the delivery of items that turn out to be of no use to them, suggesting the need for the enhancement of catalog records by inclusion of annotations or contents pages. Sloan claims that remote users may need interfaces that are different from those designed primarily for in-library users, but he gives no details on what these differences might be.

User Reactions to Library Technology

Anecdotal evidence from librarians suggests that the majority of library users fully approve of the increasing application of technology to library operations. A survey of 238 libraries of all types, undertaken by Hauptman and Anderson (1994) in 1990, found that 50% of respondents agreed that "patrons appreciate technology" and a further 28% strongly agreed with this. A mere 1% strongly disagreed. On the other hand, only 33% could agree that technology is fully utilized by patrons and only 6% could strongly agree with this. Nevertheless, the responding librarians are almost unanimous in the opinion that further technology would increase library service: 48% agree and 37% strongly agree. Direct surveys of patrons to determine their reactions to the increasing automation of services, or the effect of technology on their use of libraries, seem virtually nonexistent in the professional literature.

CHAPTER 13

Libraries and the Internet

IOIOIOIOIOIOIOIOIOIOIOIOIOIOIOIOIOIOIOIOIOIOIOIOIOIOIOIOIOIOIOIOIOIOIOIOIOIOIOI

C HAPTERS 1 - 8 dealt primarily with general management issues relating to technology and libraries, whereas chapters 9-12 dealt primarily, but not exclusively, with effects of technology on library users. Chapters 13-15 will deal with some more specialized issues in the management of technology within libraries: impact of the Internet, evaluation of automated systems, and prospects for artificial intelligence and expert system technologies. This chapter looks at the Internet, the library-related implications of which have been put concisely by Weibel (1995b):

> The rapid development of networking and electronic dissemination of information forces upon us both opportunities and burdens. The opportunity is to provide the greater flexibility and convenience that networked information affords. The burden is to integrate these services with the existing library infrastructure such that users are not confronted with two disjoint information environments. (Page 627)

The Internet is arguably the electronic resource that is now having the most significant impact on library services and operations and on the professional activities of librarians. This strength of impact is due to its multi-faceted nature since it simultaneously fulfills three important roles in library services. First, it is a resource that can be consulted and used like any other reference tool. Second, it is more dynamic and far-reaching than any other resource used in a library setting. Finally, it provides a medium of communication that has extended the potential of librarians for interaction beyond the physical library (to users, colleagues, and other professionals), beyond any previous capacity, and in a host of new ways. This chapter explores the impact of the Internet on library services, professional activities, and relationships with library users.

The Internet is actually a non-network. It is technically comprised of a group of high-speed computer networks that are interconnected by the use of a common communications protocol—TCP/IP (transmission control protocol/Internet protocol). The theoretical simplicity of this scheme, plus the rapid decrease in the cost of computing technology, have contributed to the widespread growth of connectivity to the Internet. What began as a high-speed network linking Department of Defense centers in the late 1960s has grown into a multi-purpose public communication/information vehicle, currently with very few formal restrictions on content and purpose.

A concise but rather complete description of the Internet and its resources has been provided by the Library Association (1995):

> The Internet consists of a large number of linked computer networks forming a global network. This is largely open and free, allowing users to communicate with each other for work and recreational purposes, and for corporate and personal reasons. Because the Internet is so vast and is without regulation or hierarchy, the network is a treasure-trove of information from many sources. Resources are available in all subjects; mailing is possible for all the participants; documents can be forwarded and delivered across the world; and directories and journals abound. Developments such as the World Wide Web* combine friendliness of user interface with enormously powerful information retrieval capability. Electronic mail is one of the most important services offered through the Internet, with each person having a personal mail address, enabling them to link up to another user anywhere in the world and communicate within seconds. (Page 547)

In late 1991, the High Performance Computing Act, signed into law by President Bush, authorized the establishment of the National Research and Education Network (NREN). Although libraries are specifically mentioned in few areas of this legislation, the context suggests that libraries and information services were intended to comprise a part of the network (McClure et al., 1992). On March 21, 1994 Vice President Gore addressed the International Telecommunications Union meeting, exhorting the participants to support work on building the Global Information Infrastructure (GII):

> The president and I have called for positive government action in the United States to extend the NII to every classroom, library, hospital, and clinic in the U.S. by the end of the century. I want to urge that this conference include in its agenda for action the commitment to determine how every school and library in every country can be connected to the Internet, the world's largest computer network, in order to create a Global Digital Library. (Gore, 1994, page 813)

---

*The WWW, or simply Web, is discussed later in the chapter.

It is important to recognize that the Internet's vast capability to enable the sharing of data is largely due to the efforts of individuals or groups to provide software or data files for public consumption, free or at a low cost. This "grass roots" development spirit, and U.S. government funding, is largely responsible for the availability of such a wealth of information. By the same token, this loosely coordinated growth and duplication has created one of the most complex retrieval challenges to users of online systems.

Early work by Lynch and Preston (1990) describes the resources available at that time through the Internet, and discusses the proposed impact on library services and user behavior. Within a relatively short period of time, libraries and librarians have integrated the use of the Internet into nearly all aspects of current library activities, including:

1. Communication among staff, or with colleagues or patrons, through e-mail (Cromer and Johnson, 1994); collaborative research and publication can be one facet of this (Tillman and Ladner, 1994);
2. Discussion through listservs or other electronic vehicles; this includes using the Internet to share information about the Internet itself;
3. Support of reference services of all types through search of remote databases (Ladner and Tillman, 1993) and through a cooperative approach to the answering of "difficult" questions (Batt, 1996b);
4. Exploiting the catalogs of other institutions, which may offer access points or search features not available locally (Drabenstott and Cochrane, 1994);
5. Gathering information from library users in order to create SDI profiles for them;
6. Interlibrary loan verification, requests, document delivery, and consortial file-sharing (e-journals, images, data, and text file FTP sites);
7. Cataloging;
8. Book/journal ordering;
9. Evaluation of competing online systems for purpose of selection;
10. Making locally-produced databases accessible to remote users;
11. Establishing home pages to provide information on the library, its resources, and its services (Branse et al., 1996).

In addition, some organizations have formed their own internal networks, modelled on Internet principles and often connected to the Internet. Such "intranets" can be exploited by libraries to make information and resources available (West, 1997).

Several print and electronic journals, newsletters, and listservs are now devoted to use of the Internet and its resources by librarians. The SUNY/OCLC *Internet Homesteader* (1994 on) claims as its mission: "bringing information available on the Internet to individuals with no Internet access and assisting those with access in finding their way." It typically includes a section for those with no Internet access that provides synopses of information from e-conferences and other library and technology-related Internet resources, as well as a section with reviews and training-related information for those with Internet access. The contents of this newsletter provide a particularly good example of the importance that the library profession has begun to assign to professional communication using the Internet. The synopses of e-conferences give those without Internet access the opportunity to follow in print what their colleagues have deemed important professional exchange about current issues in librarianship.

In the first "Internet Librarian" column in *American Libraries*, Schneider (1995) highlights the numerous efforts of librarians to provide organizational and access tools for Internet resources. At the 1995 annual meeting of the American Library Association, the Internet Room, which has been sponsored for several years to provide Internet access for conference-goers, was moved to the center of the exhibit hall. This is an indicator not only of the popularity of network access, but also of the growing importance librarians place on access to electronic communication to support their professional activities. An exploratory study by McClure et al. (1992) discusses key factors that affect public library use of networked resources and the potential roles for public libraries in the networked environment. The top four needs identified by public library respondents in their questionnaire survey were:

1. Awareness of what is available on the Internet;
2. Widespread library connectivity to the Internet;
3. Training in network navigational skills for librarians;
4. Librarian involvement in contributing to and organizing information on the Internet.

Getting connected to the Internet has been easier for academic and government libraries than it has for public and rural libraries, where connectivity has been a major stumbling block to Internet use. Boyce and Boyce (1995) indicate that rural library outreach programs could be greatly facilitated by Internet access such as that made available by Freenets. Holt (1995b) reinforces their point and asserts that the Internet is helping rural libraries redefine their concept of traditional limited access—"computers and networks can help rural libraries act like big libraries on a limited budget." McClure et al. (1994) recommend that public libraries coordinate their networking activities, including OCLC, regional, and national access to networked information.

Since the early 1995 privatization of the Internet, opportunities for connectivity have expanded considerably, with fierce competition in the commercial sector to market Internet services to businesses, not-for-profit organizations, and individuals. The leading vendors of online catalog systems have developed modules that incorporate Internet and Web access, including their own customized browsers. In a study of Internet connectivity costs for public libraries, McClure et al. (1995) explore five representative connectivity models that range from single workstation, single library, to multiple workstations, multiple libraries, and multimedia systems. For example, charges for a public library to connect a single workstation with text-based capabilities to the Internet are reported at a one-time cost of $1,475, with a recurring annual cost of $12,635. The study discusses costs for hardware, software, varying levels and methods of Internet connectivity, and the accompanying training and human resources support. This study presents a useful foundation that library managers can employ to establish an overview of what their investment in Internet connectivity could provide for their users.

The involvement of librarians and other information professionals in training for Internet use and in the organization of information to be used on the Internet has also increased markedly. Daniel Dern, a noted technical and networking expert, perhaps anticipated the extent of librarian involvement with the Internet when he remarked that the Internet is "the librarians' full employment act of the 1990s" (Snyder, 1994).

Impact on Library Services

Basic Internet services enable one to accomplish a number of networked information functions: connect with other computers, including library catalogs; move files of text and data using FTP commands; send and receive electronic mail; read news from many different sources; find software; search indexed databases; search for someone. Krol (1994) provides an excellent guide and resource catalog with extensive background on how these services can be used. The application of Internet services is evolving so rapidly that there is little point in providing details on specific services or functions. Liu's (1995) classified bibliography is a useful resource that examines the impact of the Internet on almost all aspects of librarianship. However, it is important to supplement print resources with information from most current discussions and documents that are available only through listservs, File Transfer Protocol (FTP) archives, and the World Wide Web (WWW), and only in electronic format.

Through access to these services, librarians have found new ways to store, move, find, and communicate about information among themselves and with users. For reference and public service librarians, this access has created many new and different service options. Kluegel's (1995) example of a search in a German online catalog through the Internet demonstrates the vast time savings possible when a librarian or user connects to a remote network to verify the existence and location of a resource. Dalrymple and Roderer (1994) characterize the Internet as "the most significant telecommunications advance affecting online searching ..." in the period of time covered by their review article—1987-1994. Ready reference can be performed with even greater speed since materials such as dictionaries, census information, U.S. government documents, and the *CIA World Fact Book* are freely available from numerous sites (Lanier and Wilkins, 1994).

Locating information through the Internet remains a challenge. Access is achieved initially through "browsers," such as the Netscape Navigator and the Microsoft Explorer, which lead to various "search engines" that have different capabilities and purposes and operate in different ways. A search on the same topic may give very different results when a user moves from one search engine to another. This whole area is changing very rapidly, with new developments occurring on almost a daily basis. "Metasearch engines" now allow searching using several search engines simultaneously and several "intelligent agents" have been developed to perform various functions for individual users (e.g., watch for new items of a particular type or automatically create specialized databases). Torok (1997) gives an excellent picture of capabilities as of September, 1996.

To aid libraries and other organizations in maintaining consistent user access to Web pages that may change physical location, OCLC has established a service called PURL (Persistent Uniform Resource Locator). Once an institution has registered its URLs (Uniform Resource Locators—the Web address of a document) with the PURL service, software freely distributed by OCLC helps Web managers to keep track of any subsequent address changes so that the user who returns to a URL that has been changed will be seamlessly routed to the new URL (OCLC Makes PURL ..., 1996).

Lanier and Wilkins note that the availability of electronic versions of print resources, as well as electronic-only sources, has increased pressure on reference librarians to stay current with Internet resources, but has also increased the likelihood that users will not leave the reference desk empty-handed. They urge that reference librarians must continue to develop their roles as "intermediaries" in the information-seeking process. Abels and Liebscher (1994) are studying the way in which electronic reference provision is changing the nature of traditional reference interaction with users.

Information professionals beyond the library have a keen interest in the development of software tools that have indexed the Web. A recent review of Web indexes places over thirty-five such tools in eight different categories, depending on the type of information desired: search engines; directories; "what's new"—sites that index Web pages that have recently been added; e-mail address finders; gopher archives; software search engines; newsgroup search engines, and metasearch engines (Conte, 1996).

The Concept of the Digital Library

The Internet has contributed to the creation of a new information environment—the digital library. At the base of the digital library is the capability to retrieve, manage, store, and publish information in numerous formats. Lucier (1995) describes an effort to build a digital library for the health sciences (DLHS) at the University of California, San Francisco. He suggests that the current structure of print-based libraries that integrate electronic resources is not sufficient to support a true digital library. He views the DLHS objectives as driven primarily by the expectations of its users, and suggests that it has three primary roles:

1. information storage, retrieval, and preservation;
2. information access and delivery;
3. the online publishing of biomedical knowledge (knowledge management).

Although these roles are consistent with current information transfer principles, Lucier emphasizes that the DLHS is not the

> ... exclusive performer of these roles. In many functions, the DLHS plays a minor role, while other collaborators, such as publishers and individual scientists, make more significant contributions. However, the DLHS adds value in partnership with others through every step of this cycle. (Page 348)

To accomplish this evolution to a digital library, Lucier outlines an approach that advocates reduction in physical storage of information, an increase in housing of personnel who manage information, and a collection development policy that focuses on filling users' critical information needs rather than on building a comprehensive collection.

Impact on Professional Roles

As Internet access has spread within the library community, professionals have begun to incorporate use of the Internet into their areas of responsibility. These changes have begun to be reflected in job titles, ranging from direct service positions to upper-level administrative jobs. Titles such as "Networked Information Resources Librarian," "Internet Services Coordinator," or "Electronic Resources Librarian" simply did not exist five years ago. Allen (1995) observes that libraries as organizations can adapt to technological change by creating new types of positions that eventually help to integrate the new technology into the mainstream of library operations. Unlike the earlier position of Online Search Coordinator established in the 1970s, Internet and networked resources positions cross over departmental boundaries, and they are equally likely to be found in the Reference or in the Library Systems departments, depending on the amount of technical skill required to perform the job.

An examination of 23 postings for librarian positions in a single issue of the *Chronicle of Higher Education* (September 15, 1995) revealed nine position descriptions in which responsibilities that include use of Internet or networked resources is a noted component of the position. Job titles include the following:

Systems Librarian (1)

Electronic Systems Librarian (1)

Law Librarian for Internet Services (1)

Network Services Librarian (1)

Public Services/Reference Librarian (with emphasis on Internet resources (2)

Database Coordinator (1)

Network Coordinator (1)

Electronic Information Services Librarian (1)

Four of the nine positions are located in the Reference or User Services departments of their respective libraries and two report to the Director of Library Systems; the other two position descriptions do not indicate a home department. The following statements were found among the qualifications required for the nine positions:

"Advanced work in computing and information science."

"Experience with online integrated library systems, campus networks, the Internet, and electronic information resources."

"Strong public service orientation, experience with searching electronic resources (online, CD-ROM, Internet), and interest in library instruction essential."

"Expert knowledge of HTML and extensive experience with Web administration and operations."

Bosseau (1995) notes that the changes brought about by the availability of networked information have affected higher level administrative positions in academic settings, resulting in the creation of combined titles for managerial positions such as "University Librarian/Associate Vice President for Information Resources," with library directors being placed in charge of "an expanded set of library and other media responsibilities." Bosseau asserts that this, among other changes, reflects recognition of the library's active role in managing technology and infrastructure services that support the delivery of effective information content to users in academic settings. He characterizes the change in the library's role in the academic setting as one that has moved from the cliche phrase "the heart of the university" to a more active and critical role as the "cardiovascular system of the university."

The presence of the Internet in the professional library arena has further blurred the traditional distinctions between technical and public service responsibilities. The major distinction may now be between primarily technical development and support skills and those that are used to help provide some method of organization and access to electronic resources. As computer and networking technologies become increasingly sophisticated, and the technical knowledge threshold is lowered, staff with traditionally lower technical skills are able to connect to and navigate the Net without assistance. Concurrently, librarians who now enter the profession seeking reference and public service positions possess more computing and networking skills than those who entered the profession as few as five years ago. This combination of simplified technologies and the increased likelihood that professionals with enhanced computing skills will enter the library market has resulted in increased professional facility with the Internet and networking resources.

Along with a shift of roles within the library profession is the overlap in training and support services between library and computing center personnel. In a recent survey of library and computing center professionals, Schiller (1994) reported more involvement by computing services staff in providing Internet access and training. However, the survey results also indicated that librarians have considerable involvement in Internet training and support. Some survey respondents reported that team training programs were being offered through collaboration between the library and the computer center. She states that a number of respondents viewed the roles as complementary, distinguishing between "physical access," which was attributed to the computing center, and "intellectual access," which was attributed to the library.

Communication

The Net in libraries has also created the potential for change in the professional communication of librarians and other staff. This change is the result of increased opportunities for communication with individuals or collegial groups — through any number of common channels, ranging from e-mail to listserv and other interactive or asynchronous discussion groups.

While the *potential* for change exists, the expansion of professional communication depends on the administrative commitment of the library to support convenient staff access to the Net and the individual's commitment to learn to use the necessary communication protocols and software (Ives, 1995). Ives includes support staff use of the Internet as an important component of how networking (electronic or non-electronic) can empower staff, and improve library service. He suggests that use of the Internet, particularly as a communication and a current awareness tool, will enable libraries to accomplish more without increasing staff and other resources. He identifies several types of Internet use that should be of value to library staff in carrying out daily responsibilities:

- E-mail: communication — in-house, group, organization, or committee communication; obtaining evaluative information about products; sharing information about policies and procedures; "electronic mail is the most pervasive means of tapping into a large number of knowledgeable people across the expanse of the planet" (Ives, 1995, page 49).
- Listservs: electronic discussion groups, usually focusing on a specific topic; there are many devoted to specific library-related topics (e.g., CDROMLAN, LIBREF-L: reference, BI-L: bibliographic instruction); listservs facilitate ongoing, daily discussion about numerous issues, but they are most useful for finding a resolution to a problem when the in-house expertise is not enough.
- Remote access: for free of fee, a large selection of library and information resources is accessible through the Internet, including remote online catalogs, software archives, full-text papers, and other documents, bibliographies, and numerous numeric and bibliographic databases.
- Use-Net newsgroups: discussion and news groups on all topics, including libraries, that require specific software for access — usually installed by the computer center for an organization. Very useful for

current awareness, they do not clutter up individual e-mail boxes as list-servs tend to.

Some library administrators harbor concerns that staff will misuse the Internet for nonwork activities, thus lowering productivity. Ives argues, however, that library administrators limit the growth potential of their organizations by not enabling staff to use the Internet to discover potentially useful work-related information. Perhaps the question is not whether to provide Internet access but, rather, what types of access are appropriate to enhance a staff member's knowledge of his or her area of specialty. This issue will likely resolve itself as library staff and administrators alike discover and exchange Internet resources that further enhance their work. Strictly limiting an employee's focus to what is already known to exist prevents the serendipitous discovery of equally or perhaps more useful information.

Listservs or e-conferences comprise a substantial portion of the mainstream methods of asynchronous communication among groups on the Internet. Based on a survey of fifty-seven library-related scholarly e-conferences, Kovacs et al. (1995) concluded that library and information science professionals used e-conferences to gather research and professional information for their personal use as well as for information to enhance service to library patrons. They suggest that participants view the information they obtain from e-conferences similarly to the more established sources upon which they rely to find and verify information—journals, conferences, mail, and telephone contacts. Most of the respondents were librarians or paraprofessionals in academic libraries.

Changing Perspectives on Service Provision

McClure et al. (1994) claim that libraries need to rethink the provision of information services for a networked environment. They suggest that libraries will need to change traditional assumptions about their clientele and their information seeking behavior. They envision that networked library services will become more demand-based than they currently are, citing the point that users will gravitate to the Internet services that best meet their needs, regardless of physical location. McCombs (1994) suggests that the provision of flexible electronic access to information that often has no physical format requires that librarians, especially those in technical services areas, will need to rethink traditional attitudes toward the access and processing of information.

Holt (1993) believes that electronic networks in general can have an important role in democratizing access to library resources. His library, the St. Louis Public Library, has already established "equity sites" in such inner city locations as YMCAs, homes for the elderly, and high schools. As Holt puts it, these:

> ... provide access to library materials for those who have trouble getting to their public library and/or those without computers in their homes. (Page 25)

Nevertheless, for various reasons, public libraries have lagged behind academic libraries in the exploitation of the Internet resources. Speaking from a British perspective, the Library Association (1995) has recommended that, given access to the Internet, public libraries should:

- use their skills to identify information, whether in text, image, or sound, and route it as appropriate to people in need of it;
- provide network access points, free or charged, as appropriate; & provide opportunities for education and training in the use of the network;
- use open information systems and broadband communications to integrate use of the network with mainstream library services;
- publish appropriate information e.g. catalogues, community information, and archives over the network;
- apply their skills to the management of the vast amounts of information on the networks;
- as appropriate and in partnership with the academic sector, provide information from the network to students and distance learners. (Pages 548-549)

Ways in which the Internet is being used by British public libraries are discussed by Batt (1996a).

Perhaps the best way to understand the impact of the Internet on libraries is not by speculation or through denial, but through examination. McClure and Lopata (1996) propose a set of evaluative methods for assessing the impact of networking on the academic environment. They suggest using standard social science research methods, such as focus groups, critical incident technique, surveys, observation and site visits, as well as collecting and analyzing standard system-generated network performance and feedback statistics. Their manual contains an overview of methods and applications, as well as sample data collection forms and information about software that can be used to measure net-work services and their level of use. A section of the manual is devoted to online catalog measures. They pose a series of questions for each area of network use in the academic environment. The overall network and library use questions center on the network's impact on a user's ability to find information, both inside the library and within the broader cam-pus community:

1. Has the network affected your use of electronic information resources (Fac-ulty, student, and librarian perception)? If yes, how?

2. Has the network affected your ability to access information in the library (Faculty, student, and librarian perception)? If yes, how?

3. Has the library provided public access to the network (Faculty, student, and librarian perception)?

4. Has the network affected your ability to find the information you need in the library (Faculty, student, and librarian perception)? If yes, how?

5. Has the network affected the types of services provided by the library (Fac-ulty, student, and librarian perception)? If yes, how?

6. Has the library been involved in developing and providing access to cam-pus information resources on the network? (Faculty, student, and librarian perception)? If yes, how? (Page 18)

Their work is further evidence of the Internet's impact in bringing ser-vice units like the library and the computer center closer together with instructional units in an academic environment.

Reid (1996) has described a "process model" for the increasing inte-gration of the Internet into library services:

The process model is divided into five phases spanning from the acquisition of Internet experience, redesign of library processes for the networked envi-ronment to a possible revision of the organization's information management processes. (Page 25)

Instruction and Training

With respect to Internet instruction and orientation, librarians appear to be finding a unique and useful niche. While Internet access providers normally furnish instructions or training in how to connect, and what general types of information are available, librarians have quickly begun to fill the void of content-based training—e.g., how to find information on a particular topic. The traditional role of bibliographic instruction has broadened to encompass Internet use as another means for gaining access to information that is available through a librarian's assistance. The recent action by the Association of College and Research Libraries (ACRL), to change the Bibliographic Instruction Section's name to simply "Instruction Section," reflects this broadened approach to instruction and training in the library profession, regardless of whether the tools are print or electronically-based.

Since the early 1990s, several Internet self-help and instructional guides have appeared. A search in the University of Illinois online catalog, in September, 1995, revealed approximately twenty books published on Internet use since late 1992, with most appearing in 1994 or later. Authors include both computer professionals and librarians. Among the "self-help" handbooks and manuals, works by Krol (1994) and Kehoe (1993) assist all types of Internet users in better understanding how to get connected to the Net and how to locate various resources. Benson (1995) provides a handbook that is tailored to the information searching activities of librarians. Jaffe (1994) provides one of the most complete training manuals that can be used for presenting Internet workshops.

Kalin and Wright (1994) describe an Internet instruction program that exemplifies how librarians have begun to collaborate with computing professionals to offer instruction and training that helps users learn both the technical and content ends of Internet use. Other approaches, such as that of Pask and Snow (1995), advocate the integration of Internet training into overall instruction for research information retrieval, particularly in the academic setting. They point out that librarians can apply their important knowledge of subject classification to the searching of the Internet.

Learning what the Internet is, and why it ought to be used, involves the teaching of database structure, information retrieval, and critical evaluation concepts, as well as the practical aspects of getting connected. Librarians have embraced the challenging task of designing instruction that combines the teaching of skills as well as evaluative techniques. Since the early 1980s, librarians involved in instruction have found themselves training on an increasingly conceptual level about the skills needed to correctly characterize an information need and to locate relevant information, whether in print or electronic form. Perhaps one of the greatest challenges in teaching use of the Internet lies in training learners to employ "work around" techniques when they encounter common communications or other network problems.

Numerous authors have commented that the two critical components of Internet training are the use of systematic search techniques and concepts, and critical evaluative skills. These skills, many suggest, are the ones that will enable Internet users to sift efficiently through the information they retrieve from disparate sources of varying degrees of validity (Pask and Snow, 1995). Connell and Franklin (1994) point out that the Internet has had a significant impact on how work and study is accomplished in academic and commercial settings. They suggest that varied approaches to instruction and training, that incorporate critical thinking and collaboration, will enable users to best locate and exploit Internet resources.

Networking, Data Sharing, and Standards

For libraries, one of the most attractive features of the Internet is its capability to support connections among remote systems. Within recent years, the library community has become increasingly involved with computer and other information professionals to create and implement standards for networking and for data sharing. Since the early 1980s, libraries have been working to implement the basic component layers of the OSI (Open Systems Interconnection) communications protocols. OSI comprises a complex set of communication protocols designed to enable different systems to communicate across a network. More recently, the ANSI Z39.50 protocol suite was developed and implemented by groups of libraries and by vendors of commercial library systems. These protocols provide guidelines and structure so that, for example, two libraries could design software that enables a user from Library 1 to formulate a search using the familiar commands of its own online catalog, execute the search across the network on Library 2's online catalog, retrieve the result set, and display it through Library 1's online catalog. A number of libraries have implemented Z39.50 in collaboration with reciprocal partners or in consortia as a means to enable users to search across different online catalog systems without having to learn the commands for the unfamiliar system. Carson and Freivalds (1993) describe one of the first such Z39.50 implementations. Numerous vendors have incorporated Z39.50 into their current OPAC systems and Z39.50 development continues, with both national and international involvement and an organized group which meets regularly to shape the content of changes and enhancements to the suite. Michael and Hinnebusch (1995) provide an excellent analysis of the development of the Z39.50 protocol and its implementation in libraries.

Cataloging, Indexing, and Metadata

The Internet has begun to affect the ways in which libraries describe and catalog resources. In 1994 the USMARC 856 field was established to provide for the description and retrieval of electronic materials on the Internet, and there is growing recognition of the need to develop methods for describing electronic sources that are not produced in the same manner as print publications and, therefore, not appropriate to the MARC format.

A critical issue that the library community now faces is that of determining how to describe literally millions of items in their collections (photographs, pictures, manuscripts, video, and so on) for which they can never hope to provide exhaustive cataloging. While our experience with cataloging and indexing places the library community in good standing to influence the types of "metadata" standards that are employed in describing Web resources, we have difficulty incorporating new approaches to information description into the existing methods of bibliographic description and control.

Librarians and computer professionals from numerous disciplines have been working to develop sets of standards for description and access to electronic information, including full text, Web-based resources, e-journals, and other resources. Current standards used to describe both print and electronic information, besides USMARC, are the TEI (Text Encoding Initiative) Header, developed by humanities computing researchers and used to describe SGML-encoded electronic texts, and the URC (Uniform Resource Citation) standard for accessing Web materials. Gaynor (1994) describes a project at the University of Virginia Library where efforts to provide bibliographic control and access through changes to traditional cataloging practices have included the use of both MARC records and TEI headers. Access to the cataloged records for electronic texts is now provided through Virginia's OPAC. This process necessitated that catalogers become familiar with the information in TEI headers. Thus, the catalogers involved in the project learned the TEI guidelines and developed a TEI header workform as well as an OCLC MARC workform (on paper) in an effort to centralize all of the available information about the electronic text to be cataloged and described. Results of the project suggested that the creation of both MARC records and TEI headers was labor- and time-intensive, with considerable duplication of work. The study recommended the purchase of better hardware and software, and also the development of an automatic SGML-MARC conversion program to convert TEI headers into MARC-like records.

Dunsire (1995) reports on Project CATRIONA (Cataloguing and Retrieval of Information Over Networks Applications), a project to investigate the cataloging of electronic information resources and the implementation of Z39.50. The Z39.50 search and retrieve protocol is being implemented so that users of OPACs at one university can retrieve records for electronic resources from another. MARC records are used for the cataloging of e-journals, CD-ROM's, and Internet resources. In principle, a range of Z39.50-based OPACs can be searched server by server, thus making feasible the implementation of a distributed catalog of Internet resources (Nicholson et al., 1995). In 1995, OCLC, along with the National Center for Supercomputing Applications (NCSA), sponsored a metadata workshop with the objective of defining a simple and usable standard for describing networked information resources (Weibel et al., 1995). Researchers at OCLC have developed an experimental system that automatically translates between MARC, TEI, and the Web-based URC. Vizine-Goetz et al. (1995) have developed the Spectrum system, which allows users to create data records in HTML (Hypertext Markup Language) format, builds a database of user-created descriptive records, and provides search and retrieval capabilities. Spectrum was built from standard Web browser components, including the Mosaic Web browser software. An interesting feature of the Spectrum system is the record creation subsystem, which processes the descriptive information input by the user and generates from it a URC (Uniform Resource Citation), TEI, or MARC record. Vizine-Goetz et al. point out that the TEI and MARC records lack required publisher data. They note that the Spectrum system will be used to create records for inclusion in OCLC's Newton database management system, which is accessible through the Mosaic Web browser software and conforms to the Z39.50 information retrieval protocol. Future plans include integrating Spectrum's functions for creating and retrieving records directly into OCLC's WebZ Server, which is currently under development.

Numerous Internet information providers are also using information organization tools, most of which provide only simple and limited subject or name access, but nevertheless are in popular use.

World Wide Web: Simplified Access to the Internet

In addition to the convenience of the Internet's global connections, the scientific community engineered the World Wide Web (Web)—a method for using graphical user interface software (now commonly referred to as *browsers*) and a form of hypertext programming language (HTML). Users of the Web can view graphical and textual information easily and legibly on the computer screen, and can move seamlessly among disparate sources and formats of information accessible from the same electronic document by means of hypertext links to files stored in various locations across the Net. Web access has popularized the Internet to an even greater extent than before. One of the more profound developments arising from Web access is the capability for individuals to become their own Internet publishers. Any individual with an Internet connection and a computer can occupy space on the Web. The Web has thus brought about the establishment of many commercial, not-for-profit, and private communication and publishing activities on the Internet. Weibel (1995a,b) provides an excellent description of Web structure and services that can be offered through the Web, including publishing. He also reviewed the access and organization tools developed for use on the Web, but developments are occurring so rapidly that his review is already rather out of date.

Commercial bibliographic vendors, including OCLC, have begun to migrate their text-based Internet services to a Web environment. The OCLC FirstSearch system, which provides access to over 55 bibliographic databases, is available through various Web browsers. The search functionality is identical to the text-based FirstSearch database, which supports features such as wordlists, Boolean operators, and search limits.

There is a need for further development of tools that provide consistent and organized access to the disparate resource types on the Internet. An entity called the Internet Engineering Task Force (IETF) was established in the early 1990s to address the formation of conventions that enable the development of these tools. Membership on the IETF includes computer professionals, scientists, and, more recently, librarians, with OCLC maintaining an active representative role. While many Web searching engines have appeared, the depth of indexing is limited, with few powerful search filters in operation. Until recently, the Web suffered from the searching condition known as "statelessness." Once a search is executed and the information from a hyperlink is delivered, the connection to the link is broken, precluding further refinement of the user's search query. Being able to build a subsequent search on the results of a previously retrieved set, as common in many searching systems, makes the Web a model closer to that which we now find familiar with library online resources. Ongoing development work on software called Common Gateway Interface (CGI) is helping to resolve the stateless Web issue in the near term, and makes it possible for the introduction of well-defined classification and searching tools that cut across the Web. CGI programming makes it possible for users to submit powerful database queries from Web browsers. Several Web-based search engines now employ CGI programming in this manner.

Further programming developments, such as the creation of Sun Microsystems' Java language, now enable the delivery of "applets" or bits of programs across the network to provide animation, audio, video, and three-dimensional displays, all available through the Web (Gordon, 1996). The impact of these technologies on knowledge management, and on the concept of document structure and content, is considerable. For example, a Web "document" can consist of text, images, audio, and video. The various media that comprise a Web document can come from local, remote, or a combination of network locations. The shape or content of that document can be changed at any time, depending on the interests of its author, or the content of its hypermedia links.

OCLC has devoted considerable research effort to the development of retrieval services on the Internet that allow for the continual verification of electronic resources. One such service, Netfirst, identifies, catalogs, and continually verifies the existence and location of Web information resources. OCLC is also sponsoring the Intercat database, an effort to create a shared database of cataloging records for Internet-accessible e-journals and other electronic resources, and has contributed to research efforts to establish standards for encoding and accessing electronic resources.

Other commercial efforts to provide subject guides and indexes to the Web include Gale (http://www.thomson.com/cyberhound.html) and SilverPlatter (http://www.silverplatter.com/). Efforts by individuals and academic institutions are numerous. Notable among these is the University of Michigan Library School and Argus Associates Subject Guides, as well as the Virtual Public Library (http://www.clearinghouse.net). Another source, the WWW Virtual Library, categorizes sources of information by use of Library of Congress subject headings (http://www.w3.org/hypertext/DataSources/bySubject/LibraryOfCongress.html). Ensor (1995) suggests that the Web holds such strong appeal that information seekers will use it regardless of the recognized organization problems. She welcomes the efforts underway to develop effective automatic Web search and retrieval engines, and suggests that librarians can provide needed assistance in Web organization by identifying subjects that are not adequately covered and by providing coverage if this seems justified. In the context of these changes, it is reasonable to state that librarians with access to Internet resources have a professional responsibility to learn to use the Internet effectively, and to evaluate whether and how it can enhance their work and service provision. That being said, it is equally important for libraries to provide the training and administrative support that librarians and library staff need to learn and evaluate Internet access for their work-related needs. Some libraries have already begun to develop their own guides to network resources (see Blinko, 1996, for one example).

While a vast amount of literature has already appeared on the subject of libraries and the Internet, surprisingly little of this is at the broadest management level—e.g., how Internet implementation and use in libraries should be managed or, conversely, how net use affects management practices in libraries. This is in contrast with the Internet literature dealing with business, government, and academia in general where such broad issues are frequently discussed.

It is legitimate, of course, to ask if the Internet has been oversold as an information access tool, since each technological development introduced into libraries since the 1960s has come with exaggerated claims for labor-saving and work-revolutionizing impact. Many Internet problems exist. Network communication problems are often encountered by Internet users regardless of their expertise in searching. Retrieval problems are common, due to lack of standardization and poor organization, and some Internet search engines cannot provide the depth of retrieval that is currently offered by many OPACs.* Moreover, the rapidly increasing volume of use is creating significant degradation of performance and response time in some cases. All these weaknesses notwithstanding, the rapid assimilation of the Internet into all aspects of library activities suggests that it will continue to develop as an important information resource and means of communication among libraries and their users.

Nevertheless, it is important to recognize that networks will continue to grow and to become more complex by virtue of their sheer size. A report from the American Association for Artificial Intelligence (Weld et al., 1995), dealing with the National Information Infrastructure, describes the situation as follows:

> Current trends in semiconductor density, processor speed, and network bandwidth suggest that the infrastructure will be thousands of times larger than existing systems such as the Internet; the array of services supported by the NII will be unimaginably vast. (Page 45)

> The NII will be orders of magnitude more complex than current systems; it could easily become a labyrinth of databases and services that is inconvenient for experts and inaccessible to many Americans. (Page 46)

Already, many scholars are frustrated by trying to find information on the Internet. Palmer (1996) quotes one research chemist as follows:

---

*Writing from the perspective of business libraries, Kelly and Nicholas (1996) identify several major problems associated with Internet use: too much information; information of poor quality, relevance or reliability; and poor organization. Their survey of information professionals working in the banking and finance sector (in the United Kingdom) revealed that less than a third claimed to use the Internet.

> It doesn't matter how marvelous the stuff is that is out there if you can't get at it—except if somebody says, "By the way, I was talking to a guy when I was at a conference last week and he says that if you go onto this computer here you can find an address to go to that computer over there where you can get what you want." Now what kind of nonsense is that? (Page 173)

The Weld et al. report emphasizes that the field of artificial intelligence has much to contribute to improving access to information within this vast network, but it is equally obvious from the report that most intelligent systems are not sufficiently robust for real life applications on a large scale. It seems, then, that librarians and other information specialists will not be replaced by knowbots in the foreseeable future.

CHAPTER 14

Evaluation of Automated Systems

IOIOIOIOIOIOIOIOIOIOIOIOIOIOIOIOIOIOIOIOIOIOIOIOIOIOIOIOIOIOIOIOIOIOIOIOIOIOIOI

AS LIBRARIES AND THEIR SERVICES grow and change, so do their automation needs. Evaluation of the performance of an automated system, whether it be for new purchase or ongoing refinement, can provide several useful types of management information on: (1) whether new or updated systems meet contract requirements; (2) whether the system is living up to the performance and output standards of its user community; (3) the point at which a new system or system refinements are needed; (4) possible future resource consumption. This chapter explores reasons for, approaches to, and types of data that can be used in the performance evaluation of online systems.

Evaluation Criteria

It is obvious that a computer system can be evaluated according to different types of criteria—ease of use, cost, reliability, integratibility, and so on. In her survey of 54 major research libraries in North America, Johnson (1991) discovered that ease of use by patrons was a major consideration in the selection of a new system—above cost and, perhaps surprisingly, ease of use by staff. The complete ranking of criteria is shown in Figure 43. The weight given to ease of use by patrons agrees with her findings (see Chapter 1) that these same libraries considered improvement of user services as the major objective of automation and improved service to users as the major accomplishment of automation.

Purposes of Evaluation

Peters (1988) identifies three types of systems evaluation: (1) functional—to determine whether a system's features meet the library's needs; (2) economic—to determine the affordability of a system; and (3) performance—to reveal whether the system capacity can meet present or anticipated future demands. These evaluation factors interact, based on the needs, political climate, and the economics involved in a library's decision to make a new purchase or to upgrade an existing system. Peters comments that a significant amount of importance is placed on performance evaluation due to the maturity of the library automation market place, which encourages healthy vendor competition. The reasons are numerous, but they can be grouped into two general categories, the first associated with buying or designing new systems, and the second with improving existing systems, summarized by Peters as follows:

> We are interested in performance evaluation because we are concerned about the long-term price/performance profile of the systems we are buying. First, we are interested in assessing whether the systems we buy meet the performance requirements expressed in our contracts and regulated through our acceptance tests and system management instruments. But we are also interested in upgrading our systems. Let's face it, we all want to add more terminals, get gifts from heaven that allow our recon programs to exceed their most optimistic projections, and otherwise receive good news that places new demands on our library automation systems. We need to know precisely whether our existing systems can be expanded to handle the load or whether new systems will be needed. We also need to learn answers to such questions in an orderly fashion (Pages 194-195).

While the expression of needs in performance evaluation may seem straightforward, Lynch (1988) cautions that interpreting the myriad of data that systems generate in order to identify appropriate measures and criteria is neither simple nor precise, and should not be based on subjective or administratively motivated aims to justify investments or change. He points out that:

> One of the greatest difficulties challenging system managers of large, complex public access information retrieval systems, where the system services a wildly varying set of searches from one day to the next, is the identification of meaningful measures of system behavior. (Page 178)

There are obviously many possible ways in which approaches to the evaluation of automated systems can be categorized. For the purposes of this chapter, two major approaches are identified:

1. Evaluation without user involvement or with less than full user involvement.
2. Evaluation with full user involvement.

The second type assumes a fully operating system in which one can evaluate not only system characteristics per se but also how a particular community makes use of the system and with what degree of success. The other type of evaluation, while it may involve user input, is concerned with the system in a more abstract sense. Indeed, this type of evaluation may be undertaken before a system has actually been selected, before it has been accepted, or before it is fully operational. Although the terms are not completely accurate, we will refer to this class of evaluation as "user-free" and the second class as "user-involved."

Criteria	Value		
	1	2	3
Ease of use by patrons	77.8	14.8	7.4
Availability of application modules and subsystems	77.8	18.5	3.7
Completeness of modules and subsystems	68.5	22.2	9.3
Cost of system	68.5	29.6	1.9
Cost of hardware	61.1	33.3	5.6
Need for local programming staff	59.3	29.6	11.1
Service reputation of vendor	53.7	37.0	9.3
Ease of use by staff	48.1	51.9	0.0
Comparable installed site	44.5	40.7	14.8
Previous experience with vendor	25.9	29.6	44.5
Training and documentation provided	22.2	66.7	11.1
Bias against vendor	5.6	25.9	68.5

Key: 1 = Seriously considered
       2 = Considered to some extent
       3 = Not considered at all

FIGURE 43

Criteria for the evaluation of automated systems as reported by respondents from 54 major academic and research libraries in North America.
Reprinted with permission of G. K. Hall & Co., an imprint of Simon & Schuster Macmillan, from *Automation and Organizational Change in Libraries* by Peggy Johnson. Copyright © 1991 by Margaret Ann Johnson.

User-Free Evaluation

This category of evaluation focuses on system features rather than on how these are exploited by a particular group of users. It may be used in the selection of a system, the acceptance of a system, or decisions relating to system enhancement or replacement.

One useful tool that can be used in the selection of systems is a check-list to determine the features present in a particular system or, more particularly, to compare the characteristics of two or more systems. Typically, checklists of desirable system features are developed, and evaluators study the system(s) of interest, noting the presence or absence of the features under investigation, and any other pertinent information. The results are frequently entered into a grid in which marks, numeric or symbolic, indicate the presence or absence of features. See Figure 44 as one example. A point value may be assigned to each feature, and a differential weighting scheme may be established to place emphasis on features that are considered more important than others. In other cases, features are assigned an equal rating of 1 or 0. System scores can be derived from the grids, with subtotals to indicate system strengths in particular areas, and total scores to indicate overall performance.

Questions	A	B	C	D	E	F	G	H	I	J	K	L
	DOBIS	Geac				NOTIS			PALS	DRA	Hom.	Hom.
1. Is there adequate logon instruction (i.e., explain which terminal types are supported	x						x		x		x	
2. Are the contents and coverage of the OPAC clearly explained?	x	x	x	x		x	x	x	x	x		x
3. Are the key equivalencies explained for remote user's keyboard?	x	NA	NA	NA	NA		NA	x	NA	x	NA	x
4. Is there adequate logoff instruction?		x	x	x	x	x	x	x	x	x	x	x
5. Is the screen display always clean? (i.e., no garbage characters)	x	x	x	x	x	x	x	x	x	x	x	x
6. (a) Is remote access unrestricted in terms of time of day?		x	x	x	x	x	x	x	x	x	x	x
(b) Does the system tell the user if there is a time limit to remote sessions?												x
(c) Does the system give a warning message of automatic logoff if there is no user input?				x	x					x	x	
7. Does the remote user have access to the same OPAC as those who use dedicated terminals in the library?	x	x		x	x	x	x	x	x	x		
8. Does the system indicate where the remote user can get additional help?	x			x						x		x
Score: (maximum 10)	6	5	4	7	5	5	6	6	6	8	6	7

Note: "NA" means "not applicable."

FIGURE 44

Example of a data summary from a checklist approach
to evaluating OPAC usability via remote access.

Reprinted from Cherry et al. (1994) by permission of the American Library Association

The checklist method of evaluation is useful for several reasons. In the case of a single system review, it helps one to arrive at a list of desirable features, and to identify the strengths and weaknesses of a particular system. In the case of a multiple system review, a comparative checklist can help to verify the existence of features across systems and thus to identify comparative strengths and weaknesses. Where a weighted scoring scheme is used, one can compare several systems on the basis of strengths and weaknesses in areas determined to be most important in meeting the needs of a particular library. The use of a checklist ensures that the same questions about system features are posed consistently across systems.

Weighting of system features is always desirable. Otherwise, the checklist scores can be deceptive. Without weighting, a system with many "superfluous" features may obtain a high overall score, but may actually be weak in features that librarians and users rate as most important. Similarly, a flat rating scheme may obscure the fact that a particular system is strong in features that users prefer, even though it may be lacking elsewhere. The challenge, then, lies in obtaining consensus on what weighting scheme equitably represents a library's preferences for system features, and in implementing the weighting scheme consistently.

Cherry et al. (1994) employed a checklist to survey features in the OPACs of twelve Canadian academic libraries. Data on each system were collected twice, by two different researchers, and the two datasets were checked a third time against the systems to resolve any disagreements. One hundred seventy features were included in the checklist, grouped into ten functional categories:

1. Database characteristics
2. Operational control
3. Searching
4. Subject search aids
5. Access points
6. Screen display
7. Output control
8. Commands
9. User assistance
10. OPAC usability via remote access

This checklist is unique among library-oriented checklists because it is based both on similar checklists for the study of OPAC features and a checklist designed for evaluating the usability of human-computer interfaces. It was found that most of the OPACs, as implemented in the libraries, possessed more than half the features that were listed as desirable on the checklist (Figure 45). All systems scored well on "screen display," and were weakest in "subject search aids," "output control," and "operational control" (Figure 46). Overall, Cherry et al. observe that, in spite of the many improvements in OPAC design, ". . . there is still a wide gap between the systems evaluated in this study and the ideal OPAC system suggested by researchers." They also recommend that the study be replicated every two to three years, and that the results in each category be compared to measure improvement in system design over time. They admit that the study would have been improved by the use of weights to reflect the relative importance of each feature, and recommend that further studies should survey online system users to determine the relative importance that they assign to specific system features.

Rank	Institution	OPAC	Percentage of Features Desirable
1	J	DRA	67.1
2	I	PALS	59.4
3	H	NOTIS	58.2
4	F	NOTIS	57.1
5	E	Geac	56.5
6	G	NOTIS	55.3
7	D	Geac	54.7
8	L	Home-grown	54.1
9	B	Geac	53.5
10	C	Geac	44.1
11	A	DOBIS	41.2
12	K	Home-grown	38.8

FIGURE 45

Ranking of OPACs as implemented in twelve Canadian academic libraries.

Reprinted from Cherry et al. (1994) by permission of the American Library Association

Rank	Characteristics	Mean Percentage of Desirable Features	Minimum Percentage of Desirable Features	Maximum Percentage of Desirable Features*
1	Screen Display	79.2	50.0	90.0
2	Database characteristics	65.6	56.3	68.8
3	Commands	64.7	38.5	76.9
4	Remote access	59.2	40.0	80.0
5	Access points	56.4	38.1	71.4
6	Searching	53.1	21.7	71.7
7	User assistance	52.9	23.5	82.4
8	Operational control	41.2	29.4	64.7
9	Output control	30.6	16.7	50.0
10	Subject search aids	26.0	12.5	37.5

* The OPAC with the highest score for screen display exhibited 90% of the features pre-identified as desirable. The OPAC with the lowest score exhibited only 50% of the features. On the average, 79.2% of the features were exhibited by the twelve systems. And similarly for the other characteristics.

FIGURE 46

**Ranking of features of twelve OPACs as implemented
in Canadian academic libraries.**

Slightly modified from Cherry et al. (1994)
by permission of the American Library Association

Because their checklist is so comprehensive, and thus of potential value to other librarians in conducting this type of comparison, it is reproduced in Appendix 1.

Acceptance testing or *benchmarking* is a process often used by libraries to verify that the new or upgraded system meets the contract requirements. Often the conditions of acceptance in a contract indicate clearly what type of performance is expected, and the acceptable level of performance, to determine whether a system works in the manner agreed upon in the contract. Although acceptance testing usually has legal implications, Lynch (1988) notes that it is difficult to bridge the gap between the contract language and the types of tests that both parties (vendor and library) agree will demonstrate whether or not the system is acceptable in all aspects. An interesting series of three articles tracks the experience of Boston University's stress test with a particular system, providing perspectives from a librarian, the system designer, and a consultant. Brown (1988) presents the library's perspective on stress tests designed to determine system performance at a 100-terminal capacity. The results indicated that immediate improvements needed to be made by the vendor; they also suggested more realistic testing parameters acceptable to both parties. Brown believes that acceptance testing may need to be made an actual part of a contract. Salmon (1988), representing the perspective of the systems designer, points out some of the unrealistic conditions that drove the stress test, although those conditions did not appear overly demanding in the contract language. Epstein (1988), the consultant for the project, focused on response time concerns, emphasizing the importance of distinguishing between response time and throughput of actual transactions to achieve the most direct searching and retrieval results for users. He also pointed out that the significant cost of acceptance testing causes vendors to enter into it only when they are interested in upscaling their operations to larger or more complex systems.

In recent years, acceptance testing has evolved into a more feasible part of systems implementation. More emphasis on trials of system performance with realistic usage loads and operating environments has succeeded in making acceptance testing less a politically and emotionally charged conflict between library and vendor and more a productive collaboration for their mutual benefit.

Once installed, monitoring of the ongoing performance of a system is crucial to the detection of subtle problems or system degradation. The installation of changes, including addition of new components, necessitates checking not only the new portion of the system, but the interaction between that and existing modules and programs. Ongoing monitoring of system performance usually takes place in the form of regularly generated system reports. Libraries typically review response time, input/output information, and network throughput on a regular basis for signals of system degradation in any one or a combination of these areas. In the case of response time, several authors have emphasized the need to perform careful ongoing system analysis before concluding that poor or decreased response time is attributable to any one factor. It is usually the case that several factors contribute to system performance degradation. When system changes or new features are added, the acceptance or stress test is normally used to evaluate the system under various conditions. Libraries, usually in consultation with vendors, develop scripts of search commands and strategies that are executed during a set period of time by an agreed upon number of participants stationed at terminals in pre-determined locations.

At times, public or staff users identify problems or make suggestions for system changes designed to refine its operation or its interaction with users. The feedback for making these changes can come from word of mouth or from the periodic review of performance logs generated by the system. For instance, librarians may observe searches failing at a critical point where the insertion of an automatically invoked help screen could render assistance. Similarly, a new version of the system software may be installed periodically, usually containing code that tunes or refines existing features. When changes are made to features or functions within an existing system, some means are needed to test how well these changes work. Stress tests are commonly used to test implementations of new features.

Capacity planning is another important element in overall evaluation. The timely allocation of resources to support the growth of a system is critical to its continued optimum performance. By tracking the size of the database, and estimating its growth rate, projections can be made about when to increase capacity, and whether this increase in size will degrade or otherwise affect response time and other performance factors. Precise capacity planning is difficult because it involves projection and prediction based on numerous complex performance factors. Lynch (1988) claims that capacity planning "usually involves a good deal of inspired guesswork." Unless there is a clear understanding of how all performance factors interact on a day-to-day basis, it is difficult to predict how they will interact in the future, given the introduction of increased, new, or different uses of the system.

Schmidt and Pobuda (1988) developed a capacity planning model for the RLIN system that they used to support hardware upgrades to the CPU. The information used in the model was based primarily on the number and types of transactions made, the resources required to process these transactions, and the "varieties in the mix of transactions over time." They obtained projections from RLIN users of the amount of cataloging, inter-library loan, acquisitions, and reference use they would make during the time period in question. These projections, as well as actual usage statistics for the three previous years, were analyzed using a PC spreadsheet program that was capable of time-series analysis. From these figures, capacity needs for the RLIN computer CPU were projected for FY 1987 (Figure 47).

13 Aug 1986 FY87 CPU Model - Constants

	Cat	CatMai	Recon	Acq	AcqMai	ILL	Print
CPU per BU	0.583	0.298	0.492	0.592	0.373	1.643	0.074

	Wylbur	Milten	Jes2
Day Utilization	4.1%	2.4%	0.6%
Peak Utilizatio	4.7%	2.9%	0.5%

	Orvyl	MVS
Day Overhead	76.9%	21.1%
Peak Overhead		19.6%

Peak to Average Ratio
127%

13 Aug 1986 FY87 CPU Model - Activity

	Sep 1986	Oct 1986	Nov 1986	Dec 1986	Jan 1987	Feb 1987	Mar 1987	Apr 1987	May 1987	Jun 1987	Jul 1987	Aug 1987	1987
fy87 budget activity													
catalog	124,929	146,056	125,985	112,511	140,825	143,306	148,039	161,614	156,849	154,848	158,273	149,707	1,722,942
catmai	124,901	144,269	124,414	106,835	134,018	138,305	145,046	158,725	149,395	148,608	161,908	164,459	1,700,883
recon	49,654	64,610	59,673	47,087	59,344	68,675	69,437	85,933	82,538	78,848	84,496	78,939	829,235
acquisitions	46,909	57,284	48,512	40,316	49,485	54,353	49,148	54,027	55,972	52,084	54,230	46,838	609,159
acqmai	55,770	64,684	55,665	47,077	61,542	64,467	64,254	71,125	69,180	67,100	67,634	57,329	745,829
tp	402,163	476,904	414,250	353,827	445,214	469,106	475,925	531,425	513,935	501,488	526,541	497,272	5,608,048
avg defq	19,151	20,735	23,014	16,849	21,201	24,690	21,633	24,156	25,697	22,795	23,934	23,680	22,294
ill	14,337	19,828	18,201	11,545	14,191	20,442	19,502	19,856	16,030	16,773	19,253	16,825	206,783
fy87 max activity													
catalog	132,815	155,276	133,938	119,614	149,715	152,352	157,384	171,816	166,750	164,623	168,264	159,158	1,831,705
catmai	134,936	156,055	134,689	115,488	144,883	149,748	157,005	172,080	161,944	161,024	175,540	178,278	1,841,670
recon	55,794	72,600	67,052	52,910	66,683	77,167	78,024	96,560	92,745	88,598	94,945	88,701	931,780
acq	51,319	62,670	53,073	44,106	54,137	59,463	53,769	59,107	61,234	56,901	59,328	51,241	666,428
acqmai	61,014	70,765	60,899	51,503	67,328	70,527	70,295	77,812	75,684	73,409	73,992	62,718	815,946
tp	435,877	517,366	449,650	383,621	482,746	509,258	516,478	577,374	558,358	544,635	572,070	540,096	6,087,529
avg defq	20,756	22,494	24,981	18,268	22,988	26,803	23,476	26,244	27,918	24,756	26,003	25,719	24,201
ill	15,464	21,386	19,631	12,452	15,306	22,049	21,035	21,416	17,290	18,091	20,766	18,148	223,034

1

13 Aug 1986 FY87 CPU Model - Utilization

	Sep 1986	Oct 1986	Nov 1986	Dec 1986	Jan 1987	Feb 1987	Mar 1987	Apr 1987	May 1987	Jun 1987	Jul 1987	Aug 1987	1987
budget utilization													
Orvyl	42.2%	45.4%	49.3%	38.5%	45.3%	51.7%	46.4%	50.1%	52.0%	47.5%	49.8%	49.0%	47.3%
HiPriority	7.0%	7.0%	7.0%	7.0%	7.0%	7.0%	7.0%	7.0%	7.0%	7.0%	7.0%	7.0%	7.0%
Batch	7.5%	7.5%	7.5%	5.0%	5.0%	5.0%	5.0%	5.0%	5.0%	5.0%	5.0%	5.0%	5.6%
MVS	12.0%	12.6%	13.4%	10.7%	12.1%	13.4%	12.3%	13.1%	13.5%	12.6%	13.0%	12.9%	12.6%
Aspen & MDF	5.0%	5.0%	5.0%	5.0%	10.0%	10.0%	12.5%	12.5%	12.5%	12.5%	12.5%	12.5%	9.6%
Total	73.7%	77.6%	82.2%	66.2%	79.4%	87.2%	83.2%	87.7%	90.0%	84.6%	87.4%	86.4%	82.1%
budget peak utilization													
Orvyl	53.6%	57.7%	62.6%	48.9%	57.6%	65.7%	58.9%	63.6%	66.1%	60.4%	63.3%	62.2%	60.1%
HiPriority	8.2%	8.2%	8.2%	8.2%	8.2%	8.2%	8.2%	8.2%	8.2%	8.2%	8.2%	8.2%	8.2%
Batch	7.5%	7.5%	7.5%	5.0%	5.0%	5.0%	5.0%	5.0%	5.0%	5.0%	5.0%	5.0%	5.6%
MVS	13.6%	14.4%	15.4%	12.2%	13.9%	15.5%	14.1%	15.1%	15.5%	14.4%	15.0%	14.8%	14.5%
Aspen & MDF	5.0%	5.0%	5.0%	5.0%	10.0%	10.0%	12.5%	12.5%	12.5%	12.5%	12.5%	12.5%	9.6%
Total	87.9%	92.8%	98.6%	79.2%	94.4%	104.3%	98.7%	104.3%	107.3%	100.4%	104.0%	102.7%	97.9%
max utilization													
Orvyl	49.1%	52.6%	56.8%	45.1%	52.4%	59.4%	53.6%	57.7%	59.8%	54.9%	57.4%	56.5%	54.6%
HiPriority	7.0%	7.0%	7.0%	7.0%	7.0%	7.0%	7.0%	7.0%	7.0%	7.0%	7.0%	7.0%	7.0%
Batch	10.0%	10.0%	10.0%	5.0%	7.5%	7.5%	7.5%	7.5%	7.5%	7.5%	7.5%	7.5%	7.9%
MVS	13.9%	14.7%	15.6%	12.0%	14.1%	15.6%	14.4%	15.2%	15.7%	14.6%	15.2%	15.0%	14.7%
Aspen & MDF	5.0%	7.5%	10.0%	10.0%	12.5%	12.5%	15.0%	15.0%	20.0%	20.0%	20.0%	20.0%	14.0%
Total	85.0%	91.8%	99.4%	79.1%	93.6%	102.0%	97.5%	102.4%	110.0%	104.0%	107.1%	106.0%	98.2%
max peak utilization													
Orvyl	62.4%	66.8%	72.1%	57.3%	66.6%	75.5%	68.2%	73.3%	76.0%	69.7%	73.0%	71.8%	69.4%
HiPriority	8.2%	8.2%	8.2%	8.2%	8.2%	8.2%	8.2%	8.2%	8.2%	8.2%	8.2%	8.2%	8.2%
Batch	10.0%	10.0%	10.0%	5.0%	7.5%	7.5%	7.5%	7.5%	7.5%	7.5%	7.5%	7.5%	7.9%
MVS	15.3%	16.2%	17.2%	13.8%	15.7%	17.4%	16.0%	17.0%	17.5%	16.3%	16.9%	16.7%	16.3%
Aspen & MDF	5.0%	7.5%	10.0%	10.0%	12.5%	12.5%	15.0%	15.0%	20.0%	20.0%	20.0%	20.0%	14.0%
Total	100.8%	108.6%	117.5%	94.2%	110.4%	121.1%	114.8%	120.9%	129.1%	121.7%	125.5%	124.1%	115.7%

FIGURE 47

FY 1987 CPU Usage Model.

From Schmidt and Pobuda (1988) by permission of the American Library Association

Schmidt and Pobuda's model makes projections for "budgeted activity" (expected level of use based on data from three previous years) and "maximum activity" (worst case highest projected usage). These figures on projected activity are then translated into projected system resource utilization. Projected resource utilization is further divided into several categories to take into consideration not only maximum projected usage, but also the projected usage during peak system load periods, which are defined as the busiest times of the day when libraries in all time zones were using RLIN. In order to validate their model, they compared their projections with an actual response time graph of the RLIN CPU that occurred during FY 1987, and obtained a fairly close matchup.

Capacity planning models can be implemented within a library environment through a combination of the information generated regularly by most online systems and the statistics normally collected within the library. Changes in transaction volume during peak and other usage times can signal the need for system expansion, involving the addition of various hardware and software resources. First, steady increases over time in the overall system usage, especially the number of simultaneous system transactions, can signal the need to increase system capacity. Secondly, increases in the aggregate numbers of transactions at specific locations can serve as indicators for a need to add more terminals.

Capacity planning has yet another facet—planning for the provision of adequate access to the online system whether through onsite terminals or remotely. Determining whether the number of physical connections to the system adequately supports the library's user base is an important component of planning. A review of system resources exploited by various user groups, and in specific locations, can assist in providing this information. Several studies have employed queuing theory in analyzing the frequency of terminal usage, and determining how many and where to place terminals. It is important to examine where increases in usage are occurring by user type, with public, staff, dial, or network access. Kaske's (1988) research demonstrates how usage patterns and levels can vary significantly within a large, decentralized academic library system.

User-Involved Evaluation

For over twenty years, a growing body of research based on information science and cognitive psychology has been performed to gain a better understanding of how users interact with systems, and how the results of that interaction can be evaluated. One practical goal of this type of research is to collect and analyze information that can be fed back into better system design. A growing body of literature in this area places heavy emphasis on the central role of the end user in the evaluation process. Benefits include the ability of librarians and systems designers to view the use of a system from a perspective that they, for all their technical or content knowledge, could not anticipate. Obvious drawbacks arise with data collection and analysis that does not include a group or groups that are representative of a system's actual user population.

The interaction between the user and the system can be the subject of study for a number of purposes. The studies discussed in this chapter are carried out to learn more about how a system is used and to improve its performance. Many possible methods are applicable. Unobtrusive measures gather data while library patrons are actually using the system. Users may or may not be aware that their keystrokes, or other actions, are being recorded or observed. The methods are unobtrusive in the sense that users are not being asked any questions and are not required to do anything they would not otherwise be doing. Obtrusive measures are used primarily to obtain feedback on user preferences for various system features and their opinions on system performance.

A primary goal of unobtrusive measurement is to be able to record and evaluate user activity in a natural environment without intervention from the researcher. Data thus collected can be useful in revealing how specific system features are exploited and in identifying features that appear to be giving users significant problems. At least three types of approach are applicable: review of transaction logs, direct observation of users operating at terminals, and video and/or audio taping of user performance. Unobtrusive data can be used to re-create exactly what occurred in a patron's encounter with the system and can complement more subjective data gathered from library users. Nielsen (1986) points out that differences may exist between what users say has happened and what actually occurred as determined by a more objective observation of their behavior.

Transaction log analysis (TLA) has been defined as the ". . . study of electronically recorded interactions between online information retrieval systems and the persons who search for the information found in those systems" (Peters et al., 1993a). After its initial application in the 1960s as a tool for evaluating system performance, transaction log analysis gathered momentum in the 1970s and 1980s as a means of analyzing the interaction between users and online catalogs. Peters (1993) lists approximately ninety studies of online systems that, since 1980, have employed TLA although he points out that relatively few researchers have performed more than one study (see also the bibliography by Peters et al., 1993b). Many TLA studies gather information on how frequently system features are used: choice of search type, use of help screens, how many hits users are willing to review, how often a search results in zero hits, the number and type of error messages that users receive, and so on. A few studies have employed TLA in conjunction with other methods to examine the affective and cognitive searching behavior of user interaction with online systems (Tenopir et al., 1989). Figures 48 and 49 present examples taken from OPAC transaction logs to show the types of data that can be collected (Flaherty, 1993).

Several studies have analyzed user errors in searching online systems and have suggested system changes or enhancements that would assist in avoiding the occurrence of these errors. Dickson (1984), in an early analysis of user errors in searching an OPAC, found that a significant number of searches failed through a combination of spelling errors, the omission of initial articles from title searches and failure to invert surnames. Jones (1986) used TLA to identify such problems as keying errors (typographical errors, or putting information in the wrong place), slow response time for known item searches, and problems following the general search path structure. Walker and Jones (1987) tested two versions of an OPAC at two different locations. One version contained additional features that provided for automatic stemming, spelling correction, and cross-reference tables to enhance subject retrieval. They found that neither group of users was aware of the corrective features that had been installed in one of the test systems, even though searching failures had decreased there. Peters (1989) used transaction logs to examine "no-hit" search results, finding that 39 percent of the items sought were not owned by the library and 21 percent of the failures occurring were the result of typographical errors. Flaherty (1990), in an examination of the reasons for search failures, tested the value of automatic space adjustment, automatic term flip (word order correction), soundex, and a spell checker, and found that the introduction of these features could correct 63 percent of the "no-hit" search failures that occurred in the OPAC. The results of these studies have yielded a set of commonly recognized system problems, many of which have been remedied by most vendors and system designers.

```
T  921012140805
U  $
C  ** start
T  921012140812
S  SCR7.1
U  THERMSA<LEFT><LEFT>AL SCIENCES<RET>
E  *14
L  thermal (209), scienc (8399),
C  Merge using 2 term(s), R = 0
C                              Merge term    np      r     wt     sv
C                               thermal     209      0     95     95
C                               scienc     8399      0     41     41
C
E  *0
O  NMPU = 25 NGW = 25 NAW = 25
U  <RET><RET>D
S  BRIEFS orig level 0 1 to 9 of 25
C  rec has AU TI PU SE CL CN SU
C  term thermal fd(s) SU
C  term scienc fd(s) TI SE
C  weight 159
R      Energy and housing : a symposium held at the Ope..  (JONES B W)        1975
C  rec has AU TI PU SE CL CN SU
C  term thermal fd(s) SU
C  term scienc fd(s) SE
C  weight 155
R      Radiant properties of materials : tables of radi.. SALA A             1986
C  rec has AU TI PU SE CL CN SU
C  term thermal fd(s) SU
C  term scienc fd(s) SE
R      Analysis of thermally stimulated processes.       CHEN R             1981
C  rec has AU TI PU SE CL CN SU
C  term thermal fd(s) SU
C  term scienc fd(s) SE
R      Retrofitting an existing wood-frame residence fo.. BURCH D M          1978
C  rec has AU TI PU SE CL CN SU
C  term thermal fd(s) TI SU
C  term scienc fd(s) SE
R      Thermal expansion of crystals.                    KRISHNAN R S        1978
C  rec has AU TI PU SE CL CN SU
C  term thermal fd(s) TI SU
C  term scienc fd(s) SE
R      The thermal performance of a two-bedroom mobile .. TIETSMA G J        1977
C  rec has AU TI PU SE CL CN SU
C  term thermal fd(s) SU
C  term scienc fd(s) SE
R      Analysis of reinforced concrete beams subjected .. ELLINGWOOD B       1976
C  rec has AU TI PU SE CL CN SU
C  term thermal fd(s) TI SU
C  term scienc fd(s) SE
R      Acoustical and thermal performance of exterior .. (SABINE H J)        1975
C  rec has AU TI PU SE CL CN SU
C  term thermal fd(s) TI SU
C  term scienc fd(s) SE
R      A proposed concept for determining the need for .. United States. ..  1975
```

Key to the Okapi log:

T = Timestamp

E = Elapsed time since last T (timestamp) or E (elapsed time)

U = Commands entered by the patron (highlighted to help you locate them). In this sample, there are three patron entries: one to start the session, another to search on "thermal sciences," and another to display the records.

O = Outcome of the search. There were 25 retrievals in this sample. (The formula shown reflects internal processing done by the system while performing the search.)

S = State of the system. The first state in this sample (SCR7.1) means that a subject search input screen was displayed. The second state (BRIEFS orig level 0 1 to 9 of 25) means that the user wishes to display the first nine of the 25 records retrieved.

R = Text of the displayed record. There are nine records displayed in this sample. Since these are brief displays, each takes just one line.

C = Comments. These were entered by the system to provide information to the Okapi system staff. The kind of information can vary from project to project; in this case, most of the comments report on which data elements were responsible for retrieving each displayed record.

FIGURE 48

Example of transaction log data from an OPAC.

Reprinted from Flaherty (1993) by permission of Pierian Press

TLA has also been employed to determine implications for bibliographic instruction programs and further system enhancement and design. Wallace (1993) studied transaction logs of eleven public access terminals in an academic library and found that the use of system-supplied help varied, that a high percentage of subject keyword searches produced ten or fewer hits, that users persist in scanning lists of titles, even in searches with large retrievals, and that system design improvements need to be complemented by increased emphasis on searching skills in bibliographic instruction programs. An annotated bibliography by Peters et al. (1993b) and a review article by Simpson (1989) serve as two excellent sources of further information about TLA. Borgman et al. (1996) provide a valuable and thorough discussion of online monitoring as a research method based on extensive experience with an online catalog for children.

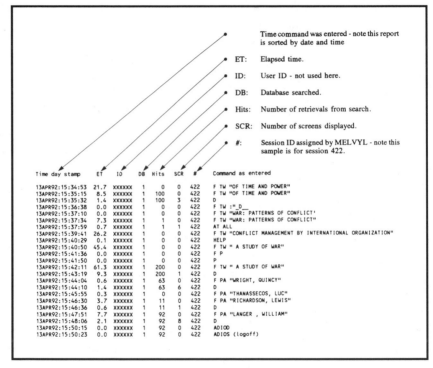

FIGURE 49

Example of data from an OPAC transaction log.

Reprinted from Flaherty (1993) by permission of Pierian Press

Commercially available systems offer various logging features. Figures 50 and 51 give examples of a "no hits" report and of use of author names in an OPAC.

Despite all of its potential benefits, transaction log analysis does have limitations. In many systems with transaction log monitoring facilities, it is either difficult or impossible to delineate individual user searching sessions. Further, the transaction log is only able to show the "footprints" of the user on the system—it cannot provide an explanation for why a searcher made the search choices that are reflected in the transaction log. It has also been shown that it is difficult to perform transaction log analysis across systems. For example, Larson (1983) attempted to compare transaction log data from four online catalogs and showed that differences in command and system structures make cross-system TLA of doubtful value.

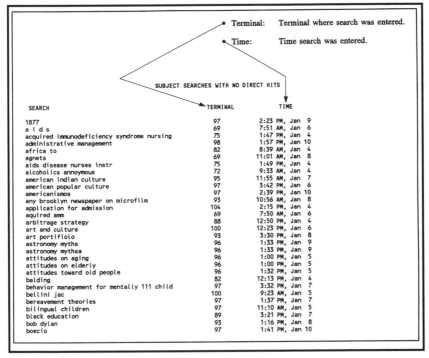

FIGURE 50
Sample "no hit" report from Innopac system.
Reproduced by permission of Innovative Interfaces Inc.

Another problem is that of cost. A comprehensive monitoring module can add a significant overhead to the cost of operating the system. Some institutions, including libraries, have discontinued use of such modules because of the additional cost of applying them and because of the fact that library managers lacked time to analyze the data on a regular basis.

Transaction log analysis collects data about system use in the aggregate and deals only with the quantitative—which commands are used how often, which headings are consulted, how much time is spent per session, and so on. But more individualized and qualitative data can also be obtained unobtrusively online. The most obvious example is the monitoring and analysis of use of a *help* command. Knowing what types of help are requested by users, especially in the case of a new system or one that has recently added new features, can be of great value in identifying problem areas that may not have been anticipated in the system design but may. in fact, be rather easy to correct.

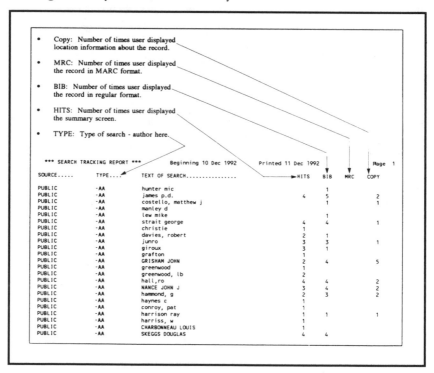

FIGURE 51
Sample author name use report from Dynix (Ameritech Library Services).
Reproduced by permission of Pierian Press

Although it is rarely acknowledged, *direct observation* is perhaps one of the most commonly employed techniques for collecting information about online system users. Critics often suggest that observation is an unscientific way of gathering only the information needed to support one's own views. The technique need not be flawed; it is the degree of consistency in what is observed, and at what intervals it is observed, that determines the reliability of the data collected. Observation of user behavior at online terminals is perhaps the easiest technique to employ because it is often a mere extension of a librarian's responsibilities in a reference or other public service setting. Observation is often the technique employed in queuing studies to determine the number of terminals that are needed in certain areas to support an optimal level of access at peak usage times. It is important to employ valid sampling techniques in conjunction with observation in order to obtain reliable data on which management decisions can be based. For example, if one wants to know how many times users have to wait in line to use terminals in the reference room, one obviously cannot rely solely on the observations of a single librarian who only staffs the reference desk fifteen hours per week, between 8 a.m. and 5 p.m., Monday through Friday. Direct observation can be useful, on its own or to supplement other methods, when appropriate sampling methods are employed and input is received from more than one observer.

A number of studies have analyzed the results of *video and/or audio taping* of the speech and actions of users during search sessions. The technique has been used to examine whether the cognitive, affective, or attitudinal behavior of users affects their performance and the outcomes of searching. Methods like protocol analysis, which employ a pre-determined framework for analyzing user comments (asking a user to "think aloud" while searching, then recording the resulting behavior and comments), can be used to classify and evaluate the relative effect of user decision-making and behavior on the success or failure of searching. Janosky et al. (1986) performed one of the first studies of this kind applied to an OPAC. Their subjects, university students, were given several searching tasks to perform. Their "thinking aloud" was recorded on tape and their interactions with the system were captured and analyzed in order to identify types of errors made. Tenopir et al. (1991) employed audio taping, in addition to transaction log analysis, in their study of users who were searching a full-text database of magazine articles. They found that users pursued mainly "single-minded" search strategies. Sandore and

Ryan (1994) employed audio taping, a survey questionnaire, TLA, and the method of protocol analysis to analyze the activity of searchers of a journal citation database. They found that users who encountered zero or one-hit retrievals often commented that they felt their searching skills and/or subject knowledge to be inadequate to undertake the searching task.

Survey questionnaires enable the collection of data about user satisfaction with a system or specific aspects of it, searching preferences and attitudes, demographic data about users, and the level of skills or knowledge that users possess. Questionnaire surveys involve contact with users; therefore, the evaluator must share with the user some information, however brief, regarding the intent of the survey, how the data will be analyzed and used, and what steps the library has taken to insure that no data will be used in such a way that it reveals the identity of individual users.

The published literature includes several studies in which online questionnaires were applied to record user attitudes and preferences for system features, or to make possible a "critical incident" approach to studying searches recently completed by users. Two such studies were completed using the University of California MELVYL system. The first, by Larson and Graham (1983), linked transaction log data to online questionnaires to determine what proportion of the searches performed were subject searches. Horres et al. (1991) used a combination of two online questionnaires, transaction logs, and a printed questionnaire to analyze user satisfaction with the MELVYL implementation of MEDLINE at several campuses. System designers wanted feedback from users on general satisfaction with the system and on the use of specific system features. Both online questionnaires used only multiple choice questions. The first received a 45% response rate, and the second, applied one year later, a 33% response rate. The printed questionnaire, used to supplement the online questionnaires by collecting open-ended comments, had a response rate of 73%. The evaluation results reported high satisfaction with and high overall use of the system. The questionnaires and the review of the transaction logs also revealed that many of the advanced searching features were rarely used. Effects on library services were also measured, and these included significant increases in reference transactions and interlibrary loan requests, with a significant decline in mediated search services (Horres et al., 1991).

Hancock-Beaulieu et al. (1990) describe online system evaluation using OLIVE, an interactive front-end system, which enables the collection of transaction log data, full-screen logging of search sessions, administering of online and offline questionnaires, and interactive questionnaires during search sessions, at specified points. Belkin et al. (1990) employ a combination of transaction log analysis, online questionnaires, observation, and interviews in their study to assess goals, tasks, and behavior of users of libraries and online catalogs. A modified version of the OLIVE front-end software is employed in their study. Sandore and Ryan (1994) administered an online questionnaire for a critical incident study of searching and to measure the working knowledge of library users on the logical elements of online bibliographic searching.

The advantage of online questionnaires over printed questionnaires is the ability to collect critical incident data about a search session immediately following the session. Response rates in the range of 30-45%, reported in some studies, are comparable to response rates for many surveys using printed questionnaires. Online questionnaires remove the problems associated with distribution and return of the instruments by mail or by other means.

In comparison with questionnaires and transaction log analysis, *interviews* can provide a more intimate view of the user's perspective on the system under examination. Interviews may be conducted on a one-to-one basis, either over the telephone or face to face. They can be structured, with specific questions and pre-specified categories in which to slot answers, or unstructured, with open-ended questions that provide the subjects with more opportunity to provide unsolicited information about the system. A study by Nitecki (1993) to identify a taxonomy of user criteria for evaluating the effectiveness of an online catalog employed unstructured interviews and used a qualitative approach in analyzing the resulting information. Another type of interview—the focus group interview—may be conducted with a small group and one or more interviewers, with video and/or audio taping, and/or assistants transcribing notes and statements during the group discussion. Focus group interviews are regularly used in marketing research to gather information from a particular, pre-selected group of users about products or potential products. The emphasis in the focus group interview rests with identifying the range of attitudes or opinions from a group of users who have certain demographic or otherwise significant points in common (gender, socio-economic status, race, age) about a series of questions related to system use. This technique helps to identify characteristics of identifiable user groups, along with attitudes. Researchers working on the NSF/ARPA/NASA-funded Digital Library Initiative at the University of Illinois have carried out focus group interviews with engineering faculty and students to determine what features they felt were important to include in a digital library for an engineering community. Further, they observed the online searching behavior of patrons working in the University of Illinois Grainger Engineering Library, noting that users experienced difficulty searching existing systems (Sandusky, 1995). The Illinois research team used this information to design a transaction log that will track the searches performed on the testbed for the project— the full text of over twenty engineering journals (Sandusky, 1996). This work is significant from the standpoint that it will enable the unobtrusive study of specific uses of networked information.

Some online systems offer the option for users to send *unsolicited comments* to librarians or system designers. In some cases, system administrators post an e-mail address to encourage users to report bugs or anomalies they encounter while searching the system. Some of these anomalies may be bibliographic in nature—typographical errors in the bibliographic record—or related to cataloging policy. Other anomalies, such as screens that are missing placeholders or are incorrectly formatted, may not be discovered in the regular system beta testing or debugging process. Therefore, the comment option is a valuable tool in problem identification. Pennsylvania State University's LIAS online catalog was one of the first systems to offer the "oops" command, which users could invoke in order to send a brief message reporting either system or bibliographic anomalies to the systems and library staff. Current systems commonly offer an option that enables users to send mail messages from within the system to system administrators or other staff who work closely with various aspects of the catalog.

For over a decade the library of the University of Illinois at Urbana-Champaign has maintained a user comment box in the public catalog area of the main library. Users regularly deposit recommended corrections for typographical errors to bibliographic records, suggestions for adding subject or name headings to particular records in order to enhance access, or general recommendations about other system needs. Once a month a librarian reviews the comments and forwards them to staff in appropriate units or to an online system advisory committee for appropriate action. Various system enhancements have been made as a result of comments received in this way.

In any study that elicits specific information about use of an online system, it is important at the outset to provide the user with a written statement on the institution's policy regarding human subjects research. Those conducting the study must do everything possible to ensure that the publicly-available results of the analysis will not disclose the identity of an individual user, or link that user with information specific to his or her information-seeking behavior.

Analysis of the use of online *help* features was mentioned earlier as an unobtrusive source of information on problems encountered by users. But users can also go to members of the library staff when they need help, and their interactions with staff members is a further source of information on system problems and weaknesses.

Many public service departments maintain statistics on the types of reference and other assistance they provide to users, including online system assistance. A recent study of the impact of locally mounted periodical citation databases on library staff, users, and collections at the University of Illinois revealed a decrease in patron assistance in locating journals, since the new system supplied call numbers and library locations with the journal citations. At the same time, however, it showed that new categories of user questions arose—related to assistance in using the citation databases and interpreting the results of searches in these (Sandore et al., 1993).

The Role of Advisory and Working Groups

Online system advisory groups or committees are often appointed to advise library administrators and system designers on what the groups feel should be the development priorities. Frequently they are organized with the intention that the appointees represent, in the organization's policy and operational matters, the perceived needs of both the librarian and user populations. The groups can also provide a forum for staff input on design and problem issues. If a computer center supports the library's online system, the inclusion of one or more representatives from this center maintains a direct channel of communication concerning developmental and organizational priorities between those who design and maintain the system and those who use it.

Groups charged with providing advice on the implementation of online systems may be developed on the basis of need. For example, an ad hoc implementation group might be appointed to assist in the implementation of a new module of an integrated system. Groups of this type have a limited and focused charge, and normally dissolve or, if needed, are reconstituted into a permanent committee once their initial work is accomplished.

Committees and working groups serve the valuable function of providing advice to administrators regarding policy and operational matters related to running online systems in a manner that is effective for users, both within and beyond the library's walls. However, it should be understood that they do not replace the need for direct user feedback on system development and implementation.

Limitations of Evaluation

Although the reasons for performance evaluation are compelling, much of the work done in systems evaluation within libraries is the exception rather than the rule. This situation can be commonly observed for a number of reasons. Sometimes system resource usage is neither the concern nor the domain of the library, but rather of the campus or city administrative computing center. In situations where the management of the computing facilities is separated from the management of the library, it is more difficult to establish a cohesive picture of the factors that affect the system's performance, much less to correct these situations when performance problems arise. Also, online systems typically generate hundreds of statistical reports about the system functions on a regular (usually monthly) basis. Often, information about system resources usage needs to be carefully analyzed and translated to a different format in order to be usable for library managers. System vendors have moved increasingly to report generation modules that can be customized by libraries in order to avoid this pitfall. The analysis of system performance data requires both skill and a commitment to ongoing analysis. Not all librarians feel they have adequate training in the use of quantitative or qualitative analysis methods. Further, it is not always clear where in the library organization the responsibility ought to rest for ongoing evaluation, beyond the annual budgeting process for equipment, software, and online contractual services. The published literature reveals that this analysis is now being performed by many different people—systems, reference, collection development, technical services, and administrative librarians.

Evaluating the Digital Library

The developments discussed in some of the earlier chapters strongly suggest that the library of the future will be dealing more and more with information resources that are network-accessible and less and less with those owned as physical artifacts. Although the evaluation of library services per se is outside the scope of the present book (the subject is covered in detail in Lancaster, 1993a, and Baker and Lancaster, 1991), it is appropriate to consider in what way the evaluation of such a "digital library" may differ from the evaluation of the more traditional library.

Traditional models for evaluating library services are largely based on whether or not the library, its resources and its tools can assist users to find the items or information they need. Technology has enabled libraries to expand access to information resources beyond the physical walls, both for library staff and for users. In some cases this has meant that the library no longer plays the role of intermediary in the delivery of information. As the locus of information resources traditionally associated with a trip to the library becomes increasingly decentralized and remotely accessible, the role of the library in providing these services will inevitably change. So too will the library's ability to evaluate its performance directly. How will the traditional model change as we move increasingly into a digital and networked environment, where users have direct access to remote information, and rely less often on the library and its resources for answers to their questions? What will become the role of the library as we now know it, with its quantifiable resources and collections? How can the library use technology to understand the needs of library users more completely, both in the traditional and the evolving digital library setting?

Figure 52 presents a model that depicts the most important current components of traditional library evaluation, and how they are employed. This traditional evaluation model has identifiable components, such as user characteristics, reasons for using the library, the size of the library collection, staff efficiency and accuracy, and whether user needs are satisfied within the necessary time frame. Characteristics, behavior, and needs of users can now be observed, to some extent at least, because most of the services offered by traditional libraries require that the user enter the library at some point to receive them. Little is known of the characteristics, behavior, and needs of nonusers in most communities.

The input predictors of the library's performance include the size of the general and reference collections and the rate at which new materials are added. Within the library, the interactions among staff processes, the library's resources and tools, and the user processes combine to produce outputs and, ultimately, outcomes. Measures of output and outcome indicate whether the information or item was obtained, whether used, and whether it had short-term (ST) or long-term (LT) impacts on the user. The most obvious output predictors of performance are circulation, number of reference questions answered, and number of literature searches performed. Libraries normally collect these data on a regular basis, either manually or through electronic monitoring. Such data quantify the services provided. True output measures relate to the effectiveness of the work done, in terms of correctness, timeliness, desired amount, and so on. While commonly accepted output measures exist (e.g., shelf availability), they require some effort to apply. Outcomes are rarely looked at: very little is known about what use is made of publications or information after users leave the library.

Some changes are needed in order to build a working model for evaluation in a digital library environment. First, it is clear that user groups will change, as will the library's ability to monitor their needs and behaviors. Since users will no longer need to come to the library to obtain access

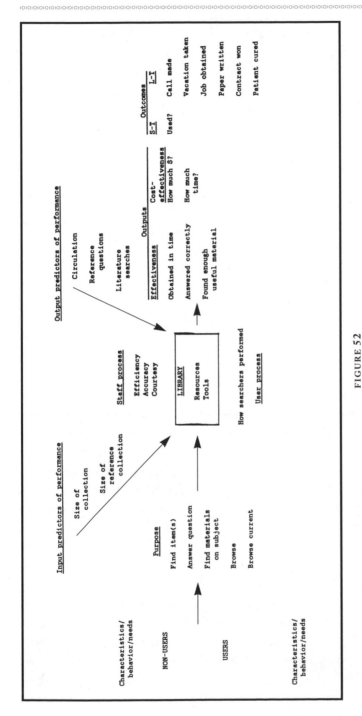

FIGURE 52

Major components of an evaluation model for traditional libraries

to library materials, they will be more remote, and more anonymous. It is likely that the group of users may widen to include previous non-users. This could occur because the library may provide convenient or cost-effective electronic access to information that formerly was not available in the library, or because the resources are now perceived to be more accessible than they were before.

Secondly, the purposes for which users seek information may change in the digital library environment. Users will have access to the electronic tools needed to build and organize their own databases of information, to create new documents incorporating or referring to that information, and to find people to communicate with or to collaborate with on future projects.

Thirdly, the role of the library in information provision will change, although it is too soon to determine in what ways, and to what degree these changes will occur. In a networked environment, a library may become merely a switching center, a switching center providing value-added interfaces and indices to electronic information, or a database builder, selecting electronic information of greatest interest to users and building databases incorporating that information.

Lastly, and perhaps most obviously, the nature of the library's "collection" will change. Resources are becoming more dispersed and intangible as the concept of a collection beyond the library's physical walls is extended. The nature of the library's "control" over the contents of these collections is also changing. Items in collections, once considered discrete pieces of information, are developing fuzzy boundaries, due to the ability of authors and users to provide hypermedia links among textual and other items in a networked digital environment. Documents can now be dynamic and interactive in nature, and may not be printable. The content of collections, or items within collections, may also change rapidly.

It is clear that such yardsticks as size of collection or number of items acquired annually have little meaning for the digital library. Also of little meaning are all output measures that relate to ownership of physical items, "shelf availability" being perhaps the most obvious example. Presumably, "items accessed" replaces "circulation" as a quantitative measure of use. However, if the actions of users can be monitored (some form of transaction logging as discussed earlier), finer measures of use become possible: how much text is accessed, how much is merely viewed, how much is downloaded to personal databases, and so on.

The fact that many users will be "remote" and "anonymous" makes evaluation more difficult. The fact that some of their actions are susceptible to monitoring makes some types of evaluation easier to implement.

If the digital library is used for the same purposes as the traditional library—to find a particular item, to find the answer to a question, to find information on a particular subject—the evaluation criteria also remain more or less the same. Nevertheless, the digital library may present special problems in evaluation, as suggested earlier; e.g., "items" may have rather fuzzy boundaries and some text may lack stability (databases, and perhaps even individual items, may be updated frequently).

If the digital library is used for other purposes—e.g., to build composite documents from several sources scattered throughout the network, to locate people with similar interests, and so on—different evaluation criteria will be needed.

In a highly developed digital information network, one can visualize a situation in which a scholar builds a personal database by downloading from network resources the text and graphics of most direct interest. This scholar may be supported by some form of institutional library (maintained perhaps by a university, college, or company) which has also downloaded from the broader network the text and graphics most likely to be of value to the institutional community. The situation is depicted in simple form in Figure 53. If an important role of the institutional library is to "feed" the personal databases of its users in a dynamic way (e.g., through some form of profile matching), the most obvious evaluation criterion would relate to the frequency with which an individual needs to go beyond personal and institutional resources to satisfy a particular need. Presumably, if the institutional library was doing an excellent job, most of the individual's needs would be satisfied from his/her own database, some from the institutional database, and very little from the wider network resources.

The digital library environment is one in which there is a high level of interaction between users and documents and perhaps between users and users. The fundamental definitions of traditional terms used to describe the library's role in information organization and delivery are being challenged, and institutional boundaries are becoming fuzzy. Many communities are developing their own databases of organized information resources in ways that enable them to access and manipulate this information optimally. Emphasis in data sharing is placed on the most convenient format for the user's needs, as opposed to the standard data formats that libraries employ in order to facilitate data exchange. The term "library" is being extended in the metaphoric sense, to the point where it will not simply refer to the traditional physical structures and collections organized and managed by library professionals. In the most basic sense, users are the builders of their own digital information environment.

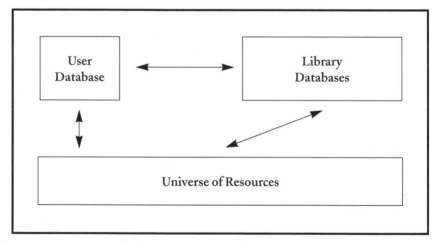

FIGURE 53
Interacting components in a digital library network

Whereas the traditional library enables users to interact simultaneously with the same materials at one physical point in time, the digital library increases the opportunities for users to make serial as well as synchronous use of the same materials in digital format, as well as enabling them to communicate with each other about the material at hand.

A debate held at the 1995 annual meeting of the Medical Library Association raised several important questions for library administrators, including one that suggests that more stringent evaluation criteria may be appropriate to the digital library environment:

> To better serve clients, do we need to change their expectations of instant gratification—i.e., information on demand—to a response time that permits more thoughtful and thorough results as is typical of other professions. (Nagle, 1996, page 662)

The development of digital libraries is accompanied by a multi-disciplinary interest in evaluation. Evaluation in the six NSF/ARPA/NASA-sponsored Digital Library Initiative projects incorporates qualitative methods developed by researchers from various fields—sociology, psychology, communications, computer science, and engineering (URL—http://dli.grainger.uiuc.edu/national.htm). Researchers in these projects are working to find out what are the most significant factors affecting use of electronic information in various areas of activity. Online system transaction monitoring is being employed widely to study the searching patterns of users, along with interviews, questionnaires, video taping, and other methods. Ironically, we may soon know more about user behavior and preferences in the digital library than we do about user behavior and preferences in the traditional library.

CHAPTER 15

Artificial Intelligence and Expert Systems

IOIOIOIOIOIOIOIOIOIOIOIOIOIOIOIOIOIOIOIOIOIOIOIOIOIOIOIOIOIOIOIOIOIOIOIOIOIOI

MUCH RESEARCH and development work has already been undertaken toward the implementation of systems able to perform many of the intellectual tasks now performed by professional librarians. This work falls in the area of research on "artificial intelligence" and "expert systems."

Any discussion of applications of artificial intelligence (AI) is complicated since no universally accepted definition of the term seems to exist. Indeed, several of the books written on artificial intelligence make no real attempt to define it.* An even worse problem is the fact that the term is used so carelessly, often referring to operations (e.g., human selection from a computer-displayed menu) in which no machine intelligence is involved at all.

While perhaps not a formal definition, Fenly (1992) has offered a clear and concise statement that illustrates what AI is, or should be, all about:

> ...computer programs have been developed which exhibit human-like reasoning, which may be able to learn from their mistakes, and which quickly and cleverly perform tasks normally done by scarce and expensive human experts. (Page 51)

In other words, one can say that AI attempts to develop systems that perform some of the tasks normally performed by experts in some area; perhaps the most obvious example is medical diagnosis. For this reason, systems of this type are frequently referred to as *expert systems*. The terms *knowledge-based systems* and *rule-based systems* seem now to be used more or less interchangeably with *expert systems* because systems of this type must be given a body of knowledge (e.g., symptoms and signs associ-

---

*The objective of artificial intelligence is at least well illustrated by Kurzweil (1991), quoting Elaine Rich, as "how to make computers do things at which, at the moment, people are better."

ated with a particular disease state) to work on and some of these knowledge bases would consist of rules, such as rules for descriptive cataloging.

In the literature of library science, the term "expert systems" is frequently linked to the term "artificial intelligence." This is somewhat misleading: a system can store and exploit knowledge or expertise without exhibiting any real intelligence (e.g., without learning from its mistakes).

Expert systems approaches to various library activities have been mentioned already at various points in this book. This chapter gives a brief overview of developments so far, and attempts to assess the promise of expert systems techniques for the immediate future. More complete surveys can be found in Alberico and Micco (1990), Bailey and Myers (1991), Drenth et al. (1991), Lancaster and Smith (1992), and Morris (1992).

Cataloging Applications

Because descriptive cataloging is rule-based, one would think that this activity would be a prime candidate for an expert systems application, and some work has been done in this area (e.g., Davies (1986); Jeng, 1986; Schwarz, 1986; Gibb and Sharif, 1988; Weibel, 1992; Ercegovac and Borko, 1992). Fenly (1992) claims that the results have so far been unconvincing. He feels that a cataloging system with genuine expertise is an order of magnitude more difficult to implement than one that merely casts cataloging rules in an automated format. As he points out:

> ... genuine expert systems, with the depth and power to solve substantial and meaningful problems, are time-consuming and costly to develop ... (Page 53)

Fenly does suggest, however, that there may exist certain descriptive cataloging problems that require an unusual amount of intellectual effort and that problems of this type might justify the expense of a full expert-systems approach. One such application is that of the cataloging of series.

Weibel (1992) seems to agree with Fenly to a very large extent. Although he, himself, has performed research at OCLC on the feasibility of automatic descriptive cataloging from images of title pages, he sees a "thread of unreality" in much of the research performed in this area so far. He claims that there exist "large obstacles to implementation of production systems." However, like Fenly, he seems to believe that certain specialized tasks in cataloging might benefit from an expert-systems treatment; one example is the detection of duplicate cataloging records. In his view, it is more important that automated approaches to cataloging should be "intelligently implemented" than that they be "intelligent."

Subject Indexing

The assignment of terms to documents, to represent the subjects dealt with, is another activity that might benefit from the expert system approach. While subject indexing cannot be as rule-based as descriptive cataloging, certain rules do have to be followed. In very large systems, such as those operated by the National Library of Medicine, these rules can be quite extensive. For example, one set of rules prescribes which subheadings are to be used with which categories of main headings.

An interactive program, MedIndEx, has been developed at the National Library of Medicine, using expert system principles, to assist the indexer in using *Medical Subject Headings* to represent the subject matter of biomedical articles. Work on this system is reported by Humphrey (1992). In essence, the system can perform two major tasks: (1) prompt the indexer to assign a particular term or type of term, and (2) correct the indexer when a term is used inappropriately. For example, an indexer who assigns a neoplasm (cancer) term reflecting the site of the disease (e.g., *bone neoplasms*) can be prompted to assign a companion term representing the histologic type of the neoplasm (e.g., *adenocarcinoma*). Or, the indexer who assigns an inappropriate combination, such as *femur* and *bone neoplasms*, can be informed that the correct term is actually *femoral neoplasms*.

Other approaches to automatic indexing or computer-aided indexing, described in the literature, also claim to use artificial intelligence or expert system techniques. However, many merely assign terms to documents on the basis of similarity between words occurring in the text (e.g., titles and abstracts) and in word "profiles" associated with each index term. While such systems could be considered "knowledge-based," they can hardly be regarded as involving artificial intelligence. On the other hand, artificial intelligence could be involved if the indexing system learned from its mistakes and was thus able to improve its own performance.

Database Searching

Much work has been done on the development of "intelligent front-ends" or "intelligent interfaces" to aid the exploitation of databases through online networks. For example, Hu (1987) has evaluated one such interface designed to help someone select the database that appears most appropriate to use to satisfy a particular information need. Hu's study indicates that this particular interface operates almost entirely through the use of menus, from which the user makes a selection, and that it exhibits no evidence of any real "intelligence" in database selection.

Other interfaces are designed to help users construct search strategies that appropriately reflect their information needs. Several interfaces of this type have been reviewed by Vickery (1992) and by Alberico and Micco (1990). Some of these operate largely through menus, some prompt the user by asking questions designed to limit the scope of the search in a useful way, and some will accept input from the user in the form of a narrative statement of information need. While many of these are ingenious and useful tools, it is not clear that they can actually be said to involve the use of artificial intelligence. Denning and Smith (1994) present some general design principles to guide the implementation of intelligent interfaces. Several are demonstrated in their prototype, ELSA (the Electronic Library Search Assistant).

Question Answering

The Association of Research Libraries survey of the use of expert systems in research libraries (Bailey and Myers, 1991) indicates that reference service is the area that has received most attention. Waters (1992) considers question answering to be an obvious application of expert system approaches because similar questions are repeated time and time again and because some libraries record questions received and answers supplied, thus creating an appropriate "knowledge base." The subject has already been thoroughly discussed and reviewed in the literature (e.g., Parrott (1986, 1989, 1992), Richardson (1989), Vedder et al. (1989), Alberico and Micco (1990), Davies et al. (1992)). The systems developed range from those restricted to highly specialized subject areas, such as AquaRef (Hanfman, 1989), to those attempting to cover the whole range of questions dealt with in a general library. Most of the systems developed operate by means of menus, but at least one does permit the use of questions in natural-language form. Typical of the general systems are Reference Expert, developed at the University of Houston (Bailey, 1992), and SourceFinder, which was developed at the Undergraduate Library of the University of Illinois at Urbana-Champaign. They do not answer questions directly but attempt to lead users to sources that will provide answers.

SourceFinder (SF), which was originally designed to support a research strategy class (Allen, 1989b), is intended to help undergraduate students to find sources to answer their reference questions when no professional librarians are available. The database contains over 2100 reference sources. SourceFinder operates through a series of menus, the first of which offers 24 broad subject categories (e.g., Art, Biographies, Law, Religion) from which a user can choose. After the subject menus lead the user to the most specific subcategories available (e.g., Performing Arts leads to the choice among Costume, Dance, Film, Musical Theatre, Television, and Theatre), further menus ask the user to restrict by type of information needed and then by type of source (e.g., handbook, dictionary). Usually, several possible sources are suggested for each question and in some cases the list may be quite long. Although the sources will usually be printed tools, the user can also be referred in other ways (e.g., to use the online catalog or a CD-ROM database).

The database of Reference Expert (RE) is much smaller—340 reference sources in printed and CD-ROM form; almost 150 are indexes and the remainder are other types of reference tools. Reference Expert operates in a way that is very similar to the way that SourceFinder works. Menus lead a user down to an appropriate level of subject heading, then offer the user various possible content types (e.g., definitions, addresses, biographies) and, possibly, formats (print or CD-ROM).

Acquisitions and Collection Development

Several expert system approaches in this area were already reviewed in Chapters 5 and 6. Pontigo et al. (1992) and Hawks (1994) have described systems capable of recommending a source to go to in order to acquire monographs, reports, or other types of publications.

The systems are able to rank the potential sources to reflect probability of success in acquisition. In the case of the system described by Pontigo et al., a learning capability is claimed.

Brown (1993) describes a system designed to determine whether a particular item is likely to be received through an approval plan, and Bianchi and Giorgi (1986) and Waldstein (1986) describe expert systems to aid library users in a variety of tasks, including document ordering.

Systems designed to aid materials selection are dealt with by Rada et al. (1987), Sowell (1989), and Meador and Cline (1992).

Achievements and Promise

Despite the activity and interest, there has been little in the way of systematic evaluation of the systems developed. This is also true of expert systems developed in other fields (Adelman, 1992). Moreover, the evaluation that has occurred has tended to concentrate on the internal functioning of the system (e.g., the completeness of the knowledge base or the logical consistency of the inference engine) rather than on the system outputs. To establish the true value of an expert system, one must compare the results achieved with the results obtained without expert system aid, using effectiveness and/or cost-effectiveness criteria (Lancaster, et al., 1996).

The few evaluations that have been performed suggest that achievements in the library field have so far been quite modest. For example, Su and Lancaster (1995), in their evaluation of two expert systems for the selection of reference sources (Reference Expert and Source Finder), conclude that they might improve the performance of only the most inexperienced of library users. Somewhat better results are reported by Richardson and Reyes (1995) in their evaluation of two expert systems but their searchers were experienced librarians, rather than unsophisticated users, and they were dealing with systems restricted to a single domain—government information. Hu (1987), in her evaluation of an interface for database selection, discovered that it could help less experienced individuals approximate the success rate of experienced searchers in the selection of databases appropriate to particular information needs, but neither the experienced searchers nor the system-aided inexperienced users performed at a very high level.

It must also be recognized that, while many prototype systems have been developed, there are few that can be considered fully operational in the sense that they have replaced previous practices or staff positions.

Fenly (1992) has usefully summarized the potential benefits of expert systems as these have been identified in the literature. They include:

1. Make scarce expertise more widely available, thereby helping non-experts achieve expert-like results.
2. Free some of the time of human experts for other activities.
3. Promote standardization and consistency in relatively unstructured tasks.
4. Provide incentives for creating a database of knowledge in a permanent form (e.g., not dependent on the availability of particular individuals).
5. Perform at a consistently high level (e.g., not influenced by fatigue or lack of concentration).

These benefits are very real and there seems little doubt that carefully designed knowledge-based systems could be of great value to the library profession when applied to highly specialized activities that are now accomplished only through the expenditure of significant amounts of the time of expensive human experts. They could also be of value in tasks, such as the document ordering activities dealt with by Pontigo et al. (1992), that can obviously benefit from learning capabilities. However, there is little to support the belief that machines with "intelligence" will soon be able to take over many of the intellectual tasks now performed by a well-trained and experienced librarian, and many writers on this subject seem much too optimistic on this point. For example, Metzler (1992) has said:

> The library of the future may be able to provide a far richer access to, and utilization of, the knowledge contained (often implicitly) in its collection. The most immediately feasible development along this line would be content-based information retrieval. This, of course, would require a far more general and robust brand of artificial intelligence and natural language understanding than what we have available now. The step beyond that would involve not only understanding text well enough to determine whether it is relevant to a general information need expressed by a user, but to understand it well enough to actually extract information that can be used by a program. (Pages 7-8)

A recent report from the American Association for Artificial Intelligence (Weld et al., 1995) suggests that the field of AI is ready to make a significant contribution to solving the information retrieval problems posed by the Internet and its successors. However, the authors of the report exaggerate the achievements of AI in such applications as medical diagnosis while, at the same time, acknowledging that many of the intelligent systems that have been developed are not sufficiently robust for transfer to a real-world environment. The report is more of a wish list, identifying areas that require further research and funding, than an accurate picture of what AI can contribute to the National Information Infrastructure today.

The enthusiasm for artificial intelligence or expert system approaches that exists in some segments of the library profession today is reminiscent of the enthusiasm for machine-aided diagnosis that existed in some segments of the medical profession about twenty years ago. Machine-aided diagnosis has not been widely accepted by the medical community (Salamon, 1989; Engle, 1992), and the performance of computer-based diagnostic systems has been less than inspiring (Berner et al., 1994; Kassirer, 1994). It is now realized that the problems are much greater than they once appeared to be. Human experts operate through a combination of knowledge, experience, and intuition. Capturing the knowledge in some electronic form is possible, if not exactly easy, but recording human experience is a problem of a greater order of magnitude, and the replacement of human intuition is unlikely to be achieved for a very long time. Most of the activities performed by librarians require less knowledge, experience, and intuition than does medical diagnosis. Nevertheless, the problems involved in automating even the "simplest" of intellectual tasks are frequently underestimated. Outside the library field, disillusionment with expert systems now seems fairly widespread (No more expert systems, 1994).

A large component of "expertise" is informal and experiential in character (Bainbridge, 1991); the recorded knowledge, however detailed and comprehensive, still requires evaluation and interpretation. People do not become experts merely by having an expert knowledge base available to them. Indeed, the very availability of such a tool can be dangerous, for it puts decisions and actions that are properly the domain of the expert into the hands of the less qualified. One of the major deterrents to the further development of expert systems in medicine is malpractice—the danger of incorrect diagnosis and treatment—with its attendant litigious consequences (Warner, 1988; Bainbridge, 1991).

The true expert is a very rare individual. There are probably less than a dozen expert neuroradiologists in the entire United States. There are rather few expert reference librarians, and they are becoming fewer. We can not use machines to replace the true expert in neuroradiology, or the truly expert reference librarian, although we may be able to design systems that would allow the worst of them to perform better. Lancaster (1993b) has asked why we refer to these systems as "expert" and suggests that "systems of mediocrity" would be a more apt description; he warns that, if our library schools concentrate on teaching students how to use such systems to exploit this mediocrity, the true expert—the expert cataloger, the expert indexer, the expert librarian—will disappear.*

It is fashionable today to claim that an important role of the librarian in the future will be that of a teacher—teaching people how to exploit information resources. Will we still have the knowledge needed to fulfill this teaching role, or will it be lost through the process of deprofessionalization as suggested by Harris (1992)? Deprofessionalization might well be accelerated by an over-reliance on expert system technologies.

The true intellectual tasks associated with the library profession—collection development, subject analysis, interpretation of information needs, search strategy, and suchlike—are not easily delegated to machines. Whatever may happen to the library as an institution (i.e., as a collection of physical artifacts), the conclusion reached in Chapter 13 still seems valid: it is unlikely that the expertise of the skilled librarian will be replaced by artificial intelligence, expert systems or other technologies in the near future.

---

*Dreyfus and Dreyfus (1986) also suggest that expert systems can not be truly expert and that "competent systems" might be a better term to describe them.

CHAPTER 16

Summary and Possible Trends

IOIOIOIOIOIOIOIOIOIOIOIOIOIOIOIOIOIOIOIOIOIOIOIOIOIOIOIOIOIOIOIOIOIOIOIOIOIOIOI

THIS CHAPTER will first summarize some of the major points made earlier in the text and then, using this discussion as a springboard, will consider possible trends in the evolution of library technology.

Computers and related technologies were first used within libraries for the convenience of the staff—applied to the internal operations of the library in the hope of saving time, economizing by reducing the number of staff or delegating more tasks to less highly qualified individuals, and generally improving efficiency. Much more recent has been the view of technology as a means of improving existing services or of offering completely new services. (Chapter 1)

Conflicting evidence exists on the effects that technology has had on staff. Although more activities have been passed from professional librarians to paraprofessional or clerical personnel, automation has not usually reduced the size of library establishments. In general, staff members do not feel that technology has made life easier for them. In fact, many believe that their jobs have become more demanding; this applies particularly to professional librarians. Some feel that the added complexity of their work needs to be reflected in improved salaries. The ability to apply new technologies has given many librarians greater job satisfaction and improved their self-image. However, there is nothing to support the belief that the general public has changed its perception of librarians for the better. Over the last thirty years, librarian attitudes toward the application of new technologies appear to have moved through three phases: resistance/mistrust, enthusiasm leading to over-enthusiasm, and (rather recently) a more realistic view of the benefits among some members of the profession. Nevertheless, there are still many who can be put in the overenthusiastic class, especially those who see a bright future for applications of artificial intelligence and expert systems, as well as a few who either resist technology or fear it. Some librarians are afraid that technology is beginning to deprofessionalize their jobs and that this could lead to the demise of the profession. (Chapter 3)

There is a widely held view that technology has had a profound effect on the organizational structure of libraries—manifested in greater levels of participative management, less rigid and formal chains of command, the blurring of traditional departmental/divisional boundaries, and much greater use of ad hoc task forces and working groups. Sweeney (1994) has used the term "post-hierarchical library" to refer to this type of organizational/ administrative structure. On the other hand, others believe that organizational change has not been as extreme as many writers claim. (Chapter 2)

Technology has had a profound effect on the training needs of both library staff and library users as well as on the way in which this training may be accomplished. (Chapter 4)

The library databases that have emerged through use of technology—of catalog, circulation, acquisition, interlibrary loan, and similar records—have the potential to yield more information of value in resource management than librarians have ever had before. (Chapter 6)

Regrettably, improved management is rarely seen as a major benefit of technology, by librarians and system vendors alike, and rather little use is made of automated systems in libraries as management information or decision support systems. (Chapter 5)

While electronic publications that are *distributed*—on tape, disk or whatever—do not radically change approaches to collection development and management, resources that are only network-accessible obviously do. A key question is whether the library of the future will be merely a switching center or, instead, will engage in such activities as database building, document creation, and even, perhaps, forms of electronic publishing. (Chapter 7)

Developments in technology have radically changed the relationship between libraries and library vendors, causing a blurring of responsibilities in some areas. Vendors use electronic access to continually expand the services they offer to libraries. (Chapter 8)

CD-ROM products have been received enthusiastically by both library staff and library users. However, many users may expect more from these tools than they can actually deliver and librarians, by and large, have not done much to encourage a more realistic/critical view of their capabilities. CD-ROM may be a temporary medium, eventually replaced by something better. (Chapter 9)

Some libraries can now choose among several access alternatives for certain sources of information: remote online search, as CD-ROM, or loaded on local mainframe computers. Use of information sources can be increased greatly by making them more widely accessible (physically and economically), such as by moving them from a limited-access CD-ROM network to a campus-wide computer network, and this increased use can greatly improve the cost-effectiveness of information provision. Libraries can establish tiers of access to electronic resources based on probable frequency of use. (Chapter 10)

Commercial document delivery services (coupled with improved capabilities in the area of electronic transmission), CD-ROM distribution and network accessibility offer viable alternatives to traditional interlibrary resource sharing and may even allow the reduction of periodical holdings for some libraries. However, problems are created for libraries by the ability of users to place orders directly with document suppliers. (Chapter 11)

The Internet is beginning to have a significant impact on libraries and library users. It has already proved its value in several areas, including reference service and professional communication. However, as with other facets of technology, it may have been oversold. Making a resource technologically accessible does not necessarily make it intellectually accessible. (Chapter 13)

Technology has had a profound effect on library users in the improvement of traditional services, in the introduction of new services, in the disintermediation of services (users doing things formerly done by library staff), and in allowing remote access to certain library resources. Remote users present new problems and challenges for the library. Although library users are generally considered to "like" technology, their attitudes toward increasing automation have rarely, if ever, been studied systematically. (Chapter 12)

There are many possible approaches and levels applicable to the evaluation of automated systems in libraries. In general, however, little serious evaluation takes place, especially in the area of user impact. The digital library presents a special set of evaluation problems. (Chapter 14)

Some librarians engaged in research and development believe that artificial intelligence/expert system technologies can produce systems capable of taking on some of the expert functions of experienced professional librarians. Except in a few highly specialized areas, there is little support for this. The few evaluations that have been performed tend to show that the performance of expert systems in library applications has so far been less than impressive. Similar findings exist in other environments such as health care. (Chapter 15)

Future of the Library

It is possible to recognize two distinct phases in the application of technology to libraries. In the first, the essential raw materials with which libraries deal—books, periodicals, and other publications—remain in traditional print-on-paper forms. Technology is used to manipulate electronic records for these items in various ways and also to facilitate their movement (e.g., through fax). This phase has been in place, to some extent at least, for about thirty years. In the second phase, the raw materials themselves are in electronic form. Through the acquisition of resources on CD-ROM, and other electronic forms, and through access to publications via the Internet, libraries are now in the early stages of the second phase. While much of this book concentrates on the first phase, the second is also dealt with.

Although some librarians still refuse to accept it (see Crawford and Gorman, 1995, as a prime example), it seems clear that, in the future, libraries will be dealing less and less with print on paper and more and more with publications in electronic form.* If this is so, and if most members of the public can access electronic resources for themselves, through workstations in the home or office, what role will remain for the library and what role for the librarian as information specialist?

While Birdsall (1994) is persuasive in his argument that the main allure of the library is as a *place*, the fact remains that remote use of library resources is becoming increasingly feasible and increasingly common.

---

*This raises the important question of "... to what extent libraries can afford to commit resources to both print access services and to electronic resources and for how long a time." (Fiscella and Proctor, 1995, p. 457).

If people do not need to visit libraries, will they really be needed? Views on the future of the library range from one extreme to the other, along a kind of continuum:

1. Libraries will not be needed at all.
2. Libraries will become nothing more than switching centers.
3. Libraries will be switching centers but will build indexes and other tools to facilitate access to network resources.
4. Libraries will take on important new roles in building databases, creating new information composites, and possibly in some electronic publishing activities.
5. Libraries will remain important as *places* that people visit, at least in the foreseeable future.

Many writers have warned that the library must change rather radically, and take on new responsibilities if it is to survive in a largely electronic publishing environment. Ungern-Sternberg and Lindquist (1995) put it this way:

> ... researchers potentially can access information resources from all over the world without even entering the library. This could be devastating for the library in its role as information provider unless it actively takes part in the changing reality. Scientific communication can take place in networks outside the library, and the increased offerings of databases can make the library a small and marginal part of the whole network. (Page 396)

Lowry (1995a,b) believes that libraries will survive if they concentrate on building a "virtual library infrastructure." To do this, they must (a) provide the technologies required to make information readily accessible to the community served, (b) create the body of electronic information that users need, and (c) solve the policy and legal (e.g., copyright) problems that now impede access to and distribution of information.

Holt (1995a) recognizes that support to remote users is becoming increasingly important, but he also believes that the public library is needed as a *place*, even in a largely electronic world—for example, to provide Internet access for those "without home or office computers." His library has already established "equity sites" to give underprivileged groups remote access to library resources and services (Holt, 1993).

Although Atkinson (1990), among others, has warned against it, some see the library of the future as nothing more than a kind of switching center in a network environment. Presumably, as a mere switching center, it would subsidize access to information for the community served (in itself, perhaps, a major justification for its existence) and would provide technological support (e.g., gateways) for this access; library staff members might also help users to identify the electronic resources they should access.

Others (e.g., Kilgour, 1993) see the library as primarily a switching center but with an important value-added function of building indexes to network resources. The indexes would be designed to facilitate access to the resources most likely to be of interest and value locally. In this role, the library would perform functions similar to those performed in the days before open access collections and cooperative/centralized cataloging—e.g., providing annotations in the catalog and tailoring subject cataloging to local needs.

Holt (1995a) believes that this type of value-added role is as important for the public library as it is for academic and special libraries:

> ... public library staff can save time for their constituents by organizing the mass of electronic information available on local, national, and international servers ... [and] can develop electronic guides to help searchers through the metadata and megafiles with which they must deal online. (Pages 555-556)

He specifically mentions the importance of providing annotations for users, and sees the public library as an information clearinghouse staffed with "information agents."

As discussed in Chapter 7, Atkinson (1990) strongly believes that librarians must go beyond this. They must facilitate access to information by building databases of importance locally through downloading from network resources, and they must be prepared to create new composite documents, as needed by users, through the drawing of text and graphics from different places in the network. He also believes that the academic library may have an important role to play in scholarly publishing if this is taken over by the academic establishment.*

---

*Elsewhere, however, he (Atkinson, 1993b) questions whether scholarly publishing in the conventional sense really has a future:

> Will formal publication survive the online age? It need not necessarily. All scholarly communication could conceivably take place through the kind of information interchanges we now see on the network discussion lists. (Page 206)

Such an informal approach to the distribution of scholarly information electronically is discussed in detail in Okerson and O'Donnell (1995).

To play a major part in electronic scholarly publishing, of course, the academic library must enter into partnerships with other entities on campus, most obviously the computer centers and university presses (Bryant, 1994). The building of electronic databases, particularly those that provide access to locally unique resources, is frequently mentioned as an activity that will become increasingly important in libraries of all types, including public libraries (Holt, 1993, 1995a; Doman, 1994; Hunter, 1994a).

While the majority of librarians seem confident that the library will survive as an institution, this view is not necessarily shared by others. For example, Arms (1994), an academic administrator, questions:

> ... whether existing library organizations have the flexibility to fulfill this role [facilitating access to the universe of electronic information resources] and whether the electronic library will develop within or outside traditional libraries ... By a strange paradox, good information has never been more important than it is today, yet the university library is declining in importance relative to other information sources. Personal computing, electronic networks, and desktop publishing allow an individual to create materials and distribute them in ways that bypass the traditional publisher and the library. (Page 168)

Woodward (1995b) points to the fact that the new campus of California State University at Monterey Bay will not have a library building. She quotes the University Chancellor as saying "You simply don't have to build a traditional library these days."*

A report on the future of the library, issued by the Benton Foundation in 1996 (*Buildings, Books, and Bytes*, 1996), indicates, perhaps not surprisingly, that the general public does not see the library as a leader in the "digital revolution." Younger Americans (the 18-24 age group), in particular, seem to see little future for the library in a more fully electronic environment.

Atkinson (1993a) believes that academic libraries will find themselves competing with publishers and other information providers in a predominantly online environment. He urges that libraries need to learn as much as possible about scholarly publishing and that they must concentrate on "personalizing and humanizing relationships with their users."

---

*A recent book by Bazillion and Braun (1995) claims to deal with the design of buildings that will allow libraries to serve as "high-tech gateways." However, their approach is conservative rather than adventurous.

One can make a case for the fact that large academic libraries are in danger of breaking down because they tend to be organized according to a model that is no longer relevant to the modern world of scholarship. The most obvious example is the departmental library structure, which tends to conform to disciplinary boundaries; this structure is becoming less and less useful to research that is becoming more and more interdisciplinary. The increasing interdisciplinarity of research, along with increasing levels of collaboration (frequently involving different departments, institutions or even countries), can be better served by collections of resources that are temporary—compiled to support a particular research project during its lifetime only. Clearly, the building of such temporary "libraries" is much easier in an electronic environment because resources can be drawn extensively from different parts of the network and organized (i.e., classified, indexed) in a way that is optimal to support a particular project.* The network-accessible electronic library, of course, also facilitates inter-institutional and international research (Qin, 1996).

Future of the Librarian

Some writers believe that the future of the librarian, as information specialist, is more secure than that of the library, as institution, since communication networks make it increasingly possible for librarians to function outside the library.**

For example, Eagle (1992) has said:

> The library of the future will likely be an on-line network of librarians—generalists and specialists. Each ... will be expert in ... indexes and searching. Each will be connected and linked to massive computer databases. (Page 99)

This view is echoed by Drabenstott (1994) and by Anders et al. (1992), among others. Drabenstott states:

> A few reference staff will be physically present in the library building to assist users in person in collection navigation. Most reference staff will be posted on the network where they will respond to user calls for assistance by monitoring a user's ongoing search. Such calls could come from users who are nav-

---

*One can also argue that a library of physical artifacts, organized according to schemes that assume that a book will always be classified in one place, is of little use to modern research which really demands libraries that can be re-organized to reflect changing perspectives, interests and needs.

**Bauwens (1993) has introduced the term "cybrarian" to refer to a librarian working in an electronic environment.

igating digital libraries from workstations in their home, dormitory rooms, or offices ... Staff could work out of their homes because they would use the capabilities of the information network to interact with users ... Public library environments would feature itinerant reference staff whose duties resemble today's information brokers. (Pages 168-169)

Anders et al. put it this way:

> When everyone is plugged in, the librarian becomes the 'gateway' ... Presently, there are so many gateways that one needs a gateway to the gateways. This is the librarian's job—to interpret the means of access ... The gateway librarian, who advises on the best route to information and interprets the language of access, will have job security for years to come. (Page 40)

The continued importance of the librarian as *intermediary* between users and information is widely accepted, whether that professional works within a library or outside it (Birchall et al., 1994). Kong (1995) claims that this role has become even more important as electronic resources proliferate:

> ... reference librarians and the services they provide, are needed more now than at any other time in the past due to the increasingly [sic] popularity and complexity of such resources as the Internet in the automated reference environment. (Page 14)

But some believe that the librarian must be an *interpreter* of information, not just an intermediary (Hunt. 1995; Scepanski, 1996). Hitchingham (1996) is one library director who believes in the importance of involvement in "filtering" and "sense-making" for users.

As discussed earlier in the book, electronic technology has had another important effect—it has reduced the need for many of the librarian's traditional services, since the initiation of interlibrary lending and the searching of electronic databases, both those accessible through networks and those in CD-ROM form, are activities that are now being taken over by library users themselves. Consequently, librarians are seeking new professional roles, and some see themselves as performing as *knowledge engineers.*

Knowledge engineering may seem a rather pretentious term but it does give something of the flavor of what some see as the future of the profession: the librarian as builder of better tools—better online catalogs, better interfaces to online resources, and better databases.

In other words, these librarians see themselves as increasingly involved in the design and construction of information systems rather than as mere users of systems created by others. Perhaps the ultimate manifestation of this is the work going on in some libraries to develop expert systems, as discussed in Chapter 15.

Views expressed in the literature concerning the knowledge engineering role of the librarian include the following:

> Librarians would engage . . . in developing the new systems and services of the virtual library, such as gateways, user interfaces, search and retrieval systems, tools for navigating the networks, and document delivery systems. (von Wahlde and Schiller, 1993, page 23)

and

> Librarians could develop expert systems to provide reference assistance to users when reference staff are not available or nearby, to capture knowledge of staff subject specialists when they are not available, to accommodate many users at the same time, to provide bibliographic instruction. (Drabenstott, 1994, page 139)

It is especially encouraging to see that such views on the changing nature of librarianship are not exclusively the domain of academia. Holt (1993), the director of a large public library system, puts it this way:

> . . . many library professionals will become as adept in programming hyperlink or utilizing artificial intelligence to speed researchers through the information maze as they are now in shelving by LC or Dewey. (Page 24)

LaGuardia (1995) is forceful in claiming that information system design is the really important function that librarians must perform:

> Reference librarians are the natural designers of the new tools for information organization, access, retrieval, and distribution: these are the functions we do best. As the information age has advanced over the past 20 years, we have been busily staffing desks at the expense of *devising* new tools for organizing and accessing information. (Page 9)

A similar sentiment is expressed by Brin and Cochran (1994):

> Librarians should become responsible for the creation and operation of systems which facilitate access, communication, and education for information management. This will involve more reference-by-appointment and more direct work with faculty and graduate students while providing less block-scheduling of librarians at the reference desks. (Page 212)

Others agree with Atkinson that the librarian of the future should be heavily involved in the repackaging of information and even in a form of electronic publishing—drawing electronic resources from different parts of the network, downloading them to local storage and creating new electronic resources through the synthesis of existing ones.

For example, DeBuse (1988) has said:

> Some librarians will become hypertext engineers . . . They will provide intellectual connections between the works of different authors or convert linear publications to hypermedia publications. (Page 17)

Even if they do not explicitly advocate the "knowledge engineer" future, others strongly believe that the librarian must be more active in at least shaping the design of information systems (e.g., Smalley, 1994) and in evaluating new information technologies for users (Raitt, 1993). In other words, librarians can and should shape the future (Swan, 1993).

Perhaps the most prevalent view, however, is that the librarian's major future role will be that of a teacher—instructing people in how to exploit information resources effectively, and Lewis (1995) suggests that this function is too important to be a mere part-time activity:

> Instruction in the use of the electronic library must become a central part of the core curriculum of the university. This will require that the teaching not be done as an add on to the duties of reference librarians. It must be done as part of regular teaching loads, by regular faculty. It is advisable that many, if not most, of these faculty should be librarians. (Page 12)

In a somewhat similar vein, Scepanski (1996) suggests that academic librarians and teaching faculty will become more alike in their activities.

Most librarians seem confident that the profession can adapt itself to take on these various new activities, although some are less sure:

> Increasingly we will need to become aware of and use tools that come from outside of the library. This will test the adaptability of staff, will require a significant upgrading of the skills of most librarians and will mean that professionals who are not librarians will have to be offered positions along side, or in place of, librarians. (Lewis, 1995, page 12)

At the very least, these new responsibilities mean that we need today, and will continue to need, a rather different approach to education for the profession. The focus of the curriculum can no longer remain the library as an institution, and the activities and services of that institution, because the information professionals of today and tomorrow need an understanding of the complete cycle by which information is transferred from producer to consumer and of their own potential roles in this cycle (Lancaster, 1994).

Arms (1994) has issued the strongest warning:

> It is clear . . . that the training of librarians must change dramatically . . . The new libraries will have to draw talent and expertise from a great range of disciplines. Yet, today, almost every library needlessly restricts its choices by requiring an MLS degree from candidates for professional positions. (Page 168)

The implications of such a statement, coming from an academic administrator, are clear: the profession must change or it will be replaced by others.*

Some librarians have issued their own warnings along the same lines. Sweeney (1994) puts it as follows:

> Professional librarians are defined by their knowledge, skills, ethics, and performance, not by what tasks they do or do not do. If a person says that they will not do something required to operate a post-hierarchical library, they are probably not a team player.
>
> Professionals are also not defined by the M.L.S. degree but by performance. The M.L.S. degree does attract people who are already interested in a library career but in no way provides an indication of that person's suitability for a truly professional position in a post-hierarchical library. Professionals are performers, highly skilled with a wide body of knowledge serving other people. The M.L.S. degree is the beginning of the process.
>
> There are fewer and fewer positions in the post-hierarchical library for people who have limited knowledge and skills. People with limited knowledge and skills cannot contribute as much nor are they flexible enough to accomplish a higher percentage of the tasks required. Low level knowledge workers moving around paper or books will disappear in the future library. (Page 89)

He emphasizes that the library leader must be a "strategist with a vision, a plan, and the will to achieve it" and that all professional staff members must be generalists as well as specialists:

> Because of the need for more knowledge, skills, and education, it might seem apparent that libraries need more specialists in narrower and narrower subject areas. There is, however, a contrasting need for libraries to be highly responsive and flexible. This means that all employees must simultaneously possess excellent specialized knowledge, skills, and education and "own" an entire process, delivering services and adapting quickly to meet customer needs.
>
> Every specialist in the post-hierarchical library must be a flexible generalist. Specialization must be augmented with even better team-playing skills. The

---

*On the other hand, Scepanski (1996) quotes another academic administrator as believing that librarians can be "transformational leaders" in the transition to an increasingly electronic environment.

specialist is not only a person with special skills but a person who can and must contribute with other more common skills outside of the specialty. The specialist must be able to see the entire process, the organization, and have some basic practical understanding of all the different tasks to compliment [sic] his/her special skills. Each new librarian is both a specialist and a generalist possessing much more knowledge and expertise than was required in the traditional library. The addition of smarter technology has actually raised the need for a higher core level of common knowledge. (Page 72)

Sweeney seems to assume that the librarians of the future will continue to work in institutions that are in some sense "libraries" although, as we have seen, others predict a de-institutionalization of the professional expertise.

What this suggests is that, at this point, the future of the librarian, as information specialist, appears to be a lot more secure than the future of the library as place, and some scholars expect the intermediary role to move from the library to elsewhere in the information distribution chain. For example, Odlyzko (1995) claims:

If the review journals evolve the way I project, . . . they will provide directly to scholars all the services that libraries used to. With immediate electronic access to all the information in a field, with navigating tools, reviews, and other aids, a few dozen librarians and scholars at review journals might be able to substitute for a thousand reference librarians. (Page 120)

Such naive statements are disturbing for they show that some scholars both completely underestimate the problems involved in providing effective intellectual access to information and show little appreciation of the important role that research libraries continue to play in improving such access.

Technology has certainly had a major impact on the library and the work of the librarian, but it does not diminish the need for human expertise. The real professional expertise of librarians lies in the role they can play as information consultants or information counsellors, and there will exist a need for such individuals for a very long time to come.

One can hardly conclude this book in a better way than to identify the questions to be considered and discussed by managers as they grapple with the problems involved in moving the library from one primarily physical to one primarily virtual. Fortunately, this has already been well done for us by Jajko (1993) and by van Gils (1995). The questions Jajko raises are reproduced in Figure 54. The list does seem to include most of the important questions facing library managers in this period of rapid technological change and many of the same questions have been raised, explicitly or implicitly, throughout this book.

Van Gils (1995) has gone one stage further and presented a plan of action for moving his library, that of the Royal Netherlands Academy of Arts and Sciences (KNAW), into a largely electronic future. It is noteworthy that the plan (see Figure 55) includes new services (including electronic publishing), recruitment of staff members with strong backgrounds in information technology, the training/retraining of existing staff, and significant increases in library funding. Govan's (1991) conclusion, first reported in Chapter 7, may well be correct: libraries must become much more expensive or they will become useless.

A New Way of Thinking

- What are the new paradigm shifts in thinking about the virtual library? Is the library, its resources, and services now defined differently?
- Will the primary mission of the library be less than a repository for materials and more the intellectual center of the organization?
- What value will the virtual library give to an organization and how can that value be maximized?
- What will information cost in the electronic environment? Will its value match its cost, and who will pay for it?

Information Management

- How can the integrity of information be protected as it goes through various mutations during electronic transfer and from electronic to print? Who will preserve the "final copy?"
- How can information on older technology be accessible as software and hardware continue to change rapidly?
- How can information be filtered effectively to deal with the voluminous amount now available?
- Will there need to be a distinction between the "formal" publications and the "gray" literature that may reside side by side?

Publishing

- How will the publishing industry change in response to increased electronic access?
- Will organizations self-publish and how would this affect peer review and the prestige of publishing in a recognized journal?
- Will publishing become interactive, allowing readers to post comments and criticisms instantly? How will this affect the research process?

Continued

FIGURE 54

Questions to be considered by managers planning for the virtual library.

From Jajko (1993) by permission of Haworth Press

- How can authoring tools be implemented to allow for the integration and manipulation of external and internal information while preserving the integrity of an author's work?

Staffing

- Will the focus shift from the virtual library to the virtual librarian?
- What is the new work in a virtual library and who will do it?
- What new skills are needed to get the work done and how will the staff either be recruited or trained?
- What is [sic] the new client/staff relationships and how can they be encouraged and supported?
- What is the balance in the librarian's roles of information manager, information navigator, educator, researcher, designer, finder, subject specialist, warehouser, and applier?
- What is the optimal organizational structure to facilitate the virtual librarian's changing roles?

User Community

- As information becomes available from all over the world, how will the end user become knowledgeable about the resources and how to access them?
- What is the optimal training support for users in basic technology and in more sophisticated information retrieval and management?
- How will support and interaction with the user community change with the virtual library?

Physical Space

- What physical space is required to support the new functions?
- How can the physical environment contribute to the greater efficiency and productivity of the virtual library?
- How can new space be designed for optimal flexibility?

FIGURE 54 *Continued*

Objective

Development of an international leading biomedical information centre by:

- optimising and extension of existing services with the help of new technologies;
- the rapid building of new services for specific target groups.

Strategic actions

- Revision of collection-building policy:
  - exclusively biomedical;
  - digital in addition to paper;

Continued

FIGURE 55

Summary of plan of action for the Library of the Royal Netherlands Academy of Arts and Sciences, 1995-1999.

From van Gils (1995) by permission of Learned Information Europe Ltd.

· critical evaluation concerning use frequency;
· attuning to associate libraries.
• Building multimedia information services via World Wide Web:
· supply of primary literature, bibliographical data and all other possibly relevant information in an *integrated* environment;
· facilities for electronic publishing;
· building of electronic depot for biomedical information;
· development of instruments for online cataloguing of Internet sources.

Outline of steps

• Upgrading local network and PCs;
• Extra and retraining courses for present staff (external and internal courses and practical training);
• Recruiting new extra staff members with a lead in the field of information technology;
• Intensifying contacts with specific (biomedical) target groups and KNAW institutes;
• Building and testing new online services;
• Extension of electronic document delivery;
• Building and realisation of marketing and public relations policy concerning the new electronic library.

Finances

(amounts in Dutch Guilders: £1.00 is approx. 2.70 guilders)
• Average annual budget Library KNAW (approx. 70 staff members):
· subsidies 5.1 million;
· receipts services 1.8 million.
• Extra financing by KNAW for Plan of Action:
· extra personnel with IT background 1995-1997: 0.4 million per year;
· extra and retraining 1995-1996: 0.2 million per year;
· investments in local network, PCs, software and databases: 1995, 0.4 million/1996, 0.6 million/ 1997, 0.2 million.

FIGURE 55 *Continued*

Evaluation Checklist for OPACs*

lOlOlOlOlOlOlOlOlOlOlOlOlOlOlOlOlOlOlOlOlOlOlOlOlOlOlOlOlOlOlOlOlOlOlOlOlOlOlOlOl

T HE CHECKLIST consisted of ten sections, each of which focused on a different functional or user interface feature of an OPAC system. It was presented in tabular form with columns for yes/no answers and comments. The checklist questions are reproduced below in sections, each one corresponding to a separate table in the study. All questions were yes/no answers. If a particular question on the checklist was not relevant to the OPAC being evaluated (e.g., a question referring to the consistency of function key definitions for systems having no function keys), then evaluators were instructed to mark the question "Not Applicable." They were also encouraged to write comments about any question in the column titles "Comments."

Section 1

Database Characteristics

1. Does the system provide the following information in either short or long record displays?

    a. call number

    b. author

    c. title

    d. subject heading(s)

    e. edition information

    f. publication info.

    g. copy information

    h. volume information

    i. location for current issues of serials

    j. name of the library where the item is located

    k. loan status

*From Cherry et al. (1994) by permission of the American Library Association.

l. document abstract

m. table of contents

n. citations within the text

o. keywords from the book index

p. book review

Section 2

Operational Control

1. a. Is there an introduction to the system?

   b. Is there a set of instructions?

2. Does the system provide a choice of command-driven or menu-driven interface throughout?

3. If menu choices are by letters, are they mnemonic?

4. In the command mode:

   a. Is a display of the commands available?

   b. Are examples of how the commands are used available?

5. Does the system allow the registered user of this library to place holds/reserves on items at the terminal?

6. Does the system allow the user of this library [to] view the list of items charged out to him/her at the terminal?

7. Does the system display system or database changes, system access notices or library news?

8. Can the user select the length of the system messages (e.g., long or short error messages, or help displays)?

9. Is there a "break" or "interrupt" key or command (e.g., Esc key)?

10. Can the user return to a previous screen and change a selection?

11. Does the system support downloading bibliographic records to the local user's personal computer?

12. Can the user communicate interactively with library staff through the OPAC whenever he/she has trouble finding material on a subject?

13. Can the user transmit search results via e-mail?

14. Does the system offer online mailboxes for user suggestions and comments?

15. Can the user send messages to a specific library staff member or department?

Section 3
Searching

1. Can the user set default values for:
   a. search type (e.g., A, T, S)?
   b. field(s) in which a keyword is to be searched?
   c. display format?
   d. dialogue mode (command or menu)?
2. Can the user reset the default values during a search session?
3. Can the user start a search anywhere?
4. Can the user continue or start a search directly from the HELP screen?
5. Does the system:
   a. permit keyword searching of the controlled vocabulary (i.e. keyword subject search & keyword author search)?
   b. support keyword title search?
6. Does the system support keyword searching anywhere in the record?
7. a. Does the system have stop words?
   b. Is there a list of stop words available for display?
   c. Does the system indicate that the word is not indexed, when the user tries to search a stop word?
8. Which of the following Boolean operators are available?
   a. AND
   b. OR
   c. NOT
9. When is Boolean searching supported?
   a. in keyword author search
   b. in keyword title search
   c. in keyword subject search
   d. in keyword search not limited to any fields
   e. in cross-fields searches (i.e. two or more fields)
10. Is there an unlimited number of Boolean operators which can be used in a single search?
11. Is a word adjacency operator available?
12. Is a word proximity operator available?

13. In multi-word searches, does the system explain that a space is the same as AND or ADJ?

14. Can a user specify:
    a. left-truncation (e.g., #ism)?
    b. right-truncation?
    c. wildcard characters (e.g., WOM#N)?
    d. variable length wildcard characters (e.g., BEHAVI#R gets both BEHAVIOR and BEHAVIOUR)?
    e. user specified limits on truncation (e.g., LIBRAR*3 to get LIBRARY and LIBRARIES but not LIBRARIANSHIP?

15. Does the system support weighted term search by ranking the search terms by:
    a. the user?
    b. the system?

16. Can searches be limited by:
    a. publisher?
    b. type of material (e.g., serials, monograph, etc.)?
    c. library location?
    d. date of publication?
    e. language of publication?

17. Does the system allow the user to indicate which of the retrieved records are relevant to the search question and use the feedback information to automatically generate searches based on some algorithm to locate other items in the collection that are similar to the relevant record?

18. Having retrieved a document record, can the user directly access another document cited in it?

19. Can the user "browse" up a list of index terms which are near the search term/phrase:
    a. in author search?
    b. in title search?
    c. in subject search?
    d. Do the indexes include cross-references?

20. Can the user save a search strategy to be used again later?

21. Can the user save search results in sets for later use?

22. Can the user easily switch from one type of search to another (e.g., author search to title search)?

Section 4
Subject Search Aids
1. Can the user browse a display of:
   a. classification outlines?
   b. classification schedules?
2. Can the user view a group of subject headings:
   a. which begin with the search term(s)?
   b. which include the search term wherever imbedded in the subject headings?
3. Does the system display the following cross-references:
   a. SEE/USE?
   b. SEE ALSO/BT/NT/RT?
4. Does the system have transparent SEE/USE references which automatically substitute the user's input term with the correct subject heading without informing the user?
5. Does the system convert an original zero hit subject search to title, keyword title or keyword subject search?

Section 5
Access Points
Does the system provide access via the following?
1. Personal author
2. Corporate author
3. Author/title
4. Title
5. Subject
6. Series
7. Notes
8. Author keyword
9. Title keyword
10. Subject Keyword
11. Notes Keyword
12. ISBN
13. ISSN
14. Government document number

15. LC card number
16. LC call number
17. Dewey Decimal Classification number
18. Circulation bar code number
19. Table of contents of books
20. Citations within the text
21. Indexes of books

Section 6
Screen Display

1. Does the display text use both UPPER and lower case?
2. Are the fields of the display labeled: (e.g., AUTHOR=)
   a. in brief bibliographic display?
   b. in long bibliographic display?
3. Is the number of hits retrieved reported before they are displayed, so that if more hits have been retrieved than are really wanted, one of the limiting devices can be used?
4. Does the system offer both brief bibliographic display and long bibliographic display?
5. Is the search request always displayed on the screen, so that the user can see what was typed while viewing the hits?
6. Is the circulation status of an item always shown on the same screen with its call number?
7. Is the total number of items to be displayed identified in the display of each item (e.g., item 1 of 100)?
8. Are items in a set numbered successively (e.g., 1 to 8, 9 to 18, etc.) when there are more items than can be displayed on one screen?
9. Are the limits to the number of hits which can be displayed equal to 150 (±50)?

Section 7
Output Control

1. Can the user select specific field(s) for display?
2. When multiple records are retrieved in a single search, can the user select:
   a. any single record for display?

b. several records not in sequence for display (e.g., record #2, #5, etc.)?

c. a range of records for display (i.e. by specifying the first and the last records. e.g., from record #5 to #9)?

3. Can the results of several searches be merged for display?

4. Can the user specify that search results be sorted by:
   a. author?
   b. title?
   c. subject?
   d. call number?
   e. date of publication?

5. Does the system support ranked document display in decreasing order of probable relevance to the search query?

6. Does the system display results by paging?

Section 8
Commands

1. Does each command have the same role in every context?

2. Are function key definitions consistent (e.g., F1 always invokes help)?

3. Can function keys be used to reduce the number of keystrokes required to enter commonly used commands?

4. Do all the commands have a standardized syntax?

5. Is the number of keystrokes kept to a minimum?

6. Is there minimal or familiar punctuation in the commands (i.e., 3)?

7. Are mnemonic abbreviations used for the commands (e.g., A for Author)?

8. Can commands be stacked (i.e. typing in several commands in a group and executing them all at once, e.g., to indicate that the search results are to be displayed in a brief format, arranged alphabetically by title)?

9. In title or title/author searches, are leading articles ignored by the system?

10. a. Can the user omit "−" for LCSH subdivisions?

    b. Does the system ignore punctuation entered by the user when they are not required?

11. Will the system accept an author's name in any order (e.g., Smith A or A Smith)?

12. Can searches be entered using a mix of UPper and lowER case?

Section 9

User Assistance

1. Does the system provide a list of accessible databases?
2. Does the system provide a list of search types?
3. Is there an online tutorial?
4. a. Are there general help messages, providing information on various aspects of search strategies, which can be called up at any point?
   b. Are they helpful?
5. a. Are there contextual help messages, specific to the point in the search reached by the user?
   b. Are they helpful?
6. a. Does the system routinely provide procedural prompts or guiding comments to indicate possible next steps during a search?
   b. Are they helpful?
7. Is an explanation of what the system is doing displayed when searching takes a long time?
8. a. Does the system provide error messages?
   b. Are they clear enough?
9. a. Does the system identify who to ask if the user needs help?
   b. Does the system identify where printed instructions are available?
10. Does the system make it clear how to edit input?
11. Is spell check software available to the user?
12. Does the system show the elapsed session time?

Section 10

Remote Access

1. Is there adequate logon instruction (i.e., explanation of which terminal types are supported)?
2. Are the contents and coverage of OPAC clearly explained?
3. Are the key equivalencies explained for remote user's keyboard?

4. Is there adequate logoff instruction?
5. Is the screen display always clean (i.e., no garbage characters)?
6. a. Is remote access unrestricted in terms of time of day?
   b. Does the system tell the user if there is a time limit to remote sessions?
   c. Does the system give a warning message for automatic logoff if there is no user input?
7. Does the remote user have access to the same OPAC as those who use dedicated terminals in the library?
8. Does the system indicate where the remote user can get additional help?

Report of the Task Force on Library Instruction*

IOIOIOIOIOIOIOIOIOIOIOIOIOIOIOIOIOIOIOIOIOIOIOIOIOIOIOIOIOIOIOIOIOIOIOIOIOIOIOIOIOI

SUMMARY

The Joint Task Force on Library Instruction proposes a modular approach to learning the campus-wide information infrastructure. The modules include a highly evolved information network providing access to information resources and instruction in their use; course integrated instruction; workshops; short domain-based courses and a three-hour course on information strategies and skills.

CONTENTS

Introduction
Recommendations
    Recommendation 1: Create and Maintain Networked Information Resources
    Recommendation 2: Bring Course Integrated Instruction to the Academic Community
    Recommendation 3: Present Multi-tiered Workshops
    Recommendation 4: Offer Short Domain-based Courses
    Recommendation 5: Teach a Semester Length Three-Hour Course
Additional Recommendations
Conclusions
Appendix A: Course Syllabus and Reading List

TEXT
Introduction
The Joint Task Force on Library Instruction is a collaborative venture between the Graduate School of Library and Information Science and

---

*University of Illinois at Urbana-Champaign, May 1995

the University Library. The charge of the Task Force was "to develop a new generation of instructional programs for the library which would largely replace Bibliographic Instruction as we know it currently."

The Task Force identified the major components of the current bibliographic instruction program, drawing on the efforts of the Reference Services and User Education subcommittee, the Task Force on Electronic Research Services, and the knowledge of its own members. The Library reaches over 5,000 students each year through programs like Rhetoric 105, Speech Communication 111, Economics 173, and numerous other course-integrated library instruction sessions. These programs, however, are targeted almost exclusively to undergraduates, with an emphasis on reaching first-year students. It was further noted that the volume of information that needs to be communicated has grown exponentially while the time and space available to the task has remained the same or shrunk. Further, the constraints of conducting the majority of these class sessions in a single room in the Undergraduate Library has added its own logistical challenge to the instructional efforts of the University Library and its faculty and staff.

Not only undergraduate students, but the entire campus community, have significant needs for becoming aware of and familiar with the campus information infrastructure and the Library's programs and services. Information access technology has fundamentally changed the possibilities for exploiting the full potential of access to information and making it available to a wider audience than ever before. These changes require new partnerships and collaborations between many different campus groups to chart the way; to ensure the appropriate presence of the information infrastructure; and to make massive bodies of information from heterogeneous sources compatible, intelligible, and accessible to very wide ranges of students and scholars of all levels. Few structures are currently in place which support such partnerships and collaborations and what links there are appear to be weak and tenuous. For example, no structure is in place to support collaboration with other faculty in incorporating knowledge about these new information technologies and services into the curriculum at the undergraduate or graduate level.

As the Task Force continued its work, the terms "library instruction" or "bibliographic instruction" came to be seen as much too limiting in describing the instructional program it was envisioning. A phrase that came closer to describing and redefining the scope of our vision was "synergistic information matrix." We were looking for a structure that could connect and unite the information community on this campus; that would establish connections between people and their information needs; and that could create an evolving mechanism for teaching the community to learn about information. This information infrastructure cannot be built by one campus-unit acting alone, but requires the combined action of contributing campus community members. We see major roles for the faculty of the Library and other academic units, for university-wide computing services, and for the utilization of the vast resources of the Internet to integrate disparate information sources into a syndetic community. The primary role for librarians will be as information managers and as information advocates, establishing connections between people and their information needs and helping people to exploit the full potential of access to information.

Networks and networked information allow for the possibility of distributed education delivered to learners at a time and place convenient to them. The Task Force notes that this is an auspicious time for its work. There are several campus-wide initiatives, including Academic Plan 2000, the Campus Working Group on Academic Information and Library Information, and SCALE: Sloan Center for Asynchronous Learning Environments which focus on the integration of computer technologies with instruction and information delivery. The kind of physical access to information that the network offers needs to be matched by strategies for providing intellectual access. Through closer ties with other campus information service providers like the Computing and Communications Services Office, the Library and the Graduate School of Library and Information Science can create and deliver an integrated instructional program which will meet the needs of the campus now, in the year 2000 and beyond.

The Task Force identified three major goals for configuring a new instructional program for the campus: information literacy, increased collaboration between librarians and other faculty, and the development and coordination of a campus-wide integrated information infrastructure.

The first goal, information literacy, has been defined by the American Library Association Presidential Committee on Information Literacy in their Final Report, January, 1989. "To be information literate, a person must be able to recognize when information is needed and have the ability to locate, evaluate, and use effectively the needed information." American Library Association. Presidential Committee on Information Literacy, *American Library Association Presidential Committee on Information Literacy: Final Report* (Chicago: American Library Association, [1989]), 1. The Library must play a major collaborative role in helping students, faculty and staff acquire the necessary abilities by which they can achieve information literacy. The acquiring of information literacy requires a carefully honed partnership if it is to be realized. The vast resources of the Library, the University, and the Internet are of little value to those who cannot recognize their information needs and who do not know how to solve their information problems. These same resources are merely a source of frustration to those who know they need information but lack the tools, skills, and strategies to find, assess, and use the information.

Establishing and maintaining collaborative roles between librarians and other faculty is crucial to the development and implementation of any new integrated information instruction program. Librarians have a significant expertise to share with other faculty in the continued development of curricula and courses that include research and writing as important elements. Part of the urgency in meeting this goal is the realization that librarians can directly meet only a very small part of the information literacy needs of the students of this campus through traditional course-integrated instructional sessions. These sessions have traditionally focused very narrowly on the tools needed to meet the pressing needs of an assignment. Other crucial aspects of information literacy such as assessing and evaluating materials or recognizing information needs independently are omitted due to constraints of time, space, and human resources available to the task. A further constraint is the sheer number of courses which might benefit from the participation of librarians. A more effective and efficient information instruction program would provide the foundation for librarians to work with other faculty in designing the integration of information literacy skills into the entire fabric of a course. Information literacy skills need to be viewed as an integral aspect of learning a discipline and need to be incorporated throughout the curricula. Only by working together, with librarians and other faculty contributing from their spheres of expertise can this integration be accomplished. Finding new structures to support this collaboration will be an important aim. The third goal identified by the Task Force is the development and maintenance of the information infrastructure. This includes the development of human resources within the Library to enable each member to reach high and sustained levels of information expertise in all formats and media. It also includes the development and maintenance of the physical supports of the information infrastructure. Many librarians are inhibited in their development by the lack of access to suitable equipment and technical support. It is hard to create a program based on the use of software and network developments if one has to travel to another unit, building, or site to even view the software. It is even harder if there is no local support for the effective use of the software. The Library needs to work with the Computing and Communications Services Office, the Graduate School of Library and Information Science, and other units on campus, such as the Office of Instructional Resources and Administrative Information Systems and Services, to develop and implement this information infrastructure.

RECOMMENDATIONS

The Task Force has created a modular plan with a number of components designed to meet the information instructional needs of the campus community. The central point from which all other components revolve and radiate is a strong presence on the World Wide Web. This presence is a starting point for those who wish to discover what information resources and services are available to them and also provides a minimal level of instruction and support in using those resources and services. It provides an environment in which exploratory or discovery learning may flourish. For those who wish, independently, to further their information skills, there are a variety of basic workshops which focus primarily on information tools. For those wishing a more conceptual approach to information skills and strategies, there are short domain-based courses of half a semester; and for those who wish to have more formal instruction and guidance the modular approach offers a semester-length three-hour course. At the heart of this plan are strong recommendations for collaboration between librarians and other faculty to integrate information literacy into courses and our recommendations provide a number of avenues by which this can come to fruition. Information that will be used in many different ways needs to be taught in many different ways.

Recommendation 1:
Create and Maintain Networked Information Resources

Networked information resources, the nucleus of our instructional program, will allow the campus community to approach learning about information diachronically. The user will be able to explore and to discover information, not limited by the imposition of time and scheduling constraints. The Library will develop and maintain a virtual presence within the campus community (and beyond) where users can turn for necessary information at the time of need on the use of traditional materials and electronic resources and where users can access useful networked information sources that have been identified, collected, organized, and authorized as trustworthy by librarians. A networked information resource will reach the greatest number of users in the most efficient and effective way and provide the fundamentals necessary to begin to use the campus information system in an intelligent manner.

The strength of this system will derive from partial overlapping of many different threads of connectedness across the information landscape. A large variety of resources will be created and maintained by librarians to create this information infrastructure and will include, but will not be limited to the following: library orientation materials, such as interactive online tours, information related to the library system, its units, its services, policies and collections. Locally produced library guides, bibliographies, etc. will also be mounted with appropriate links, leading the user to discover other information as he or she explores the information infrastructure.

Librarians will also play a principal role in collaboration with campus units to organize information which is currently scattered among multiple offices and units and difficult to access via the campus network. Campus information includes information produced and statistics compiled by various administrative units; calendars of events; deadlines; library workshop announcements; etc.

In addition to those sources and resources created and produced by librarians, other sources, available through a variety of different means, both commercial and non-profit, such as electronic dictionaries, encyclopedias, and other reference sources, will also be carefully selected, mounted and maintained.

As part of the instructional component, computer assisted instruction (CAI) modules related to library use and the research process (possibly commercially produced, locally adapted and modified) will also be included. As more and more hypertextual learning tools become available they too will be mounted. Other instruction programs available through e-mail (e.g., Crispen's "Roadmap") and gopher client/server protocols (e.g., UIC's "Ride the Etrain") and Web-based programs will also be made available.

Recommendation 2:
Bring Course Integrated Instruction to the Academic Community

A second component, equally important, of networked information resources will be geared towards individual information needs and particular courses. Working closely with other faculty, librarians will play a more active role in the provision of information, in support of course assignments and activities. Being a member of a problem-solving team, librarians will be readily and easily available through asynchronous learning networks, such as *FirstClass* and *PacerForum*, to help both faculty and students solve their information problems on an as-needed basis.

Currently, most course integrated instruction consists of a one-time, one-hour presentation to a class. At UIUC, primarily these hours consist of making students aware that the library exists (overviews of the library, of the arrangement/location of materials, hours, etc.) and of the services which it offers. This current practice, however, does not fall within the intended domain of course integrated instruction, or if it does, only by virtue of the fact that it takes place in an hour which has been reserved by an instructor for the purpose of "library instruction." The informational aspects of this hour need to be obtained through other means since it is neither efficient nor cost-effective to have librarians utilizing an hour of time when a simple, well-designed hand-out or a Web page could provide students with the same information. Rather than looking towards students as primary clientele, librarians need to see other faculty as their primary clientele, collaborating with them to meet the information needs of the students within a particular course and helping to guide the instructor in the best utilization of the information infrastructure to meet the information needs of the students. Librarians can take the lead in designing portions of the curriculum which will be information needs relevant to the students. This may involve, for example, providing students with a lecture or two on the intellectual topography and the structure of information as it relates to the subject matter of the course; helping students grasp the character of a body of literature; or providing students with a basis for independent evaluation both of a body of literature and of the status of "authorities in the field."

The potential for collaboration using asynchronous learning networks is boundless, but needs to be carefully exploited.

Recommendation 3:
Present Multi-tiered Workshops

As students advance in their skills and knowledge of the information infrastructure, it seems most appropriate to expend greater human resources to help those with serious information needs learn in more depth important access tools for finding information and solving information problems. Workshops are one such vehicle for providing more in-depth training on an informal basis as students discover their own gaps and limitations in navigating the information infrastructure. We are proposing a series of workshops to be presented on a regular basis and as demand warrants.

A three-tiered approach is recommended:

- Tier one will offer basic orientation to the campus information infrastructure and to campus information services by means of tours (primarily via the World Wide Web), videos, and multimedia presentations.
- Tier Two will offer tool-based workshops, including instruction in the use of the local online catalog and its various interfaces; indexing and abstracting tools; and the Internet in collaboration with the Computing and Communications Services Office.
- Tier Three will offer concepts-based workshops and will have as prerequisites Tier Two workshops. Some examples of Tier Three workshops topics are pre-research papers, discussing topic selection, types and formats of information, the publication cycle, etc.; finding information on potential employers; finding statistical information; finding biographical information; finding government information; researching current events; etc.

The above workshops are geared toward the undergraduate, but the entire campus community is welcome to attend. However, graduate students and faculty often have information needs far different from those of undergraduates, and special workshops will need to be tailored to meet their needs. These faculty-graduate student workshops will provide some of the necessary marketing and public relations work which this Task Force deems necessary to revitalize the collaborative relationship between librarians and other faculty. One workshop might be entitled, "Collaborating with Librarians to Meet Research and Teaching Needs." Possible topics are using the Internet for current awareness in [name the discipline] and scholarly communication; issues in electronic publishing for faculty; publishing on the Internet, issues and trends. Other workshops might be on new software packages to enhance research capabilities; for example, using *Pro-Cite* to maintain a large bibliographic database; up-loading records from online catalogs and locally-mounted indexes and abstracts to a personal bibliographic database. With increased collaboration, other workshops that can best serve the needs of the faculty will be identified.

Recommendation 4:
Offer Short Domain-based Courses

Designed to address areas of information literacy beyond skills and tools, one-credit courses will be taught during the academic year by librarians. Students will undertake study and discussion on concepts that are important for many types of professional work or graduate work. Issues addressed will have minimal overlap with the skills covered in workshops or short courses offered to departments and will generally be at a more conceptual level. Topics to be addressed include: the nature of information; the organization of information; patterns of scholarly communication; patterns of business communications; publishing and the publications sequence; the value of information; teaching information use skills.

Course format will generally be lecture/discussion. Students will be evaluated on the basis of their contribution to class discussion and the writing of brief, analytic papers.

Courses will be specific to broad academic disciplines and will span over one half of a semester; course content will vary somewhat by semester. For example, one semester might focus on the practical use of journal literature in business; another semester might focus on the changing nature of scholarly communication as a result of electronic information exchange. Another course might address the information uses of mass media.

These short courses will be open to any student at UIUC. In order to be useful as credit for graduate students, the Task Force recommends courses at the 300 level. Taught by librarians in order to bring a conceptual basis to the study of information infrastructures, the course will meet in a regular UIUC classroom equipped with a network connection, projection equipment, etc.

Recommendation 5:
Teach a Semester Length Three-Hour Course

The Library and the Graduate School of Library and Information Science will collaboratively offer *Information Seeking Strategies and Skills*, a semester-long, three-hour course, providing undergraduate students with an opportunity to acquire critical strategies and skills necessary for effective and efficient information problem-solving in an integrated and supportive classroom- based environment, characterized by ongoing instructor feedback. The students who are reached by this course will become highly sophisticated thinkers about and end users of information: how it is created, produced, distributed, accessed and used. There are, however, opportunities for reaching a larger student community through the use of asynchronous learning systems. The Task Force sees no reason why asynchronous learning systems might not also serve this course well, allowing it to reach a larger audience. We recommend that this become an important realm for further exploration. A sample syllabus and reading list is included in Appendix A.

Additional Recommendations

The Library currently has the talent on which to draw to implement such an instruction program, yet a number of obstacles stand in the way of a fully integrated information infrastructure, a synergistic information matrix, on this campus. One is a basic lack of a library network and the necessary computing tools on every librarian's desktop to carry through this vision. Another impediment appears to be that there is no one person who has a sense of the campus information needs as a whole and we suggest that a librarian be appointed whose business it would be to know about those campus information needs. There appear to be many groups on this campus who have charges and interests of a nature quite similar to this Task Force but with different focuses. By joining forces and resources with these groups, librarians would be in a better position to serve the needs of the campus community. Some resources could indeed come from restructuring library services and the way that librarians currently utilize their time and place their efforts. Careful thought and consideration must be given to the models and paradigms that are currently in place for providing information services to the campus community and look to new models and paradigms as our awareness of how information technologies can be utilized for more effective and efficient service provision grows. This vision, perhaps, implies a retooling of the library staff infrastructure and argues for a pro-active stance to be taken.

Conclusion

By following this modular approach, different components can be combined in a variety of ways to meet the information needs and learning styles of the greatest number of members of the campus community. The modular approach also allows flexibility in implementation, based on resources and staff. The first module to be supported should be the creation and maintenance of networked-based resources and instruction. Some of the modules currently in place for example, the catalog workshops, can be continued and augmented over time. A majority of resources should, at this time, be directed towards the creation and maintenance of networked-based resources and instruction, the nucleus of our recommendations.

Respectfully submitted,
Marcella Genz, Chair
Library Instruction Task Force

Lori Foulke
Lisa Janicke
Shellie Jeffries
Kathleen Kleugel
Gregory B. Newby
Beth Woodard
Joyce Wright

Appendix A:
Course Syllabus and Reading List

LIS 2XX: Information Seeking Strategies and Skills

Course Description: Provides the critical strategies and skills needed by students to undertake effective and efficient information problem solving within formally structured systems and informal situations. Focuses on the exploration, discovery, management, use, and evaluation of information and information sources in any discipline. Uses and explores print and electronic resources including those found in the library and on the Internet.

Intended Audience: Upper-Division undergraduate students, with selected major(s), and anticipated research needs.

Course Outline

Week One
Class 1   Introduction/Orientation
Class 2   The Nature of Information
Class 3   Organization of Information

Week Two
Class 1   The UIUC Library and Its Resources
Class 2   Online Catalog Workshop
Class 3   Patterns of Scholarly Communication

Week Three
Class 1   Discipline & Interdisciplinary Scholarship
Class 2   What Libraries are Trying to Accomplish

Class 3   Publishing and The Publication Sequence

Week Four
Class 1   Information Needs Analysis
Class 2   The Research Process and Search Strategies
Class 3   Information Problem Solving and Conceptual Frameworks

Week Five
Class 1   Documenting Information Strategies; Finding Finding Tools
Class 2   Nature of Non-Scholarly Communication; Unpublished
           Information
Class 3   Authority/Validity/Evaluation

Week Six
Class 1   Finding Information on Current Events
Class 2   Research Literature in a Discipline
Class 3   Periodical Indexes

Week Seven
Class 1   Electronic Databases
Class 2   IBIS Workshop
Class 3   Research Literature in Another Discipline

Week Eight
Class 1   Electronic Information Sources
Class 2   Using the Internet to Find Information, Part 1
Class 3   Using the Internet to Find Information, Part 2

Week Nine
Class 1   Using the Internet to Find Information, Part 3
Class 2   Intellectual Property and Copyright
Class 3   Statistics and Data Overview

Week Ten
Class 1   Government Statistics
Class 2   Social Science Data

Class 3   Biographical Information

Week Eleven
Class 1   Corporate and Industry Information
Class 2   Information about Organizations
Class 3   Reviews & Criticisms

Week Twelve
Class 1   Government Information - Hearings & Laws
Class 2   Government Information - Regulations
Class 3   Interacting with the Government, e.g. Student Loans, Taxes, Social Security

Week Thirteen
Class 1   Locating Places in Print
Class 2   Locating Places Electronically
Class 3   Map Room Tour

Week Fourteen
Class 1   Fugitive literature
Class 2   Archival materials
Class 3   "Alternative Literature"

Week Fifteen
Class 1   Information Analysis Revisited
Class 2   "What I Know Now"
Class 3   Summary; Course Evaluation

Reading List for LIS 2XX: Information Seeking Strategies and Skills:

Altheide, David L. "The Culture of Information." *Journal of Education for Library and Information Science*, 31, no.2 (1990): 113-121.

Biblio-Tech: Survival Skills for the Information Age. Waterbury, VT: Community College of Vermont, 1987.

Boorstin, David J. *Gresham 's Law, Knowledge or Information?: Remarks at the White House Conference on Library and Information Services, November 19, 1979*. Washington, DC: Library of Congress, 1980.

Garvey, William D. & Griffith, Belver C. "Scientific Communication: Its Role in the Conduct of Research and Creation of Knowledge." *American Psychologist* (1971): 349-362.

ıoıoıoıoıoıoıoıoıoıoıoıoıoıoıoıoıoıoıoıoıoıoıoıoıoıoıoıoıoıoıoıoıoıoıoıoıoıoıoıoıoıoıoıoıoıoıoıoıoıoıoıoıoıoıoıoıoıoıoıoıoıoıoıoıoıoıoıoı

Kronick, David A. "Writing, Publication Cycle" in *The Literature of the Life Sciences*, 68-70. Philadelphia: ISI Press, 1985.

Lee, Martin A. and Norman Solomon. *Unreliable Sources: A Guide to Detecting Bias in News Media*. New York: Carol Publishing Group, l990.

Mann, Thomas. *Library Research Models: A Guide to Classification, Cataloging, and Computers*. New York: Oxford University Press, 1993.

McCarthy, Michael J. *Mastering the Information Age: A Course in Working Smarter, Thinking Better, and Learning Faster*. New York: St. Martin's Press, 1991.

The Encyclopedia of Library and Information Science, s.v. "Scientific Literature."

West, Charles K. *The Social and Psychological Distortion of Information*. Chicago: Nelson-Hall, 1981.

Wurman, Richard Saul. *Information Anxiety*. New York: Doubleday, 1989.

Principal Abbreviations or Acronyms in the Text

IOIOIOIOIOIOIOIOIOIOIOIOIOIOIOIOIOIOIOIOIOIOIOIOIOIOIOIOIOIOIOIOIOIOIOIOIOIOIOIOI

ACQNET-L	An Internet listserv devoted to acquisitions topics
ACRL	Association of College & Research Libraries
ADONIS	(Originally an acronym for) Article Delivery Over Network Information Systems, now a full-text journal article service on CD-ROM
AI	Artificial intelligence
ALA	American Library Association
ANSI	American National Standards Institute
ARPA	Advanced Research Projects Agency
ASCII	American Standard Code for Information Interchange
BI-L	A listserv devoted to the topic of bibliographic instruction
BRS	Bibliographic Retrieval Services
CAI	Computer-assisted instruction
CATRIONA	Cataloguing And Retrieval of Information Over Network Applications
CBI	Collection balance indicator
CBT	Computer-based training
CD-ROM	Compact disk, read-only memory
CGI	Common Gateway Interface
CIC	Committee on Institutional Cooperation
CIP	Cataloging in publication
CPU	Central processing unit
DIALOG	A commercial online search service
DLHS	Digital Library for the Health Sciences
E-conference	An electronic discussion group that communicates over the Internet

EDI	Electronic Data Interchange
ELSA	Electronic Library Search Assistant
ERIC	Educational Resources Information Center
ETS	Electronic Text Service
Free-net	A not-for-profit, usually community-based Internet access organization
FTP	File transfer protocol
GII	Global Information Infrastructure
HEGIS	Higher Education General Information Survey
HTML	Hypertext markup language
IETF	Internet Engineering Task Force
ILCSO	Illinois Library Computer Systems Organization
ILL	Interlibrary loan
INNOPAC	The online public access catalog system produced by Innovative Interfaces, Inc
IPEDS	Integrated Postsecondary Education Data System
ISBN	International Standard Book Number
ISU	Illinois State University
JSTOR	(Journal Storage), a project that creates high quality bit-mapped images of back issues of important journals
KNAW	Royal Netherlands Academy of Arts and Sciences
LAN	Local area network
LC MARC	Library of Congress Machine readable cataloging format
LC	Library of Congress
LCD	Last circulation date
LCSH	Library of Congress Subject Headings
LIAS	Pennsylvania State University's online catalog system
LIRT	Library Instruction Round Table, a section within the American Library Association
Listserv	An electronic discussion group that communicates over the Internet
LOEX	Library Orientation and Exchange, a clearinghouse for instructional materials

LUIS	Library User Information System: the public access module of the NOTIS online catalog system (now Ameritech Library Systems)
MARC	Machine-Readable Cataloging
MEDLINE	Medical Literature Analysis and Retrieval System (MEDLARS) Online
MELVYL	The online union catalog of the University of California system
NASA	National Aeronautics and Space Administration
NCSA	National Center for Supercomputing Applications
NETTRAIN	An electronic listserv devoted to teaching the use of the Internet
NII	National Information Infrastructure
NLM	National Library of Medicine
NREN	National Research and Education Network
NSF	National Science Foundation
NTIS	National Technical Information Service
OCLC	Online Computer Library Center
OCR	Optical character recognition
OLIVE	An experimental interactive online system developed in England
OPAC	Online public access catalog
OSI	Open Systems Interconnection
PC	Personal computer
PEU	Percentage of expected use
PLA	Public Library Association
RBH	Ratio of borrowings to holdings
RLG	Research Libraries Group
RLIN	Research Libraries Information Network
SDI	Selective dissemination of information
SGML	Standard generalized markup language
SUNY	State University of New York
TCP/IP	Transmission control protocol/Internet protocol
TEI	Text encoding initiative
TLA	Transaction log analysis
TOC	Table of contents

IOI

TULIP	The University Licensing Program
URC	Uniform Resource Citation
Web, WWW	World Wide Web
X12	A set of standard protocols approved by ANSI and used in the electronic transmission of book ordering information among publishers, vendors, and libraries
Z39.50	A set of protocols that enable the search and retrieval of bibliographic records across different online systems

REFERENCES

Abbott, C. and Smith, N. Resourcing issues. In: *CD-ROM in Libraries: Management Issues*; ed. by T. Hanson and J. Day, pp. 39-55. London, Bowker-Saur, 1994.

Abels, E. G. and Liebscher, P. A new challenge for intermediary-client communication: the electronic network. *Reference Librarian*, 41/42, 1994, 185-196.

Adelman, L. *Evaluating Decision Support and Expert Systems*. New York, Wiley, 1992.

Aguilar, W. The application of relative use and interlibrary demand in collection development. *Collection Management*, 8(1), 1986, 15-24.

Aguilar, W. *Relationship Between Classes of Books Circulated and Classes of Books Requested on Interlibrary Loan*. Doctoral dissertation. Urbana-Champaign, University of Illinois, Graduate School of Library and Information Science, 1984.

Alberico, R. Remarks at the Symposium on the Role of Network-Based Electronic Resources in Scholarly Communication and Research; ed. by C. W. Bailey, Jr., and D. Rooks. *Public-Access Computer Systems Review*, 2, 1991, 152-198.

Alberico, R. and Micco, M. *Expert Systems for Reference and Information Retrieval*. Westport, CT, Meckler, 1990.

Allen, B. Academic information services: a library management perspective. *Library Trends*, 43, 1995, 645-662.

Allen, G. Patron response to bibliographic databases on CD-ROM. *RQ*, 29, 1989a, 103-110.

Allen, M. B. Focusing the one-shot lecture. *Research Strategies*, 7, 1989b, 100-105.

Anders, V. et al. A glimpse into a crystal ball: academic libraries in the year 2000. *Wilson Library Bulletin*, 67(2), 1992, 36-40.

Ankeny, M. L. Evaluating end-user services: success or satisfaction? *Journal of Academic Librarianship*, 16, 1991, 352-356.

Annual Review of OCLC Research July 1991-June 1992. Dublin, OH, OCLC Inc., 1992.

Arms, W. Y. The institutional implications of electronic information. *Leonardo*, 27, 1994, 165-169.

Arnold, K. Acquisitions policy in an electronic world. In: *Electronic Documents and Information: from Preservation to Access*; ed. by A. H. Helal and J. W. Weiss, pp. 68-77. Essen, Essen University Library, 1996.

Arnold, K. Virtual transformations: the evolution of publication media. *Library Trends*, 43, 1995, 609-626.

Atkinson, R. The acquisitions librarian as change agent in the transition to the electronic library. *Library Resources & Technical Services*, 36, 1992, 7-20.

Atkinson, R. The coming contest. *College & Research Libraries*, 54, 1993a, 458-460.

Atkinson, R. Library functions, scholarly communication, and the foundation of the digital library: laying claim to the control zone. *Library Quarterly*, 66, 1996, 239-265.

Atkinson, R. Networks, hypertext, and academic information services: some longer-range implications. *College & Research Libraries*, 54, 1993b, 199-215.

Atkinson, R. Text mutability and collection administration. *Library Acquisitions: Practice & Theory*, 14, 1990, 355-358.

Bailey, C. W., Jr. The Intelligent Reference Information System project: a merger of CD-ROM LAN and expert system technologies. *Information Technology and Libraries*, 11, 1992, 237-244.

Bailey, C. W., Jr. and Myers, J. E., eds. *Expert Systems in ARL Libraries*. Washington, DC, Association of Research Libraries, 1991. SPEC Kit 174.

Bainbridge, D. I. Computer-aided diagnosis and negligence. *Medicine, Science and the Law*, 31, 1991, 127-136.

Baker, B. A conceptual framework for teaching online catalog use. *Journal of Academic Librarianship*, 12, 1986, 90-96.

Baker, B. et al., eds. *The Evolving Educational Mission of the Library*. Chicago, Association of College & Research Libraries, Bibliographic Instruction Section, 1992.

Baker, S. L. and Lancaster, F. W. *The Measurement and Evaluation of Library Services*. Second edition. Arlington, VA, Information Resources Press, 1991.

Barbour, B. and Rubinyi, R. Remote access to CD-ROMs using generic communications software. *CD-ROM Professional*, 5(2), 1992, 62-65.

Barden, P. Multimedia document delivery—the birth of a new industry. *Online & CDROM Review*, 19, 1995, 321-323.

Batt, C. The libraries of the future: public libraries and the Internet. *IFLA Journal*, 22, 1996a, 27-30.

Batt, C. Public libraries, public Internet. *Electronic Library*, 14, 1996b, 127.

Batterbee, C. and Nicholas, D. CD-ROMs in public libraries: a survey. *Aslib Proceedings*, 47, 1995, 63-72.

Bauwens, M. The emergence of the "cybrarian": a new organisational model for corporate libraries. *Business Information Review*, 9(4), 1993, 65-67.

Bayne, P. S. et al. Implementing computer-based training for library staff. *Library Administration & Management*, 8, 1994, 78-81.

Bazillion, R. J. and Braun, C. *Academic Libraries as High-Tech Gateways: a Guide to Design and Space Decisions*. Chicago, American Library Association, 1995.

Beheshti, J. Retrieval interfaces for CD-ROM bibliographic databases. *CD-ROM Professional*, 4(1), 1991, 50-53.

Belkin, N. J. et al. Taking account of user tasks, goals and behavior for the design of online public access catalogs. *Proceedings of the American Society for Information Science*, 27, 1990, 69-79.

Bellamy, L. M. et al. Remote access to electronic library services through a campus network. *Bulletin of the Medical Library Association*, 79, 1991, 53-62.

Bennett, V. M. and Palmer, E. M. Electronic document delivery using the Internet. *Bulletin of the Medical Library Association*, 82, 1994, 163-167.

Benson, A. C. *The Complete Internet Companion for Librarians*. New York, Neal Schuman, 1995.

Bergen, C. *Instruments to Plague Us? Human Factors in the Management of Library Automation.* Bradford, UK, MCB University Press Ltd., 1988.

Berner, E. S. et al. Performance of four computer-based diagnostic systems. *New England Journal of Medicine,* 330, 1994, 1792-1796.

Berry, J. W. Digital libraries: new initiatives with worldwide implications. *IFLA Journal,* 22, 1996, 9-17.

Bianchi, G. and Giorgi, M. Towards an expert system as intelligent assistant for the design of an online documentation service. *Proceedings of the Tenth International Online Information Meeting,* pp. 199-208. Oxford, Learned Information, 1986.

Bills, L. G. and Helgerson, L. W. User interfaces for CD-ROM PACs. *Library Hi Tech,* 6(2), 1988, 73-115.

Birchall, A. et al. Knowledge automation and the need for intermediaries. *Journal of Librarianship and Information Science,* 26, 1994, 181-192.

Birdsall, W. F. *The Myth of the Electronic Library: Librarianship and Social Change in America.* Westport, CT, Greenwood Press, 1994.

Blinko, B. B. Academic staff, students and the Internet: the experience at the University of Westminster. *Electronic Library,* 14, 1996, 111-116.

Bobay, J. et al. Library services for remote users with LINKWAY. *Reference Services Review,* 18(3), 1990, 53-57.

Bonn, G. S. Evaluation of the collection. *Library Trends,* 22, 1973-1974, 265-304.

Borgman, C. L. et al. Rethinking online monitoring methods for information retrieval systems: from search product to search process. *Journal of the American Society for Information Science,* 47, 1996, 568-583.

Borman, S. Advances in electronic publishing herald changes for scientists. *Chemical & Engineering News,* 71, June 14, 1993, 10-24.

Bosch, V. M. and Hancock-Beaulieu, M. CDROM user interface evaluation: the appropriateness of GUIS. *Online & CDROM Review,* 19, 1995, 255-270.

Bosseau, D. L. The formerly virtually neutral library. *Journal of Academic Librarianship,* 21, 1995, 121-122.

Bothwell, I. and Lovejoy, F. Technological change: experiences and opinions of library workers. *Australian Academic & Research Libraries,* 18, 1987, 41-47.

Boyce, J. I. and Boyce, B. R. Library outreach programs in rural areas. *Library Trends,* 44, 1995, 112-128.

Bradley, P. *UKOLUG Quick Guide to CD-ROM Networking.* London, UK Online User Group, 1996.

Brahmi, F. A. The effect of CD-ROM MEDLINE on online end user and mediated searching. *Medical Reference Services Quarterly,* 7(4), 1988, 47-56.

Branse, Y. et al. Libraries on the Web. *Electronic Library,* 14, 1996, 117-121.

Brichford, M. and Maher, W. Archival issues in network electronic publications. *Library Trends,* 43, 1995, 701-712.

Brin, B. and Cochran, E. Access and ownership in the academic environment: one library's progress report. *Journal of Academic Librarianship,* 20, 1994, 207-212.

Bristow, A. Academic reference service over electronic mail. *College & Research Libraries News,* 53, 1992, 631-632, 637.

Britten, W. A. Remarks at the Symposium on the Role of Network-Based Electronic Resources in Scholarly Communication and Research; ed. by C. W. Bailey, Jr., and D. Rooks. *Public-Access Computer Systems Review*, 2, 1991, 152-198.

Britten, W. A. A use statistic for collection management: the 80/20 rule revisited. *Library Acquisitions: Practice & Theory*, 14, 1990, 183-189.

Britten, W. A. and Webster, J. D. Comparing characteristics of highly circulated titles for demand-driven collection development. *College & Research Libraries*, 53, 1992, 239-248.

Brown, J. Measuring system performance: the library's perspective. *Information Technology and Libraries*, 7, 1988, 184-185.

Brown, L. C. B. An expert system for predicting approval plan receipts. *Library Acquisitions: Practice & Theory*, 17, 1993, 155-164.

Brownson, C. W. Modeling library materials expenditure: initial experiments at Arizona State University. *Library Resources & Technical Services*, 35, 1991, 87-103.

Brudvig, G. L. Tailoring a journal article database to local needs: planning and management issues. *Journal of Library Administration*, 15 (3/4), 1991, 85-100.

Bryant, E. Reinventing the university press. *Library Journal*, 119 (14), 1994, 147-149.

Buckland, M. K. *Book Availability and the Library User*. New York, Pergamon Press, 1975.

Buckland, M. K. An operations research study of a variable loan and duplication policy at the University of Lancaster. *Library Quarterly*, 42, 1972, 97-106.

Buckland, M. K. and Hindle, A.. Loan policies, duplication and availability. In: *Planning Library Services*; ed. by A. G. Mackenzie and I. M. Stuart, pp. 1-16. Lancaster, UK, University of Lancaster Library, 1969.

Buildings, Books, and Bytes. Washington DC, Benton Foundation, 1996.

Bush, C.C. et al. Toward a new world order: a survey of outsourcing capabilities of vendors for acquisitions, cataloging and collection development services. *Library Acquisitions: Practice & Theory*, 18, 1994, 397-416.

Butcher, K. S. and Scott, S. R. Effects of CD-ROM in a university library. *Journal of Educational Media & Library Sciences*, 27, 1990, 257-269.

Butler, B. Electronic course reserves and digital libraries: progenitor and prognosis. *Journal of Academic Librarianship*, 22, 1996, 124-127.

Byrd, G. D. et al. Collection development using interlibrary loan borrowing and acquisitions statistics. *Bulletin of the Medical Library Association*, 70, 1982, 1-9.

Cain, M. Periodical access in an era of change: characteristics and a model. *Journal of Academic Librarianship*, 21, 1995, 365-370.

Campbell, N. Michigan State tested PromptCat prototype in fall 1993. http://www.oclc.org/oclc/new/n212/spreport.htm#sprart06, 1994.

Cargill, J. Automation and the change process: the human factors. In: *Proceedings of the Conference on Integrated Online Library Systems*; ed. by D. C. Genaway, pp. 197-218. Canfield, OH, Genaway Associates, 1987.

Carrigan, D. P. Data-guided collection development: a promise unfulfilled. *College & Research Libraries*, 57, 1996, 429-437.

Carson, S. M. and Freivalds, D. I. Z39.50 and LIAS: Penn State's experience. *Information Technology and Libraries*, 12, 1993, 230-237.

Caswell, J. V. et al. Importance and use of holding links between citation databases and online catalogs. *Journal of Academic Librarianship*, 21, 1995, 92-96.

CD-ROM Consistent Interface Committee. CD-ROM consistent interface guidelines: a final report. *CD-ROM Librarian*, 7(2), 1992, 18-29.

CEU addresses long-term access to electronic publications: collaboration with DATF welcomed. *Newsletter of the Commission on Preservation and Access*, Number 86, February 1996, 1, 3.

Chang, A. A database management system for interlibrary loan. *Information Technology and Libraries*, 9, 1990, 135-143.

Charles, S. K. and Clark, K. E. Enhancing CD-ROM searches with online updates: an examination of end-user needs, strategies, and problems. *College & Research Libraries*, 51, 1990, 321-328.

Chaudhry, A. S. Automation systems as tools of use studies and management information. *IFLA Journal*, 19, 1993, 397-409.

Cherry, J. M. et al. OPACs in twelve Canadian academic libraries: an evaluation of functional capabilities and interface features. *Information Technology and Libraries*, 13, 1994, 174-195.

Chrzastowski, T. E. Do workstations work too well? An investigation into library workstation popularity and the "principle of least effort." *Journal of the American Society for Information Science*, 46, 1995, 638-641.

Chrzastowski, T. E. Journal collection cost-effectiveness in an academic chemistry library: results of a cost/use survey at the University of Illinois at Urbana-Champaign. *Collection Management*, 14(1/2), 1991, 85-98.

Cibbarelli, P. R. et al. Choosing among the options for patron access databases: print, online, CD-ROM, or locally mounted. *Reference Librarian*, 39, 1993, 85-97.

Clement, G. Evolution of a species: science journals published on the Internet. *Database*, 17(5), 1994, 44-54.

Cline, N. M. Local or remote access: choices and issues. In: *Electronic Access to Information: a New Service Paradigm*; ed. by W.-S. S. Chiang and N. E. Elkington, pp. 17-24. Mountain View, CA, Research Libraries Group, 1994.

Cochenour, D. CICNet's electronic journal collection. *Serials Review*, 22(1), 1996, 63-68.

Collier, M. W. A model license for acquisition of electronic materials. In: *Electronic Documents and Information: from Preservation to Access*; ed. by A. H. Helal and J. W. Weiss, pp. 51-67. Essen, Essen University Library, 1996.

Collier, M. W. A model for the electronic university library. In: *Toward a Worldwide Library: a Ten Year Forecast*; ed. by A. H. Helal and J. W. Weiss. Essen, Essen University Library, 1997 (*in press*).

Connell, T. H. and Franklin, C. The Internet: educational issues. *Library Trends*, 42, 1994, 608-625.

Conte, R., Jr. Guiding lights. *Internet World*, 7(5), 1996, 41-44.

Conway, P. *Preservation in the Digital World*. Washington, DC, Commission on Preservation and Access, 1996.

Coulter, C. ALCTS creative ideas in technical services discussion group, Midwinter, 1996. *ACQNET*, 7, 7, February 27, 1996. (Email to ACQNET-L listserv, February 9, 1996 (Cynthia.Coulter@uni.edu)).

Cowan, B. M. and Usherwood, B. Automation routes past and present: the training implications. *Journal of Librarianship and Information Science*, 24, 1992, 139-148.

Cox, J. The CD-ROM market. In: *CD-ROM in Libraries: Management Issues*; ed. by T. Hanson and J. Day, pp. 5-21. London, Bowker-Saur, 1994.

Cox, J. Making your electronic information products promote and pay for each other. *Proceedings of the Fifteenth International Online Information Meeting*, 421-428. Medford, NJ, Learned Information, 1991.

Cox, J. and Hanson, T. Setting up an electronic current awareness service. *Online*, 16(4), 1992, 36-43.

Craghill, D. et al. *The Impact of IT on Staff Deployment in UK Public Libraries*. Boston Spa, British Library, 1989. British Library Research Paper 69.

Crawford, W. and Gorman, M. *Future Libraries: Dreams, Madness, & Reality*. Chicago, American Library Association, 1995.

Creth, S. D. Beyond technical issues: the impact of automation on library organizations. In: *Questions and Answers: Strategies for Using the Electronic Reference Collection*; ed. by L. C. Smith, pp. 4-13. Urbana-Champaign, University of Illinois, Graduate School of Library and Information Science, 1989.

Creth, S. D. A changing profession: central roles for academic librarians. *Advances in Librarianship*, 19, 1995, 85-98.

Creth, S. D. Personnel realities in the university library of the future. In: *The Future of the Academic Library: Proceedings of the Conference Held at the University of Wisconsin in September 1989*; ed. by E. P. Trani, pp. 45-62. Urbana-Champaign, University of Illinois, Graduate School of Library and Information Science, 1991. Occasional Papers 188 and 189.

Cromer, D. E. and Johnson, M. E. The impact of the Internet on communication among reference librarians. *Reference Librarian*, 41/42, 1994, 139-157.

Current Research and Development in Scientific Documentation, Number 15. Washington, DC, National Science Foundation, Office of Science Information Service, 1969.

Cutright, P. and Girrard, K. M. Remote access to CD-ROM for the distant learner. *CD-ROM Professional*, 4(6), 1991, 80-82.

Dainoff, M. J. Learning from office automation: ergonomics and human impact. In: *Human Aspects of Library Automation*; ed. by D. Shaw, pp. 16-29. Urbana-Champaign, University of Illinois, Graduate School of Library and Information Science, 1986.

Dalrymple, P. W. Clinical uses of MEDLINE on CD-ROM: a composite report of a panel discussion on five sites. In: *MEDLINE on CD-ROM*; ed. by R. M. Woodsmall et al., pp. 25-33. Medford, NJ, Learned Information, 1989.

Dalrymple, P. W. and Roderer, N. K. Database access systems. *Annual Review of Information Science and Technology*, 29, 1994, 137-178.

Dannelly, G. N. Resource sharing in the electronic era: potentials and paradoxes. *Library Trends*, 43, 1995, 663-678.

Davies, R. Expert systems and cataloguing: new wine in old bottles? In: *Expert Systems in Libraries*; ed. by F. Gibb, pp. 67-82. London, Taylor Graham, 1986.

Davies, R. et al. Expert systems in reference work. In: *The Application of Expert Systems in Libraries and Information Centres*; ed. by A. Morris, pp. 91-132. London, Bowker-Saur, 1992.

Davis, S. Dial access users of online catalogs: responding to the needs of BI's newest user group. *Illinois Libraries*, 70, 1988, 638-644.

Day, M. and Revill, D. Towards the active collection: the use of circulation analyses in collection evaluation. *Journal of Librarianship and Information Science*, 27, 1995, 149-157.

DeBuse, R. So that's a book ... advancing technology and the library. *Information Technology and Libraries*, 7, 1988, 7-18.

DeGennaro, R. JSTOR: the Andrew W. Mellon Foundation's journal storage project. In: *Toward a Worldwide Library: a Ten Year Forecast*; ed. by A. H. Helal and J. W. Weiss. Essen, Essen University Library, 1997 (*in press*).

de Klerk, A. and Euster, J. R. Technology and organizational metamorphoses. *Library Trends*, 37, 1989, 457-468.

de Kock, M. Remote users of an online public access catalogue (OPAC): problems and support. *Electronic Library*, 11, 1993, 241-244.

Demas, S. et al. The Internet and collection development: mainstreaming selection of Internet resources. *Library Resources & Technical Services*, 39, 1995, 275-290.

Denning, R. and Smith, P. J. Interface design concepts in the development of ELSA, an intelligent Electronic Library Search Assistant. *Information Technology and Libraries*, 13, 1994, 133-147.

Dickinson, G. K. *Selection and Evaluation of Electronic Resources*. Englewood, CO, Libraries Unlimited, 1994.

Dickson, J. An analysis of user errors in searching an online catalog. *Cataloging & Classification Quarterly*, 4(3), 1984, 19-38.

DiMattia, E. A., Jr. New technologies and the library. A remote access perspective. *Microcomputers for Information Management*, 8, 1991, 45-51.

DiMattia, E. A., Jr. Total quality management and servicing users through remote access technology. *Electronic Library*, 11, 1993, 187-192.

Doman, D. MAGGIE'S PLACE: connecting with the community at the Pikes Peak Library District. In: *Emerging Communities: Integrating Networked Information into Library Services*; ed. by A. P. Bishop, pp. 32-38. Urbana-Champaign, University of Illinois, Graduate School of Library and Information Science, 1994.

Dougherty, R. M. and Hughes, C. *Preferred Futures for Libraries*. Mountain View, CA, Research Libraries Group, 1991.

Dowlin, K. E. The neographic library: a 30-year perspective on public libraries. In: *Libraries and the Future: Essays on the Library in the Twenty-first Century*; ed. by F. W. Lancaster, pp. 29-43. New York, Haworth Press, 1993.

Dowlin, K. E. and Magrath, L. Beyond the numbers—a decision support system. In: *Library Automation as a Source of Management Information*; ed. by F. W. Lancaster, pp. 27-58. Urbana-Champaign, University of Illinois, Graduate School of Library and Information Science, 1983.

Drabenstott, K. M. *Analytical Review of the Library of the Future*. Washington, DC, Council on Library Resources, 1994.

Drabenstott, K. M. and Cochrane, P. A. Improvements needed for better subject access to library catalogs via the Internet. In: *Emerging Communities: Integrating Networked Information into Library Services*; ed. by A. P. Bishop, pp. 70-83. Urbana-Champaign, University of Illinois, Graduate School of Library and Information Science, 1994.

Drenth, H. et al. Expert systems as information intermediaries. *Annual Review of Information Science and Technology*, 26, 1991, 113-154.

Dreyfus, H. L. and Dreyfus, S. E. *Mind Over Machine: the Power of Human Intuition and Expertise in the Era of the Computer*. New York, Free Press, 1986.

Dunsire, G. CATRIONA: netting the cat and PACing the Net. *Catalogue and Index*, number 115, Spring 1995, 1-3.

Duranceau, E. et al. Electronic journals in the MIT Libraries: report of the 1995 e-journal subgroup. *Serials Review*, 22(1), 1996, 47-61.

Dyer, H. The effects of CD-ROM on library services. *Health Libraries Review*, 7, 1990, 196-203.

Dyer, H. The impact of technology on library staff. *An leabharlann (The Irish Library)*, 8(1), 1991, 3-17.

Eagle, M. The librarian of the future: image storage and transmission. In: *Proceedings of the Seventh National Conference on Integrated Online Library Systems*, pp. 99-103. Medford, NJ, Learned Information, 1992.

Edwards, C. et al. Impel project: the impact on people of electronic libraries. *Aslib Proceedings*, 47, 1995, 203-208.

Engel, G. User instruction for access to catalogs and databases on the Internet. *Cataloging & Classification Quarterly*, 13(3/4), 1991, 141-156.

Engle, R. L., Jr. Attempts to use computers as diagnostic aids in medical decision making: a thirty-year experience. *Perspectives in Biology and Medicine*, 35, 1992, 207-219.

Ensor, P. Organizing the Web: a contradiction in terms? *Technicalities*, 15(9), 1995, 1, 6-7.

Enssle, H. R. Reserve on-line: bringing reserve into the electronic age. *Information Technology and Libraries*, 13, 1994, 197-201.

Entlich, R. Networked delivery of full-text electronic journals: diverse options, shared limitations. In: *Emerging Communities: Integrating Networked Information into Library Services*; ed. by A. P. Bishop, pp. 241-252. Urbana-Champaign, University of Illinois, Graduate School of Library and Information Science, 1994.

Epstein, S. B. Measuring system performance: the consultant's perspective. *Information Technology and Libraries*, 7, 1988, 190-193.

Ercegovac, Z. and Borko, H. Design and implementation of an experimental cataloging advisor—Mapper. *Information Processing & Management*, 28, 1992, 241-257.

Evans, G. T. and Beilby, A. A library management information system in a multi-campus environment. In: *Library Automation as a Source of Management Information*; ed. by F. W. Lancaster, pp. 164-196. Urbana-Champaign, University of Illinois, Graduate School of Library and Information Science, 1983.

Everett, D. Full-text online databases and document delivery in an academic library: too little, too late? *Online*, 17(2), 1993, 22-25.

Ewing, K. and Hauptman, R. Is traditional reference service obsolete? *Journal of Academic Librarianship*, 21, 1995, 3-6.

Fairman, R. Networking CD-ROMs: theory and practical experience. *Aslib Information*, 19, 1991, 356-362.

Farber, E. I. Plus ça change. *Library Trends*, 44, 1995, 430-438.

Fenly, C. Technical services processes as models for assessing expert system suitability and benefits. In: *Artificial Intelligence and Expert Systems: Will They Change the Library?*; ed. by F. W. Lancaster and L. C. Smith, pp. 50-66. Urbana-Champaign, University of Illinois, Graduate School of Library and Information Science, 1992.

Final Report of the Cataloging Task Force, April 15, 1990. Internal document, University Library, University of Illinois at Urbana-Champaign.

Fine, S. F. Terminal paralysis or showdown at the interface. In: *Human Aspects of Library Automation*; ed. by D. Shaw, pp. 3-15. Urbana-Champaign, University of Illinois, Graduate School of Library and Information Science, 1986.

Fiscella, J. B. and Proctor, E. An approach to assessing faculty use of locally loaded databases. *College & Research Libraries*, 56, 1995, 446-458.

Fisher, W. A brief history of library-vendor relations since 1950. *Library Acquisitions: Practice & Theory*, 17, 1993, 61-69.

Flaherty, P. *An Investigation into the "Zero Match" Searches in the MSUS/PALS Online Catalog*. Master's thesis, Mankato State University, 1990.

Flaherty, P. Transaction logging systems: a descriptive summary. *Library Hi Tech*, 11(2), 1993, 67-78.

Fox, E. A. et al., eds. Digital libraries. *Communications of the ACM*, 38(4), 1995, 15-110.

Gaines, B. R. Dimensions of electronic journals. In: *Computer Networking and Scholarly Communication in the Twenty-First Century University*; ed. by T. M. Harrison and T. Stephen, pp. 315-334. Albany, State University of New York Press, 1996.

Gaunt, M. I. Literary text in an electronic age: implications for library services. *Advances in Librarianship*, 19, 1995, 191-215.

Gaunt, M. I. Machine-readable literary texts: collection development issues. *Collection Management*, 13(1/2), 1990, 87-96.

Gaynor, E. Cataloging electronic texts: the University of Virginia Library experience. *Library Resources & Technical Services*, 38, 1994, 403-413.

Geffert, B. Beginning with MARC: providing a foundation for electronic searching. *Research Strategies*, 13, 1995, 26-33.

Geldenhuys, A. CD-ROM networking in an academic library—two case studies: trial, tribulation and success at the University of Pretoria. *Electronic Library*, 13, 1995, 371-376.

Getz, M. Document delivery. *Bottom Line*, 5(4), 1991-1992, 40-44.

Ghikas, M. W. Collection management for the 21st century. *Journal of Library Administration*, 11(1/2), 1989, 119-135.

Gibb, F. and Sharif, C. A. Y. Catalyst: an expert assistant for cataloging. *Program*, 22, 1988, 62-71.

Gillentine, J. et al. *Evaluating Library Services*. Santa Fe, New Mexico State Library, 1981.

Gleeson, M. E. and Ottensmann, J. R. Using data from computerized circulation and cataloging systems for management decision making in public libraries. *Journal of the American Society for Information Science*, 44, 1993, 94-100.

Glogoff, S., ed. Staff training in the automated library environment: a symposium. *Library Hi Tech* 7(4), 1989, 61-83.

Goehlert, R. The effect of loan policies on circulation recalls. *Journal of Academic Librarianship*, 5, 1979, 79-82.

Golden, B. A method for quantitatively evaluating a university library collection. *Library Resources & Technical Services*, 18, 1974, 268-274.

Goodram, R. J. The E-RBR: confirming the technology and exploring the law of "electronic reserves": two generations of the digital library system at the SDSU Library. *Journal of Academic Librarianship*, 22, 1996, 118-123.

Gordon, B. Java: a new brew for educators, administrators and students. *Educom Review*, 31(2), 1996, 44-46.

Gore, A., Vice President of the United States. As quoted in *American Libraries*, 25, 1994, 813.

Gorman, M. The organization of academic libraries in the light of automation. *Advances in Library Automation and Networking*, 1, 1987, 151-168.

Gosling, W. A. et al. Cooperative efforts in new methods of information delivery: the Michigan experience. *Advances in Librarianship*, 19, 1995, 23-42.

Govan, J. F. Ascent or decline? Some thoughts on the future of academic libraries. In: *The Future of the Academic Library: Proceedings of the Conference Held at the University of Wisconsin in September 1989*; ed. by E. P. Trani, pp. 24-44. Urbana-Champaign, University of Illinois, Graduate School of Library and Information Science, 1991. Occasional Papers 188 and 189.

Graham, P. S. Requirements for the digital research library. *College & Research Libraries*, 56, 1995, 331-339.

Haar, J. M. The reference collection development decision: will new information technologies influence libraries' collecting patterns? *Reference Librarian*, 22, 1988, 113-124.

Halperin, M. and Renfro, P. Online vs. CD-ROM vs. onsite: high volume searching—considering the alternatives. *Online*, 12 (6), 1988, 36-42.

Hancock-Beaulieu, M. et al. *Evaluation of Online Catalogues: an Assessment of Methods*. London, British Library Research and Development Department, 1990. British Library Research Paper 78.

Hanfman, D. AquaRef: an expert advisory system for reference support. *Reference Librarian*, 23, 1989, 113-133.

Hansen, E. A computerized serials list as a management tool. *Technicalities*, 6(4), 1986, 12-15.

Hanson, T. CD-ROM, downloading and related management issues. In: *CD-ROM in Libraries: Management Issues*; ed. by T. Hanson and J. Day, pp. 193-206. London, Bowker-Saur, 1994a.

Hanson, T. A future for CD-ROM as a strategic technology? In: *CD-ROM in Libraries: Management Issues*; ed. by T. Hanson and J. Day, pp. 241-253. London, Bowker-Saur, 1994b.

Hanson, T., ed. *Bibliographic Software and the Electronic Library*. Hatfield, University of Hertfordshire Press, 1995.

Haricombe, L. J. and Lusher, T. J. You want it when? Document delivery in the 1990s. In: *Continuity and Transformation: the Promise of Confluence*; ed. by R. AmRhein, pp. 357-364. Chicago, Association of College & Research Libraries, 1995.

Harris, R. Information technology and the de-skilling of librarians. *Computers in Libraries*, 12, 1992, 8-16.

Harrison, T. M. and Stephen, T. D. The electronic journal as the heart of an online scholarly community. *Library Trends*, 43, 1995, 592-608.

Harsin, S. E-mail communication, February 27, 1996 <SHARSIN@wpo.it.luc.edu>.

Harter, S. P. and Kim, H. J. Accessing electronic journals and other e-publications: an empirical study. *College & Research Libraries*, 57, 1996, 440-456.

Hauptman, R. and Anderson, C. L. The people speak: the dispersion and impact of technology in American libraries. *Information Technology and Libraries*, 13, 1994, 249-256.

Hawbaker, A. C. and Wagner, C. K. Periodical ownership versus fulltext online access: a cost-benefit analysis. *Journal of Academic Librarianship*, 22, 1996, 105-109.

Hawks, C. P. Expert systems in technical services and collection management. *Information Technology and Libraries*, 13, 1994, 203-212.

Hawks, C. P. The Geac acquisitions system as a source of management information. *Library Acquisitions: Practice & Theory*, 10, 1986, 245-253.

Hawks, C. P. Management information gleaned from automated library systems. *Information Technology and Libraries*, 7, 1988, 131-138.

Hawley, L. M. Faster and cheaper document delivery with online searching skills. *Online*, 16(4), 1992, 45-48.

Haynes, C. *Providing Public Services to Remote Users*. Washington, DC, Association of Research Libraries, 1993. SPEC Kit 191.

Heller, P. Remote access: its impact on a college library. *Electronic Library*, 10, 1992, 287-289.

Helsel, S. K. and Roth, J. P., eds. *Virtual Reality: Theory, Practice, and Promise*. Westport, CT, Meckler, 1991.

Herala, M. K. et al. Automated SDI service using CDROM databases. *Online & CDROM Review*, 19, 1995, 137-141.

Hickox, C. R. *Training for the Internet: Stages of Concern Among Academic Library Staff in the AMIGOS Consortium*. Doctoral dissertation. Commerce, East Texas State University, 1994.

Higginbotham, B. B. and Bowdoin, S. *Access Versus Assets: a Comprehensive Guide to Resource Sharing for Academic Librarians*. Chicago, American Library Association, 1993.

Hitchingham, E. Collection management in light of electronic publishing. *Information Technology and Libraries*, 15, 1996, 38-41.

Hoffman, M. M. et al. The RightPages™ service: an image-based electronic library. *Journal of the American Society for Information Science*, 44, 1993, 446-452.

Holt, G. E. Computers and public libraries: the future is now. *OCLC Newsletter*, No. 206, November/December, 1993, 24-25.

Holt, G. E. On becoming essential: an agenda for quality in twenty-first century public libraries. *Library Trends*, 44, 1995a, 545-571.

Holt, G. E. Pathways to tomorrow's service: the future of rural libraries. *Library Trends*, 44, 1995b, 190-215.

Horner, J. and Michaud-Oystryk, N. The efficiency and success rates of print ready reference vs. online ready reference searches in Canadian university libraries. *Journal of Academic Librarianship*, 21, 1995, 97-102.

Horres, M. et al. MELVYL® MEDLINE®: a library services perspective. *Bulletin of the Medical Library Association*, 79, 1991, 309-320.

Horwitz, S. Reference service delivered through an online medium. *Proceedings of the Tenth National Online Meeting*, pp. 197-202. Medford, NJ, Learned Information, 1989.

Hu, C. *An Evaluation of Online Database Selection by a Gateway System with Artificial Intelligence Techniques*. Doctoral dissertation. Urbana-Champaign, University of Illinois, Graduate School of Library and Information Science, 1987.

Huang, S. T. CD-ROM database searching vs. traditional online database searching. *Proceedings of the Twelfth National Online Meeting*, pp. 139-148. Medford, NJ, Learned Information, 1991.

Huang, S. T. and McHale, T. J. A cost-effectiveness comparison between print and online versions of the same frequently-used sources of business and financial information. *Proceedings of the Eleventh National Online Meeting*, pp. 161-168. Medford, NJ, Learned Information, 1990.

Humphrey, S. M. Interactive knowledge-based systems for improved subject analysis and retrieval. In: *Artificial Intelligence and Expert Systems: Will They Change the Library?*; ed. by F. W. Lancaster and L. C. Smith, pp. 81-117. Urbana-Champaign, University of Illinois, Graduate School of Library and Information Science, 1992.

Hunt, P. J. Interpreters as well as gatherers: the librarian of tomorrow ... today. *Special Libraries*, 86, 1995, 195-204.

Hunter, I. Desktop publishing: new opportunities for public libraries. In: *Changing Information Technologies: Research Challenges in the Economics of Information*; ed. by M. Feeney and M. Grieves, pp. 81-91. London, Bowker-Saur, 1994a.

Hunter, K. Issues and experiments in electronic publishing and dissemination. *Information Technology and Libraries*, 13, 1994b, 127-132.

Hunter, K. Publishing for a digital library—what did TULIP teach us? *Journal of Academic Librarianship*, 22, 1996, 209-211.

Hurt, C. Building the foundations of Virginia's virtual library. *Information Technology and Libraries*, 14, 1995, 50-53.

Internet Homesteader. Published monthly since April 1994 by the OCLC Network and Office of Library Services, State University of New York.

Ison, J. Rural public libraries in multitype library cooperatives. *Library Trends*, 44, 1995, 129-151.

Ives, D. J. Staff empowerment and library improvement through networking. *Journal of Education for Library and Information Science*, 36, 1995, 46-51.

Jackson, M. E. Document delivery over the Internet. *Online*, 17(2), 1993a, 14-21.

Jackson, M. E. Integrating document delivery services with electronic document delivery technologies. *Law Library Journal*, 85, 1993b, 609-618.

Jackson, M. E. Integrating ILL with document delivery: five models. *Wilson Library Bulletin*, 68(1), 1993c, 76-78.

Jackson, M. E. Stand and deliver. *Wilson Library Bulletin*, 66(8), 1992, 86-88.

Jackson, M. E. and Croneis, K. *Uses of Document Delivery Services.* Washington, DC, Association of Research Libraries, 1994. SPEC Kit 204.

Jacsó, P. *CD-ROM Software, Dataware, and Hardware: Evaluation, Selection, and Installation.* Englewood, CO, Libraries Unlimited, 1992.

Jaffe, L. D. *Introducing the Internet: a Trainer's Workshop.* Berkeley, CA, Library Solutions Press, 1994.

Jain, A. K. *Report on a Statistical Study of Book Use.* Lafayette, IN, Purdue University, School of Industrial Engineering, 1967.

Jain, A. K. *A Sampled Data Study of Book Usage in the Purdue University Libraries.* Lafayette, IN, Purdue University, 1965.

Jain, A. K. Sampling and data collection methods for a book-use study. *Library Quarterly*, 39, 1969, 245-252.

Jain, A. K. Sampling and short-period usage in the Purdue Library. *College & Research Libraries*, 27, 1966, 211-218.

Jajko, P. Planning the virtual library. *Medical Reference Services Quarterly*, 12(4), 1993, 51-67.

Janosky, B. et al. Online library catalog systems: an analysis of user errors. *International Journal of Man-Machine Studies*, 25, 1986, 573-592.

Jaros, J. Training endusers/remote users. *Journal of Library Administration*, 12(2), 1990, 75-88.

Jeapes, B. Digital library projects: where they are now. *Electronic Library*, 13, 1995, 551-554; 14, 1996, 62-64.

Jeng, L.-H. An expert system for determining title proper in descriptive cataloging: a conceptual model. *Cataloging & Classification Quarterly*, 7(2), 1986, 55-70.

Jenks, G. M. Circulation and its relationship to the book collection and academic departments. *College & Research Libraries*, 37, 1976, 145-152.

Jennings, L. Regrowing staff: managerial priority for the future of university libraries. *Public-Access Computer Systems Review*, 3, 1992, 76-86.

Jensen, A. and Sih, J. Using E-mail and the Internet to reach users at their desktops. *Online*, 19(5), 1995, 82-86.

Johnson, P. Adding computer files to the research library: issues in collection management and development. In: *Computer Files and the Research Library*, ed. by C. C. Gould, pp. 3-13. Mountain View, CA, Research Libraries Group, 1990a.

Johnson, P. *Automation and Organizational Change in Libraries.* Boston, G. K. Hall, 1991.

Johnson, P. Why do libraries automate and what are they missing? *Technicalities*, 10(12), 1990b, 5-8.

Jones, D. E. Library support staff and technology: perceptions and opinions. *Library Trends*, 37, 1989, 432-456.

Jones, R. M. Improving Okapi: transaction log analysis of failed searches in an online catalogue. *Vine*, 62, May 1986, 3-13.

Kahn, P. Making a difference: a review of the user interface features in six CD-ROM database products. *Optical Information Systems*, 8(4), 1988, 169-183.

Kalin, S. W. Support services for remote users of online public access catalogs. *RQ*, 31, 1991, 197-213.

Kalin, S. W. and Wright, C. Internexus: a partnership for Internet instruction. *Reference Librarian*, 41/42, 1994, 197-209.

Kaske, N. K. A comparative study of subject searching in an OPAC among branch libraries of a university library system. *Information Technology and Libraries*, 7, 1988, 359-372.

Kassirer, J. P. A report card on computer-assisted diagnosis—the grade: C. *New England Journal of Medicine*, 330, 1994, 1824-1825.

Kehoe, B. P. *Zen and the Art of the Internet: a Beginner's Guide*. Second edition. Englewood Cliffs, NJ, Prentice Hall, 1993.

Kelly, S. and Nicholas, D. Is the business cybrarian a reality? Internet use in business libraries. *Aslib Proceedings*, 48, 1996, 136-144.

Kennedy, R. A. Computer-derived management information in a special library. In: *Library Automation as a Source of Management Information*; ed. by F. W. Lancaster, pp. 128-147. Urbana-Champaign, University of Illinois, Graduate School of Library and Information Science, 1983.

Kilgour, F. G. The metamorphosis of libraries during the foreseeable future. In: *Libraries and the Future: Essays on the Library in the Twenty-first Century*; ed. by F. W. Lancaster, pp. 131-146. New York, Haworth Press, 1993.

Kirby, H. G. Public library case study: CD-ROM at Croydon Central Library. In: *CD-ROM in Libraries: Management Issues*; ed. by T. Hanson and J. Day, pp. 217-231. London, Bowker-Saur, 1994.

Kirby, M. and Miller, N. MEDLINE searching on Colleague: reasons for failure or success of untrained end users. *Medical Reference Services Quarterly*, 5(3), 1986, 17-34.

Kircher, P. PromptCat, OCLC's new copy cataloging option to be introduced in April. URL: http://www.oclc.org/oclc/new/n212/spreport.htm#sprart06, 1994.

Kluegel, K. M. Trends in electronic reference services: opportunities and challenges. In: *Reference and Information Services: an Introduction*; ed. by R. E. Bopp and L. C. Smith, pp. 123-151. Second edition. Englewood, CO, Libraries Unlimited, 1995.

Kobelski, P. and Reichel, M. Conceptual frameworks for bibliographic instruction. *Journal of Academic Librarianship*, 7, 1981, 73-77.

Kohl, D. F. Revealing UnCover: simple, easy article delivery. *Online*, 19(3), 1995, 52-60.

Kong, L. M. Reference service evolved. *Journal of Academic Librarianship*, 21, 1995, 13-14.

Kountz, J. What's in a library? Comparing library holdings to the constituencies served. *Library Hi Tech*, 9(2), 1991, 31-48, 61.

Kovacs, D. K. et al. A model for planning and providing reference services using Internet resources. *Library Trends*, 42, 1994, 638-647.

Kovacs, D. K. et al. Scholarly E-conferences on the academic networks: how library and information science professionals use them. *Journal of the American Society for Information Science*, 46, 1995, 244-253.

Kriz, H. M. and Queijo, Z. K. An environmental approach to library staff training. *Library Hi Tech*, 7(4), 1989, 62-66.

Krol, E. *The Whole Internet: User's Guide & Catalog*. Second edition. Sebastopol, CA, O'Reilly, 1994.

Krueger, M. W. *Artificial Reality*. Reading, MA, Addison-Wesley, 1983.

Kurzweil, R. Machine intelligence: the first 80 years. *Library Journal*, 116 (13), 1991, 69-71.

Ladner, S. J. and Tillman, H. N. Using the Internet for reference. *Online*, 17 (1), 1993, 45-51.

LaGuardia, C. *Desk Set* revisited: reference librarians, reality, & research systems' design. *Journal of Academic Librarianship*, 21, 1995, 7-9.

Lamolinara, G. Metamorphosis of a national treasure. *American Libraries*, 27(3), 1996, 31-33.

Lancaster, F. W. The curriculum of information science in developed and developing countries. *Libri*, 44, 1994, 201-205.

Lancaster, F. W. *Evaluation of On-line Searching in MEDLARS (AIM-TWX) by Biomedical Practitioners*. Urbana-Champaign, University of Illinois Graduate School of Library Science, 1972. Occasional Paper 101. (ERIC Document Reproduction Service ED 062989)

Lancaster, F. W. Has technology failed us? In: *Information Technology and Library Management*; ed. by A. H. Helal and J. W. Weiss, pp. 1-13. Essen, Essen University Library, 1991.

Lancaster, F. W. *If You Want to Evaluate Your Library...* Second edition. Urbana-Champaign, University of Illinois, Graduate School of Library and Information Science, 1993a.

Lancaster, F. W. Librarians, technology and mediocrity. In: *Opportunity 2000: Understanding and Serving Users in an Electronic Library*; ed. by A. H. Helal and J. W. Weiss, pp. 99-113. Essen, Essen University Library, 1993b.

Lancaster, F. W. *Libraries and Librarians in an Age of Electronics*. Arlington, VA, Information Resources Press, 1982.

Lancaster, F. W. ed. *Library Automation as a Source of Management Information*. Urbana-Champaign, University of Illinois, Graduate School of Library and Information Science, 1983.

Lancaster, F. W., ed. Networked scholarly publishing, *Library Trends*, 43(4), Spring 1995 (entire issue).

Lancaster, F. W. and Loescher, J. The corporate library and issues management. *Library Trends*, 43, 1994, 159-169.

Lancaster, F. W. and Smith, L. C., eds. *Artificial Intelligence and Expert Systems: Will They Change the Library?* Urbana-Champaign, University of Illinois, Graduate School of Library and Information Science, 1992.

Lancaster, F. W. et al. Evaluation of interactive knowledge-based systems: overview and design for empirical testing. *Journal of the American Society for Information Science*, 47, 1996, 57-69.

Lancaster, F. W. et al. The relationship between literature scatter and journal accessibility in an academic special library. *Collection Building*, 11(1), 1991, 19-22.

Lancaster, F. W. et al. Searching databases on CD-ROM: comparison of the results of end-user searching with results from two modes of searching by skilled intermediaries. *RQ*, 33, 1994, 370-386.

Lanham, R. The implications of electronic information for the sociology of knowledge. *Leonardo*, 27, 1994, 155-164.

Lanier, D. and Wilkins, W. Ready reference via the Internet. *RQ*, 33, 1994, 359-368.

Lantz, B. Evaluation of technical services functions: towards a management information system. *Journal of Librarianship*, 18, 1986, 257-279.

Larson, R. R. *Users Look at Online Catalogs: Part 2. Interacting with Online Catalogs*: Final Report to the Council on Library Resources. Berkeley, University of California, Library Studies and Research Division, 1983. (ERIC Document Reproduction Service ED 231 401)

Larson, R. R. and Graham, V. Monitoring and evaluating MELVYL. *Information Technology and Libraries*, 2, 1983, 93-104.

Leach, R. G. and Tribble, J. E. Electronic document delivery: new options for libraries. *Journal of Academic Librarianship*, 18, 1993, 359-364.

Lee, D. C. and Lockway, L. A. Using an online comprehensive library management system in collection development. *Collection Management*, 14(3/4), 1991, 61-73.

Leimkuhler, F. F. Systems analysis in university libraries. *College & Research Libraries*, 27, 1966, 13-18.

LePoer, P. M. and Mularski, C. A. CD-ROM's impact on libraries and users. *Laserdisk Professional*, 2(4), 1989, 39-45.

Lewis, D. W. Inventing the electronic university. *College & Research Libraries*, 49, 1988, 291-304.

Lewis, D. W. Traditional reference is dead, now let's move on to important questions. *Journal of Academic Librarianship*, 21, 1995, 10-12.

Lewontin, A. Providing online services to end users outside the library. *College & Research Libraries News*, 52, 1991, 21-22.

Library Association. Information superhighways: library & information services and the Internet. *Electronic Library*, 13, 1995, 547-550.

Line, M. B. Libraries and information services in 25 years' time: a British perspective. In: *Libraries and the Future: Essays on the Library in the Twenty-first Century*; ed. by F. W. Lancaster, pp. 73-83. New York, Haworth Press, 1993.

Lippincott, J. K. End-user instruction. In: *Conceptual Frameworks for Bibliographic Education: Theory into Practice*; ed. by M. Reichel and M. A. Ramey, pp. 183-191. Littleton, CO, Libraries Unlimited, 1987.

Liu, L.-G. *The Internet and Library and Information Services: a Review, Analysis and Annotated Bibliography*. Urbana-Champaign, University of Illinois, Graduate School of Library and Information Science, 1995. Occasional Paper 202.

Lowry, A. Electronic texts in English and American literature. *Library Trends*, 40, 1992, 704-723.

Lowry, A. Machine-readable texts in the academic library: the Electronic Text Service at Columbia University. In: *Computer Files and the Research Library*, ed. by C. C. Gould, pp. 15-23. Mountain View, CA, Research Libraries Group, 1990.

Lowry, C. B. Preparing for the technological future: a journey of discovery. *Library Hi Tech*, 13(3), 1995a, 39-53.

Lowry, C. B. Putting the pieces together—essential technologies for the virtual library. *Journal of Academic Librarianship*, 21, 1995b, 297-300.

Lucier, R. E. Building a digital library for the health sciences: information space complementing information place. *Bulletin of the Medical Library Association*, 83, 1995, 346-350.

Luijendijk, W. Archiving electronic journals: the serial information provider's perspective. *IFLA Journal*, 22, 1996, 209-210.

Lynch, C. A. Response time measurement and performance analysis in public access information retrieval systems. *Information Technology and Libraries*, 7, 1988, 177-183.

Lynch, C. A. and Preston, C. M. Internet access to information resources. *Annual Review of Information Science and Technology*, 25, 1990, 263-312.

Lynn, P. and Bacsanyi, K. CD-ROMs: instructional methods and user reactions. *Reference Services Review*, 17(2), 1989, 17-25.

MacEwan, B. and Geffner, M. The Committee on Institutional Cooperation electronic journals collection (CIC-EJC): a new model for library management of scholarly journals published on the Internet. *Public-Access Computer Systems Review*, 7(4), 1996 (http://www.lib.ncsu.edu./stacks/p/pacsr/pr-v7n04—macewan—committee.txt).

Machovec, G. S. et al. Choices: collection management issues of the IOLS. *Proceedings of the Sixth National Conference on Integrated Online Library Systems*, pp. 83-91. Medford, NJ, Learned Information, 1991.

Malinconico, M. Electronic documents and research libraries. *IFLA Journal*, 22, 1996, 211-225.

Mancini, A. D. Evaluating commercial document suppliers: improving access to current journal literature. *College & Research Libraries*, 57, 1996, 123-131.

Marchant, M. P. and England, M. M. Changing management techniques as libraries automate. *Library Trends*, 37, 1989, 469-483.

Marks, C. Case study: the use of CD-ROM for library catalogue production and distribution at Staffordshire University. In: *CD-ROM in Libraries: Management Issues*, ed. by T. Hanson and J. Day, pp. 183-192. London, Bowker-Saur, 1994.

Martyn, J. et al, eds. *Information UK 2000*. London, Bowker-Saur, 1990.

Massey-Burzio, V. The MultiPlatter experience at Brandeis University. *CD-ROM Professional*, 3(3), 1990, 22-26.

McAbee, S. Personal email communication, ACQNET-L Listserv, Wed, 28 Feb 1996 (smcabee@jsucc.jsu.edu).

McClellan, A. W. *The Logistics of Public Library Bookstock*. London, Association of Assistant Librarians, 1978.

McClellan, A. W. New concepts of service. *Library Association Record*, 58, 1956, 299-305.

McClung, P. A. *Digital Collections Inventory Report.* Washington, DC, Commission on Preservation and Access and Council on Library Resources, 1996.

McClure, C. R. and Lopata, C. L. *Assessing the Academic Networked Environment: Strategies and Options.* Washington, DC, Coalition for Networked Information, 1996.

McClure, C. R. et al. *Internet Costs and Cost Models for Public Libraries.* Washington, DC, National Commission on Libraries and Information Science, 1995.

McClure, C. R. et al. *Libraries and Internet/NREN: Perspectives, Issues, and Challenges.* Westport, CT, Meckler, 1994.

McClure, C. R. et al. *Public Libraries and the Internet/NREN: New Challenges, New Opportunities.* Syracuse, NY, Syracuse University, School of Information Studies, 1992.

McCombs, G. M. The Internet and technical services: a point break approach. *Library Resources & Technical Services*, 38, 1994, 169-177.

McGrath, W. E. Measuring classified circulation according to curriculum. *College & Research Libraries*, 29, 1968, 347-350.

McGrath, W. E. The significance of books used according to a classified profile of academic departments. *College & Research Libraries*, 33, 1972, 212-219.

McGrath, W. E. et al. Ethnocentricity and cross-disciplinary circulation. *College & Research Libraries*, 40, 1979, 511-518.

Meador, J. M. Jr. and Cline, L. Displaying and utilizing selection tools in a user-friendly electronic environment. *Library Acquisitions: Practice & Theory*, 16, 1992, 289-294.

Metz, P. *The Landscape of Literatures: Use of Subject Collections in a Library.* Chicago, American Library Association, 1983.

Metzler, D. P. Artificial intelligence: what will they think of next? In: *Artificial Intelligence and Expert Systems: Will They Change the Library?*; ed. by F. W. Lancaster and L. C. Smith, pp. 2-49. Urbana-Champaign, University of Illinois, Graduate School of Library and Information Science, 1992.

Meyer, R. W. Management, cost and behavioral issues with locally mounted databases. *Information Technology and Libraries*, 9, 1990, 226-241.

Meyer, R. W. Personal communication, March 19, 1996.

Meyer, R. W. Selecting electronic alternatives. *Information Technology and Libraries*, 12, 1993, 173-180.

Michael, J. J. and Hinnebusch, M. *From A to Z39.50: a Networking Primer.* Westport, CT, Mecklermedia, 1995.

Michalko, J. Foreword. In: Dougherty, R. M. and Hughes, C. *Preferred Futures for Libraries.* Mountain View, CA, Research Libraries Group, 1991.

Miller, T. Early user reaction to CD-ROM and videodisc-based optical information products in the library market. *Optical Information Systems*, 7, 1987, 205-209.

Mills, T. R. *The University of Illinois Film Center Collection Use Study.* Urbana-Champaign, University of Illinois, Graduate School of Library and Information Science, 1982. (ERIC Document Reproduction Service ED 227 821).

Mitchell, E. and Walters, S. A. *Document Delivery Services: Issues and Answers.* Medford, NJ, Learned Information, 1995.

Mogge, D., ed. *Directory of Electronic Journals, Newsletters and Academic Discussion Lists.* Sixth edition. Washington, DC, Association of Research Libraries, 1996.

Moody, M. K. The impact of CD-ROM on resource sharing. *Advances in Library Resource Sharing,* 1, 1990, 154-165.

Mooers, C. N. Mooers' law or, why some retrieval systems are used and others are not. *American Documentation,* 11(3), 1960, ii.

Morris, A. ed. *The Application of Expert Systems in Libraries and Information Centres.* London, Bowker-Saur, 1992.

Mostyn, G. R. The use of supply-demand equality in evaluating collection adequacy. *California Librarian,* 35, 1974, 16-23.

Mountifield, H. M. Electronic current awareness service: a survival tool for the information age? *Electronic Library,* 13, 1995, 317-323.

Mushrush, J. L. Options in learning: instructor led and computer based training (CBT). *Journal of Library Administration,* 12(2), 1990, 47-55.

Nagle, E. The new knowledge environment: quality initiatives in health sciences libraries. *Library Trends,* 44, 1996, 657-674.

Nash, S. and Wilson, M. C. Value-added bibliographic instruction: teaching students to find the right citations. *Reference Services Review,* 19(1), 1991, 87-92.

Neavill, G. B. and Sheblé, M. A. Archiving electronic journals. *Serials Review,* 21(4), 1995, 13-21.

Negroponte, N. *Being Digital.* New York, Knopf, 1995.

Newhouse, J. P. and Alexander, A. J. *An Economic Analysis of Public Library Services.* Lexington, MA, Lexington Books, 1972.

Newkirk, J. G. and Jacobson, T. E. CD-ROM search strategy analysis: a pilot study. In: *CD-ROM for Library Users: a Guide to Managing and Maintaining User Access;* ed. by. P. Nicholls and P. Ensor, pp. 83-89. Medford, NJ, Learned Information, 1994.

Nicholson, D. et al. *Cataloguing the Internet: CATRIONA Feasibility Study.* London, British Library, 1995. Library and Information Research Report 105.

Nielsen, B. Teacher or intermediary: alternative professional models in the Information Age. *College & Research Libraries,* 43, 1982, 183-191.

Nielsen, B. What they say they do and what they do: assessing online catalog use instruction through transaction monitoring. *Information Technology and Libraries,* 5, 1986, 28-34.

Nielsen, B. and Baker, B. Educating the online catalog user: a model evaluation study. *Library Trends,* 35, 1987, 571-585.

Nimmer, R. J. Circulation and collection patterns at the Ohio State University Libraries 1973-1977. *Library Acquisitions: Practice & Theory,* 4, 1980, 61-70.

Nisonger, T. E. Collection management issues for electronic journals. *IFLA Journal,* 22, 1996, 233-239.

Nitecki, D. User criteria for evaluating the effectiveness of the online catalog. In: *Research in Reference Effectiveness;* ed. by M. E. Murfin and J. B. Whitlatch, pp. 8-28. Chicago, American Library Association, 1993. RASD Occasional Paper Number 16.

No more expert systems? The intelligent technology that got left behind. *Critical Technology Trends*, Report No. 3, March 1994.

Noble, R. Document delivery and full text from OCLC. *Electronic Library*, 14, 1996, 57-60.

Norbie, D. The electronic library emerges at US West. *Special Libraries*, 85, 1994, 274-276.

Nutter, S. K. Online systems and the management of collections. *Advances in Library Automation and Networking*, 1, 1987, 125-149.

Oberman, C. Unmasking technology: a prelude to teaching. *Research Strategies*, 13, 1995, 34-39.

OCLC makes PURL software available free of charge on the World Wide Web (press release, June 2, 1996. URL: http://www.oclc.org./oclc/press/960621.htm).

Odlyzko, A. M. Tragic loss or good riddance? The impending demise of traditional scholarly journals. *International Journal of Human-Computer Studies*, 42, 1995, 71-122.

O'Donovan, K. Management issues. In: *CD-ROM in Libraries: Management Issues*; ed. by T. Hanson and J. Day, pp. 23-37. London, Bowker-Saur, 1994.

Okerson, A. S. and O'Donnell, J. J., eds. *Scholarly Journals at the Crossroads: a Subversive Proposal for Electronic Publishing*. Washington, DC, Association of Research Libraries, 1995.

Olsgaard, J. N. Automation as a socio-organizational agent of change: an evaluative literature review. *Information Technology and Libraries*, 4, 1985, 19-28.

Olsgaard, J. N. *The Relationship Between Administrative Style and the Use of Computer-Based Systems: an Attitudinal Study of Academic Library Professionals*. Doctoral dissertation. Urbana-Champaign, University of Illinois, Graduate School of Library and Information Science, 1984.

Onsi, P. W. et al. Dial-in access to CD-ROM databases: beyond the local area network. *Bulletin of the Medical Library Association*, 80, 1992, 376-379.

Orchard, S. Document delivery: towards the year 2000. In: *Toward a Worldwide Library: a Ten Year Forecast*; ed. by A. H. Helal and J. W. Weiss. Essen, Essen University Library, 1997 (*in press*).

Ottensmann, J. R. and Gleeson, M. E. Implementation and testing of a decision support system for public library materials acquisition budgeting. *Journal of the American Society for Information Science*, 44, 1993, 83-93.

Pagell, R. A. The virtual reference librarian: using desktop videoconferencing for distance reference. *Electronic Library*, 14, 1996, 21-26.

PALINET announces table of contents pilot project. *Advanced Technology/ Libraries*, 24(3), 1995, 5.

Palmer, C. L. Information work at the boundaries of science: linking library services to research practices. *Library Trends*, 45, 1996, 165-191.

Palmini, C. C. The impact of computerization on library support staff: a study of support staff in academic libraries in Wisconsin. *College & Research Libraries*, 55, 1994, 119-127.

Parang, E. and Saunders, L. *Electronic Journals in ARL Libraries: Issues and Trends*. Washington, DC, Association of Research Libraries, 1994a. SPEC Kit 202.

Parang, E. and Saunders, L. *Electronic Journals in ARL Libraries: Policies and Proce-dures.* Washington, DC, Association of Research Libraries, 1994b. SPEC Kit 201.

Parrott, J. R. Expert systems for reference work. *Microcomputers for Information Management,* 3, 1986, 155-171.

Parrott, J. R. Reference expert systems: foundations in reference theory. In: *Artificial Intelligence and Expert Systems: Will They Change the Library?;* ed. by F. W. Lancaster and L. C. Smith, pp. 118-160. Urbana-Champaign, University of Illinois, Graduate School of Library and Information Science, 1992.

Parrott, J. R. Simulation of the reference process, Part II: REFSIM, an implementation with expert system and ICAI modes. *Reference Librarian,* 23, 1989, 153-176.

Pask, J. M. and Snow, C. E. Undergraduate instruction and the Internet. *Library Trends,* 44, 1995, 306-317.

Payne, P. and Willers, J. M. Using management information in a polytechnic library. *Journal of Librarianship,* 21(1), 1989, 19-35.

Peek, R. P. and Newby, G. B., eds. *Scholarly Publishing: the Electronic Frontier.* Cambridge, MA, MIT Press, 1996.

Penniman, D. W. Shaping the future for libraries through leadership and research. In: *Libraries and the Future: Essays on the Library in the Twenty-first Century;* ed. by F. W. Lancaster, pp. 5-15. New York, Haworth Press, 1993.

Peters, P. E. A framework for the development of performance measurement standards. *Information Technology and Libraries,* 7, 1988, 193-197.

Peters, T. A. The history and development of transaction log analysis. *Library Hi Tech,* 11(2), 1993, 41-66.

Peters, T. A. When smart people fail: an analysis of the transaction log of an online public access catalog. *Journal of Academic Librarianship,* 15, 1989, 267-273.

Peters, T. A. et al. Transaction log analysis. *Library Hi Tech,* 11(2), 1993a, 37.

Peters, T. A. et al. Transaction log analysis. *Library Hi Tech Bibliography,* 8, 1993b, 151-183.

Peterson, E. Management decisions—beyond the OPAC. *Journal of Academic Librarianship,* 21, 1995, 43-45.

Petrowski, M. J. et al. Designing the Electronic Village—First Year Seminar 028 (course syllabus and personal communication, October, 1995).

Pimentel, K. and Teixeira, K. *Virtual Reality: Through the New Looking Glass.* Second edition. New York, McGraw-Hill, 1995.

Pontigo, J. et al. Expert systems in document delivery: the feasibility of learning capabilities. In: *Artificial Intelligence and Expert Systems: Will They Change the Library?;* ed. by F. W. Lancaster and L. C. Smith, pp. 254-266. Urbana-Champaign, University of Illinois, Graduate School of Library and Information Science, 1992.

Poole, H. *Theories of the Middle Range.* Norwood, NJ, Ablex, 1985.

Potter, W. G. Expanding the online catalog. *Information Technology and Libraries,* 8, 1989, 99-104.

Power, C. J. and Bell, G. H. Automated circulation, patron satisfaction, and collection evaluation in academic libraries - a circulation analysis formula. *Journal of Library Automation,* 11, 1978, 366-369.

Preece, B. G. and Henigman, B. Shared authority control: governance and training. *Technical Services Quarterly*, 11(3), 1994, 19-31.

Presley, R. L. Firing an old friend, painful decisions: the ethics between librarians and vendors. *Library Acquisitions: Practice & Theory*, 17, 1993, 53-59.

Prince, B. and Burton, P. F. Changing dimensions in academic library structures: the impact of information technology. *British Journal of Academic Librarianship*, 3, 1988, 67-81.

Puttapithakporn, S. Interface design and user problems and errors: a case study of novice searchers. *RQ*, 30, 1990, 195-204.

Qin, J. *Levels and Types of Collaboration in Interdisciplinary Research in the Sciences*. Doctoral dissertation. Urbana-Champaign, University of Illinois, Graduate School of Library and Information Science, 1996.

Quinn, F. A role for libraries in electronic publication. *Serials Review*, 21(5), 1995, 27-30.

Ra, M. Technology and resource sharing: recent developments and future scenarios. *Advances in Library Resource Sharing*, 1, 1990, 141-153.

Rada, R. et al. Computerized guides to journal selection. *Information Technology and Libraries*, 6, 1987, 173-184.

Raitt, D. The library of the future. In: *Libraries and the Future: Essays on the Library in the Twenty-first Century*, ed. by F. W. Lancaster, pp. 61-72. New York, Haworth Press, 1993.

Reed-Scott, J. Information technologies and collection development. *Collection Building*, 9(3/4), 1989, 47-51.

Reese, J. CD-ROM: a successful format in the education library. In: *Public Access CD-ROMs in Libraries: Case Studies*, ed. by L. Stewart et al., pp. 39-57. Westport, CT, Meckler, 1990.

Reese, J. The challenge of CD-ROM end-user instruction: what works? what doesn't? In: *CD-ROM for Library Users: a Guide to Managing and Maintaining User Access*, ed. by P. Nicholls and P. Ensor, pp. 91-100. Medford, NJ, Learned Information, 1994.

Reid, E. O. F. Exploiting Internet as an enabler for transforming library services. *IFLA Journal*, 22, 1996, 18-26.

Reid, M. T. Evaluating the work of a vendor. In: *Understanding the Business of Library Acquisitions*, ed. by K. A. Schmidt, pp. 123-135. Chicago, American Library Association, 1990.

Rheingold, H. *Virtual Reality*. New York, Summit Books, 1991.

Richardson, J. V., Jr. Toward an expert system for reference service: a research agenda for the 1990s. *College & Research Libraries*, 50, 1989, 231-248.

Richardson, J. V., Jr. and Reyes, R. B. Government information expert systems: a quantitative evaluation. *College & Research Libraries*, 56, 1995, 235-247.

Rimmer, A. and Miller, R. B. Psychological preparation for automation. In: *Proceedings of the Conference on Integrated Online Library Systems*, ed. by D. C. Genaway, pp. 373-383. Canfield, OH, Genaway Associates, 1987.

Roberts, E. P. ILL/document delivery as an alternative to local ownership of seldom-used scientific journals. *Journal of Academic Librarianship*, 18, 1992, 30-34.

Roche, M. M. *ARL/RLG Interlibrary Loan Cost Study*. Washington, DC, Association of Research Libraries, 1993.

Rosen, L. CD-ROM user interfaces: consistency or confusion? *Database*, 13(2), 1990, 101-103.

Rowland, F. et al. ELVYN: the delivery of an electronic version of a journal from the publisher to libraries. *Journal of the American Society for Information Science*, 47, 1996, 690-700.

Rowland, F. et al., eds. *Project ELVYN: an Experiment in Electronic Journal Delivery*. London, Bowker-Saur, 1995.

Rubin, R. *Inhouse Use of Materials in Public Libraries*. Urbana-Champaign, University of Illinois, Graduate School of Library and Information Science, 1986.

Salamon, R. Expert systems in medicine. *World Health*, August/September 1989, 12-13.

Salmon, S. R. Measuring system performance: the vendor's perspective. *Information Technology and Libraries*, 7, 1988, 185-189.

Sandore, B. and Ryan, K. Evaluating electronic resources: a study using three concurrent methods. In: *Resource Sharing: New Technologies as a Must for Universal Availability of Information*; ed. by A. H. Helal and J. W. Weiss, pp. 61-84. Essen, Essen University Library, 1994.

Sandore, B. et al. *The Effect of Expanded Electronic Access to Periodicals Literature on Library Users, Collections and Operations*. Final Report of the Measurement and Evaluation Subcommittee, Online Catalog Advisory Committee, University of Illinois Library at Urbana-Champaign. April 4, 1993. (ERIC Document Reproduction Service ED 360 987)

Sandusky, R. J. Observations of bibliographoc tool use at the Grainger Engineering Library. 1995. URL - http://anshar.grainger.uiuc.edu/ dlisoc/grainger-sum.html

Sandusky, R. J. Software instrumentation and user registration. 1996. URL - http://anshar.grainger.uiuc.edu/dlisoc/logs-sum.html

Scepanski, J. M. Public services in a telecommuting world. *Information Technology and Libraries*, 15, 1996, 41-44.

Schiller, N. Internet training and support—academic libraries and computer centers: who's doing what? *Internet Research*, 4(2), 1994, 35-47.

Schmidt, J. G. and Pobuda, M. Capacity modeling at RLG. *Information Technology and Libraries*, 7, 1988, 173-177.

Schneider, K. G. Lean, mean searching machines. *American Libraries*, 26, 1995, 568-569.

Schultz, K. and Salomon, K. End users respond to CD-ROM. *Library Journal*, 115(2), 1990, 56-57.

Schwarz, H. Expert systems and the future of cataloguing: a possible approach. *LIBER Bulletin*, 26, 1986, 23-50.

Seaman, D. The Electronic Text Center: on-line archive of electronic texts. In: *Scholarly Publishing on the Electronic Networks*; ed. by A. Okerson, pp. 101-106. Washington, DC, Association of Research Libraries, 1993.

Secor, J. R. A growing crisis of business ethics: the gathering stormclouds. *Serials Librarian*, 13(2/3), 1987, 67-84.

Secor, J. R. Why some vendors will endure and others will not. *Against the Grain*, 8(1), 1996, 20-24.

Sellers, M. and Beam, J. Subsidizing unmediated document delivery: current models and a case study. *Journal of Academic Librarianship*, 21, 1995, 459-466.

Senge, P. M. *The Fifth Discipline: the Art and Practice of the Learning Organization*. New York, Doubleday, 1990.

Sharpe, K. UWired—cooperative effort brings technology to the classroom. *Windows on Computing*, Number 16, Winter/Spring 1995, 21-24.

Shreeves, E. Between the visionaries and the Luddites: collection development and electronic resources in the humanities. *Library Trends*, 40, 1992, 579-595.

Siddiqui, M. A. Compact disk indexes effect on interlibrary loan at a university library. *Libri*, 45, 1995, 178-185.

Simpson, C. W. OPAC transaction log analysis: the first decade. *Advances in Library Automation and Networking*, 3, 1989, 35-67.

Slater, M. *Non-use of Library-Information Resources at the Workplace*. London, Aslib, 1984.

Sloan, B. G. Remote access: design implications for the online catalog. *Cataloging & Classification Quarterly*, 13(3/4), 1991, 133-140.

Smalley, T. N. Computer systems in libraries: have we considered the tradeoffs? *Journal of Academic Librarianship*, 19, 1994, 356-361.

Snyder, J. Diving into the Internet: online while outta' town. *Internet World*, 5(3), 1994, 62-64.

Somers, S. W. Life in a gold fish bowl: or the changing nature of acquisitions work in an integrated online environment. *Acquisitions Librarian*, 1, 1989, 45-56.

Sowell, S. L. Expanding horizons in collection development with expert systems: development and testing of a demonstration prototype. *Special Libraries*, 80, 1989, 45-50.

Spaulding, F. H. and Stanton, R. O. Computer-aided selection in a library network. *Journal of the American Society for Information Science*, 27, 1976, 269-280.

Steffey, R. J. and Meyer, N. Evaluating user success and satisfaction with CD-ROM. *Laserdisk Professional*, 2(5), 1989, 35-45.

Stern, B. T. and Compier, H. C. J. ADONIS—document delivery in the CD-ROM age. *Interlending and Document Supply*, 18(3), 1990, 79-87.

Stevens, P. Acquisitions home page, University of Washington, 1996. URL: http://weber.u.washington.edu/~acqdiv/; Date: Wed, 28 Feb 1996, ACQNET-L listserv communication.

Stevens, P. Vendor selection policy. University of Washington Libraries. (13 March 1996) URL: http://weber.u.washington.edu/~acqdiv/vensel.html.

Stewart, L. and Olsen, J. Compact disk databases: are they good for users? *Online*, 2(3), 1988, 48-52.

Stoffle, C. J. et al. Choosing our futures. *College & Research Libraries*, 57, 1996, 213-225.

Stoller, M. E. Electronic journals in the humanities: a survey and critique. *Library Trends*, 40, 1992, 647-666.

Story, G. A. et al. The RightPages image-based electronic library for alerting and browsing. *Computer* 25(9), 1992, 17-26.

Stratton, B. The transiency of CD-ROM? A reappraisal for the 1990s. *Journal of Librarianship and Information Science*, 26, 1994, 157-164.

Su, S.-F. Attitudes of academic library professionals towards computer-based systems in Taiwan. *Journal of Librarianship and Information Science*, 25, 1993, 143-152.

Su, S.-F. and Lancaster, F. W. Evaluation of expert systems in reference service applications. *RQ*, 35, 1995, 219-228.

Summerhill, C. A. Remarks at the Symposium on the Role of Network-Based Electronic Resources in Scholarly Communication and Research; ed. by C. W. Bailey, Jr., and D. Rooks. *Public-Access Computer Systems Review*, 2, 1991, 152-198.

Swan, J. The electronic straitjacket. *Library Journal*, 118(17), 1993, 41-44.

Sweeney, R. T. Leadership in the post-hierarchical library. *Library Trends*, 43, 1994, 62-94.

Sykes, P. Automation and non-professional staff: the neglected majority. *Serials*, 4(3), 1991, 33-43.

Sylvia, M. A dial-in gateway to the CD-ROM network: support for off-campus and non-traditional students. In: *CD-ROM for Library Users: a Guide to Managing and Maintaining User Access*; ed. by P. Nicholls and P. Ensor, pp. 107-115. Medford, NJ, Learned Information, 1994.

Task Force on Library Instruction. University of Illinois at Urbana-Champaign. Final Report to the Dean, Graduate School of Library and Information Science and to the University Librarian. May 18, 1995.

Tennant, R. The virtual library foundation: staff training and support. *Information Technology and Libraries*, 14, 1995, 46-49.

Tenopir, C. and Neufang, R. The impact of electronic reference on reference librarians. *Online*, 16(3), 1992, 54-60.

Tenopir, C. et al. Magazines online: users and uses of full text. *Proceedings of the American Society for Information Science*, 26, 1989, 172-176.

Tenopir, C. et al. Strategies and assessments online: novices' experience. *Library & Information Science Research*, 13, 1991, 237-266.

Tiefel, V. M. Library user education: examining its past, projecting its future. *Library Trends*, 44, 1995, 318-338.

Tillman, H. N. and Ladner, S. J. Special librarians and the Internet: a descriptive study. In: *Emerging Communities: Integrating Networked Information into Library Services*; ed. by A. P. Bishop, pp. 156-172. Urbana-Champaign, University of Illinois, Graduate School of Library and Information Science, 1994.

Toren, N. Deprofessionalization and its sources. *Sociology of Work and Occupations*, 2, 1975, 323-337.

Torok, A. G. Internet search engines: are users ready? In: *Toward a Worldwide Library: a Ten Year Forecast*; ed. by A. H. Helal and J. W. Weiss. Essen, Essen University Library, 1997 (*in press*).

Trochim, M. K. et al. *Measuring the Circulation Use of a Small Academic Library Collection: a Manual*. Chicago, Associated Colleges of the Midwest, 1980. [An updated version was issued by the Office of Management Studies, Association of Research Libraries in 1985.]

Truesdell, C. B. Is access a viable alternative to ownership? A review of access performance. *Journal of Academic Librarianship*, 20, 1994, 200-206.

Tuck, B. and Moulton, R. Electronic document delivery: technical aspects and future developments. In: *Electronic Library and Visual Information Research: Elvira 1*, ed. by M. Collier and K. Arnold, pp. 66-75. London, Aslib, 1995.

TULIP. Final Report. New York, Elsevier Science, 1996.

Tyckoson, D. Electronic databases, information pricing, and the role of the library as a collective information utility. *Technicalities*, 9(6), 1989a, 11-13.

Tyckoson, D. The 98% solution: the failure of the catalog and the role of electronic databases. *Technicalities*, 9(2), 1989b, 8-12.

Ungern-Sternberg, S. von and Lindquist, M. The impact of electronic journals on library functions. *Journal of Information Science*, 21, 1995, 396-401.

University of Pennsylvania Libraries. Providing local access to machine-readable data files: choices and tradeoffs. In: *Computer Files and the Research Library*, ed. by C. C. Gould, p. 59. Mountain View, CA, Research Libraries Group, 1990.

van Brakel, P. A. Electronic journals: publishing via Internet's World Wide Web. *Electronic Library*, 13, 1995, 389-396.

van Gils, W. The precarious position between content and technology: libraries seeking their future. *Electronic Library*, 13, 1995, 533-537.

Van House, N. A. et al. *Output Measures for Public Libraries: a Manual of Standardized Procedures*. Second edition. Chicago, American Library Association, 1987.

Vedder, R. G. et al. Five PC-based systems for business reference: an evaluation. *Information Technology and Libraries*, 8, 1989, 42-54.

Vickery, B. C. Intelligent interfaces to online databases. In: *Artificial Intelligence and Expert Systems: Will They Change the Library?*; ed. by F. W. Lancaster and L. C. Smith, pp. 239-253. Urbana-Champaign, University of Illinois, Graduate School of Library and Information Science, 1992.

Vizine-Goetz, D. et al. Spectrum: a Web-based tool for describing electronic resources. In: *Proceedings of the Third International WWW Conference, Darmstadt, Germany, April, 1995* (URL: http://www.igd.fhg.de/www/www95/ proceedings/papers/59/spectrum.final. html).

von Wahlde, B. and Schiller, N. Creating the virtual library: strategic issues. In: *The Virtual Library: Visions and Realities*; ed. by L. M.. Saunders, pp. 15-46. Westport, CT, Meckler, 1993.

Waldstein, R. K. *Library*—an electronic ordering system. *Information Processing & Management*, 22, 1986, 39-44.

Walker, S. and Jones, R. M. *Improving Subject Retrieval in Online Catalogues: 1. Stemming, Automatic Spelling Correction and Cross-Reference Tables*. London, British Library, 1987. British Library Research Paper 24.

Wallace, P. M. How do patrons search the online catalog when no one's looking? Transaction log analysis and implications for bibliographic instruction and system design. *RQ*, 33, 1993, 239-252.

Wanger, J. Education and training for online systems. *Annual Review of Information Science and Technology*, 14, 1979, 219-245.

Warner, E. Expert systems and the law. *High Technology Business*, 8, October 1988, 32-35.

Waters, D. New technology & job satisfaction in university libraries. *LASIE*, 18, 1988, 103-108.

Waters, S. T. Expert systems at the National Agricultural Library: past, present, and future. In: *Artificial Intelligence and Expert Systems: Will They Change the Library?*; ed. by F. W. Lancaster and L. C. Smith, pp. 161-177. Urbana-Champaign, University of Illinois, Graduate School of Library and Information Science, 1992.

Webb, T. D. The frozen library: a model for twenty-first century libraries. *Electronic Library*, 13, 1995, 21-26.

Weibel, S. L. Automated cataloging: implications for libraries and patrons. In: *Artificial Intelligence and Expert Systems: Will They Change the Library?*; ed. by F. W. Lancaster and L. C. Smith, pp. 67-80. Urbana-Champaign, University of Illinois, Graduate School of Library and Information Science, 1992.

Weibel, S. L. Trends in World Wide Web development: May, 1995. *Library Hi Tech*, 13(3), 1995a, 7-10.

Weibel, S. L. The World Wide Web and emerging Internet resource discovery standards for scholarly literature. *Library Trends*, 43, 1995b, 627-644.

Weibel, S. L. et al. *OCLC/NCSA Metadata Workshop Report*. OCLC, 1995. (http://www.oclc.org:5046/oclc/research/conferences/metadata/dublin−core−report.html)

Weingand, D. E., ed. Marketing of library and information services. *Library Trends*, 43(3), Winter 1995. (Complete issue)

Weld, D. S. et al., eds. The role of intelligent systems in the National Information Infrastructure. *AI Magazine*, 16(3), 1995, 45-64.

Weller, A. C. A study of remote users' satisfaction with online services before and after procedural modifications. *Bulletin of the Medical Library Association*, 73, 1985, 352-357.

Welsch, E. K. Remarks at the Symposium on the Role of Network-Based Electronic Resources in Scholarly Communication and Research; ed. by C. W. Bailey, Jr., and D. Rooks. *Public-Access Computer Systems Review*, 2, 1991, 152-198.

Welsh, J. J. Evaluation of CD-ROM use in a government research library. *Laserdisk Professional*, 2(6), 1989, 55-61.

Wenger, C. B. et al. Monograph evaluation for acquisitions in a large research library. *Journal of the American Society for Information Science*, 30, 1979, 88-92.

Wessling, J. E. Benefits from automated ILL borrowing records. *RQ*, 29, 1989, 209-218.

West, J. A. The intranet: using the World Wide Web to disseminate company information over the Internet. In: *Toward a Worldwide Library: a Ten Year Forecast*; ed. by A. H. Helal and J. W. Weiss. Essen, Essen University Library, 1997 (*in press*).

Widdicombe, R. P. Eliminating all journal subscriptions has freed our customers to seek the information they really want and need: the result—more access, not less. *Science & Technology Libraries*, 14(1), 1993, 3-13.

Wilson, T. C. Training reference staff for automation in a transitional environment. *Library Hi Tech*, 7(4), 1989, 67-70.

Woodsmall, R. M. et al. eds. *MEDLINE on CD-ROM*. Medford, NJ, Learned Information, 1989.

Woodward, H. Electronic journals in libraries. In: *Project ELVYN: an Experiment in Electronic Journal Delivery*; ed. by F. Rowland et al., pp. 49-64. London, Bowker-Saur, 1995a.

Woodward, J. A. Auto aces or accident victims: librarians on the info superhighway. *American Libraries*, 26, 1995b, 1016-1018.

Wu, Z. et al. The user perspective of the ELINOR electronic library. *Aslib Proceedings*, 47, 1995, 13-22.

Wynne, P. M. Experimentation with electronic document delivery in the BIBDEL Project at the University of Central Lancashire. *Electronic Library*, 14, 1996, 13-20.

Xu, H. The impact of automation on job requirements and qualifications for catalogers and reference librarians in academic libraries. *Library Resources & Technical Services*, 40, 1996, 9-31.

Zager, P. and Smadi, O. A knowledge-based expert systems application in library acquisitions: monographs. *Library Acquisitions: Practice & Theory*, 16, 1992, 145-154.

Zhao, D. G. The ELINOR electronic library system. *Electronic Library*, 12, 1994, 289-294.

Zink, S. D. Toward more critical reviewing and analysis of CD-ROM user software interfaces. *CD-ROM Professional*, 4(1), 1991, 16-22.

Zipf, G. K. *Human Behavior and the Principle of Least Effort*. New York, Hafner, 1965 (1949).

INDEX